WARRIORS
OF THE
CAGE

THE UK'S MIXED MARTIAL ARTS FIGHT CLUB!

WARRIORS
OF THE
CAGE

Research and Interviews by
Jonathan Buffong

Written by
Brenda Downes

First published in hardback 2009
by Pennant Books

British Library Cataloguing-in-Publication Data:
A catalogue record for this book is available on request
from The British Library

ISBN 978-1-906015-42-8

Design & Typeset by Envy Design Ltd

Printed and bound in the United Kingdom by
CPI William Clowes, Beccles NR34 7TL

Pictures reproduced with kind permission of Frank Mensah/Ringpics,
'Demon' Lee/Demon Photography, Jonathan Buffong and David Ellis.

Front cover image: Damien Riccio pins down his opponent Marios
Zaromskis during Cage Rage Championship 20 at Wembley Arena,
10 February 2007. Copyright © Daniel Berehulak/Getty Images.

Pennant Books
PO Box 5675
London W1A 3FB

www.pennantbooks.com

Contents

WARRIORS OF THE CAGE

Acknowledgements by Jonathan Buffong

I would like to thank:

My fiancée and children, for being there when I've been absent. I love you dearly.

Terence Merchant, a.k.a. Super T, and Khan McSween for technical support.

Auntie Hailor and Auntie Theresa, for your support from the start.

Uncle Sidney and Uncle Stephen, for giving me your encouragement.

Matthias Merchant for the music downloads, from Beethoven to Rick James, which kept me awake all through those nights.

Michael Offo – keep up the training, I want to see you in UFC!

To the rest of my bloodline – thank you.

Brenda and Roger, you've been fantastic.

To everyone that I've interviewed, who gave me contacts or pushed me along on this journey, thank you. To Grant Beglan – without your support, I may not have got there so soon. To Paul Downes – what can I say? To Rob Nutley – you've been a brother to me. To Team Titan, Wolfslair, Mark Weir's Academy, London Shootfighters, Angrr Management, Chris & Mark – you've all been so very supportive from the start. To Mark 'the Beast' Epstein – I owe you a Nando's. To Darryl Jackson (a.k.a. Stan the fan), Martin Annor and Christopher Sibia – for those midnight calls. To Joe

Long, all at Fighters Inc and Chris Rose – keep the fire burning! To Dave and Andy – the pioneers of UK MMA.

To all at Ultimate Challenge, UWC, FX3, UFC, and everyone who used to be at Cage Rage. To Wendy Sanford – you're a gem, even though you witnessed me hobbling along. To Judge Dread, Joel Campbell, Mickey Gooch, Mr 1 Finger and anyone I've not mentioned – you know who you are. You have all played a magnificent part in this project.

To all those who lay to rest, RIP. I know you've been watching over me, so God bless. Finally, a sincere dedication to Mark Aplin – the husband of Lorraine Campbell Aplin, known as Lue – whose contribution to the MMA scene as an announcer had a great impact. His life, from 4/12/56 to 4/9/09, should be joyfully celebrated.

Frustration and stress equals success, but MMA is like a game of chess. Before you move, you must think first!

Acknowledgements by Brenda Downes

Thanks to:

Roger (to bits!)

Dave, Anne, John & Dawn – for their patience, encouragement and practical help.

Marion and Betty – for many things.

Paul Downes – who got me into this in the beginning.

Johnny Buffong – for a fabulous learning experience!

Evelyn – who has always believed.

Dan and Adie for the rescue.

In memory of John Downes, who woke me up to listen to Terry's fights, and of Bertha Downes, who thought I shouldn't go to school tired. I listened and learned, in and out of the classroom. They taught me never to stop doing either.

Johnny and Brenda would both like to thank Cass, Paul and the whole team for making an idea a reality.

1

The Beginning

Expect to hear the sounds of agonising pain sometimes; to feel the odd spattering of warm, spurting blood; to hear the noise of flesh ripping, ligaments tearing and bones crunching.

No, they haven't brought back fox hunting yet – this is Mixed Martial Arts, at an arena near you! Encouraged by a crowd of thousands of screaming, excited fight fans, gladiators fight to the point of knockout or submission using every technique from every known martial art. The enclosed indoor arena heightens the human – and sometimes frankly subhuman – noises coming from the cage.

Just when the tension has become unbearable, the one-to-one combat seemingly impossible to withstand, just when you know there's no more oxygen getting into that fighter's lungs, that it looks like he's beaten, it flips – the choke is broken; the other guy's shoulder blades are digging into the canvas; now *he's* tapping to indicate his submission, or being rescued by the ref.

The first round ends and the girls in sequins are back. Pop music blares and all appears normal. Then *blam!* It's round two and your blood's up again. The fighters are kicking and punching, each trying to force the other into submission. Suddenly you're on your feet, screaming stuff that you've never heard yourself say before, urging the warriors to go for the kill. And all this for a few quid.

This is not a sport for the fainthearted. Whether watching, training or fighting, it's full-on unarmed combat. Mixed Martial Arts is a fast, gripping, skilled, composed, exciting, intimidating tango of moves, counter-moves, attacks, ambushes, defeats and triumphs.

As soon as the last side of the octagon is locked, the tension rises. For the crowd, there's just time for a last prediction and a shout-out to a mate; for the officials, there's only time to remind the warriors to stick to the rules. For the fighters, there's no time at all. No turning back. There are now just those three five-minute rounds. The click of the lock on the cage flicks the switch in their minds to ON. Nothing outside the cage exists any longer – they hear only the sounds of the octagon, of each other, the referee, the trainers and the horn. Beyond the wire, all else is silence

So what is the appeal of *Mixed* Martial Arts? Well, what's so attractive about a box of chocolates? It has something for everyone, a blend of old favourites with new experiences. All wrapped up in a shiny box that screams fun and excitement! It's easy to see why aficionados of kickboxing, jiu-jitsu, karate, tai-chi, Thai-boxing, wrestling and boxing have embraced the octagon. For those who train or simply watch these sports, the sheer discipline needed by competitors to reach the MMA standard commands respect. Most fighters have studied in at least three disciplines and also incorporate moves from others. Take Anderson Silva: he started in taekwondo before studying kickboxing and wrestling. (He also throws a mean punch.)

Fighters enjoy the challenge of extending their range of skills and the punters are kept guessing, entertained because they're never quite sure about what's coming next. Bouts turn on a knife-edge, as a taekwondo specialist grapples with a karate expert, both using skills from another discipline. The cage doesn't have to be eight-sided; it doesn't even have to be a cage per se. It's just a way to define the space. And that's the first rule of MMA: stay in the space.

Hybrid sports need new rules. In the UK the rules have been drawn up by the National Fighting Arts Commission, led by renowned referee Grant Waterman. Drawing from the full range of martial arts, the rules of MMA contain the expected referees, and corners, and weight classes. They also deal with the unfamiliar: the bout must take place in a locked octagon; contestants must wear protective gloves weighing no more than six ounces, shorts and no footwear. Other rules address the 32 varieties of fouls which might be committed – one of which is 'timidity' and avoiding contact with an opponent – and the conditions under which a bout may be brought to an early close – for example, a contestant may submit or the referee may stop a bout.

THE BEGINNING

So here we are. We've been to the arena, taken a look at the girls and the concession stalls, yelled and screamed a bit, had a drink and gone home. At this point, a lot of people may wonder where the fighters go home to. Who do they say goodnight to? Have they always been fighters?

We wondered about all this too, which led to the interviews and the totally unexpected answers to the questions in this book. Who would have imagined that some of these fighters live with their parents, or work in a bank? That some were born with a silver spoon while others had to borrow a plastic one? That the referees and the doctors and the police would all be keen to talk about their involvement in the events?

But first, a bit of history. MMA was brought to England by a fighter called Lee Hasdell, known to many as 'the Godfather'. Lee had been fighting internationally in single discipline and mixed events, and winning whenever he fought. Concerned at the lack of opportunities for fighters at home, Lee put together the first UK event. Milton Keynes may have seemed an odd choice of location for the first British MMA event, which took place in 1997, but as Lee was a local boy it was ideal for him. Milton Keynes remains an important centre for the sport.

The first major event in England was held in September 2002 at the Elephant and Castle, south London. The now legendary Dave O'Donnell and Andy Geer promoted the event as Cage Rage, and the name stuck to English and European MMA until 2008. Dave had been fighting for many years – indeed, he trained with all the big names, including the Gracie brothers. After devising an expanded training programme of his own, Elite Fighting System, which included moves from the full range of martial arts, he needed a vehicle for his new skills. And so a new UK sport was born, with the cage as its cradle. Dave's still the daddy.

Cage Rage went from strength to strength, pulling crowds of up to 10,000 in venues as prestigious as Wembley Arena. Fighters from the international circuit – which had established itself in the USA in the mid-1990s – became desperate to take part in the new scene in England. English MMA very quickly became a regular feature on national and international television, with huge sponsorship from the likes of *Nuts* magazine, Sky Sports and the *Daily Star*.

As the revenue and the reputation of Cage Rage grew, so did the interest from other promoters. One day we all woke up to find our bus stops plastered with adverts for something called Ultimate

Fighting Championship – a cage event held in Manchester Arena, on the same day that Wembley was to host Cage Rage. UFC was, and is, the largest promoter of MMA in America, and the very first time it crossed the ocean it made a direct play for the Cage Rage audience in the UK. A lot of people remember that Saturday night because England went down three-one after penalties to Portugal in the quarter final of the World Cup, but Cage Rage fans also remember it as the night the Americans arrived

Since that night, both Cage Rage and UFC have promoted events to thrill the fans. MMA has also been successfully promoted beyond London and the southeast in one guise or another. For some of us, watching the bobbing and weaving between the competitors from this side of the wire, it's been a long and fascinating bout and nobody's certain of the final outcome for CR or UFC yet. In fact, in 2008 British MMA was re-branded, with Dave O'Donnell deciding to drop the old Cage Rage name for the more dynamic Ultimate Challenge. What we do know is that either way the fans win, with more events and better fighters brought in by competing promoters.

So, what's it all about? Love? Money? Fame? Power?

On this journey through the lives of those who get their kicks through this most passionate and yet most disciplined of sports, we intend to get some answers.

LORRAINE CAMPBELL

Lorraine Campbell – or Lue, as she's known to her friends – was in on the ground floor of MMA in England, as part of the group who formed the original Elite Fighting Club. These days she still trains and runs classes for children. She is well qualified to do so, having won many competitive trophies herself. Lue also holds down a job as an Early Years practitioner.

Lue lives in Lambeth in southwest London with her husband Mark and their five children.* They've all seen her tattoo of the Elite logo and eyes. Lue would never hide this. She's proud of her connection to Elite and of the part she played in its formation. She speaks the with authority and confidence of a woman who's damned good at everything she does.

THE BEGINNING

How did Elite begin, Lue?

David O'Donnell opened the club on 14th October 1997 in memory of his brother Joe, who died in August of that year. Joe was my own brother-in-law. As it started to come up popular we were all starting to do more. Initially, he'd come away from his martial arts training with Lajos Jacob and just left it there. A club was what he wanted, but he didn't do anything about it. I don't know, but I think things got together in his brain and that was why the club was opened. Joe's death sort of pushed him to do it, and after that there was just no stopping David. There were about 30 people there on the first night. Over the weeks it built up. More people started to come along and there was no doubt that it would be a success. The club was just like, *bang*, it started growing. It was never dribbling-drabbling. No, it was just *crash*, straight into it.

Who were your students in those days?

When we started it was just family and friends, no known criminals among us! Probably some who, if it fell off the back of a lorry, they'd buy it! It was just normal, everyday people. It depends what age you came in. I mean, when the club started I was in my thirties. Those that came later were people who saw the posters. Wherever you went, you saw *Elite Fight System, first lesson free.* That brought curious people into the club thinking, "Oh, here's something for nothing." That was good publicity for us. Looking back, people have come in, married each other and had a family together. Everybody was welcome. It didn't matter. You came in, if you liked it you stayed. We never discriminated against anyone. You could never really tell if anyone who walked in the door had an attitude, though some of them looked a bit cocky. Because of how that first class was run, Then, as time went on and you got to know people, you might get to hear why they came. It would be, "I want to come in here because I really want to hang off the street." Or they'd say, "I was this, I was that, I was into drugs." Everybody who's walked in that door, their lives have changed in some way or another. People have been noticed, been recognised. The amount of women who came was brilliant.

How did Elite develop?

Dave advertised for members to get it going. Soon he needed fights, and we started on some small fights over at Hornchurch in Essex. We started doing open combat and kickboxing and little matches.

Then we seemed to just start winning all the time; even when we went down with the kids from the club we were winning and we started getting a name. We were in *MMA and Fighters*. After that more people got interested in us. We started to get invited to places and then we got into doing seminars and performing. We were performing and then going out and winning medals and giving demonstrations. At the beginning, the whole of Elite was united like a family. It is totally different now, but the original Elite members still have contact and that's a good thing. Any time there's a gathering we get together and see each other at the event.

What was the importance of Elite in those days?
We did so many different things. After David had come up with the name Elite we got our logo. It was based on the No Fear eye and one of the young kids, Tom, drew it. From the start we had that and the *yin-yang*. We also did a lot of other things. The local newspaper, the *Southwark News,* really became interested. Later, we started the children's classes and the newspaper felt that we were helping the community. The paper got more involved and wrote about everything we did. About a year later Steve Cooper decided to train with Dave, and Aubrey Henry was up with us too, so all three instructors were up there. The next year Aubrey changed from Self Defence to Elite Fighting System, and a year later Steve opened a club up South Norwood way. It just started growing from there. All three clubs are still active.

What was your own part in Elite?
All the time with Elite is always in my brain. I was one of the originals. When I think back to when we first started and all the original guys – like Eric, the Pillar, Hal, Dougie, all the north London guys, Chris Cummings and Rob Nutley, Richard Barker, Tommy Gunn, Alvin Delmico, Paul Griffiths and obviously me, Mel O'Donnell, Glen Appleby and Danniella Smith – I realise there were only ever three girls in Elite that stuck through it really. That was me, Mel and Danniella.

At Elite, you started to go to seminars and demonstrations held with people like the Gracie's and other great MMA legends. How did that come about?
Yeah, we've had quite a few of them. David always had an interest in and always followed the MMA, no matter what. He was always into the

UFC too, and anything that was about martial arts. He started to get known by the top people and we started to get invited everywhere and to have seminars, we had some of the top names come over to Elite, like Ian McShee.

We used to go to seminars with the old Elite abroad. Once we went to Portugal and that was just awesome. We'd do demonstrations, and at the time we'd just got into the grappling and everything. All we did was sort of grapple on the sand and we had all the tourists and the locals watching, they were interested in coming over to see it. We always used to have an audience.

But Elite's involvement was through Paul Griffin of the British National Martial Arts Association. You'd get, say, ten to 20 different styles and clubs from around the country. Every instructor would run a seminar for half an hour. So David and Steve would be on at the start of the seminar, and everybody was just in awe of what they said and did. It looked realistic. We were good at it, we showed off with it, everybody just told us how good it was.

You went to France too, didn't you?
Yeah, a couple of times we did seminars in France. It was great, they're all massive memories for everyone. The night before one of them, me and Mel and Danniella snuck into the guys' room. Chris Cummins and Rob Nutley were asleep, so we painted their toenails with nail varnish and I think we put lipstick over Chris. He was in a dead sleep so he was really easy, but Rob woke up. It was funny, because the next day when we went down to the seminar there was no nail varnish remover, so they had to keep it on!

Weren't you were also part of Tongue 'n' Cheek entertainment, which did shows and demonstrations as Charlie's Angels?
Yeah. A lot of the demos that we did were like real-life situations. Say Mel and me would be acting as two women walking down the road – you know, on a late night out, having had a drink – and then some lager louts come up behind us, giving abuse and trying to molest us. We would use this pretend situation to display a few techniques and put them to the floor. We did things like showing women walking down the road with a buggy and getting harassed. A lot of stuff we did was from real life and we did a lot of fun stuff.

Don't tell the men – well, you can do – but they were really good, they were just so awesome at everything. When you look at these guys and how they teach and perform, they put all their heart and soul and their love into the Elite Fighting System. They don't just stand around as instructors, saying, "You do this and you do that." Whatever any of their students can do, they can do. None of them are boastful; none of them have ever shown off.

Tell me a bit more about the early days at Elite.
A lot of people that came into Elite were younger than us, like Rob Nutley and Richard Barker. A lot of them came in because they were street fighters, and wanted to fight anyone. They were 21 and 22 when they came, and now they're in their thirties and forties. It was Chris that brought them into it, he met them up at the Uni. That was the thing, it didn't matter where you went, you'd find a stranger and you'd bring them into the Elite.

Whenever we used to go down to Portsmouth for competitions there was a whole coach full of Elite people, down to support each other. They still do it, especially the original crowd – not so much the new fighters from Elite, who just want to come in and fight at Cage Rage, but the old guys come no matter what. If there was one fighter fighting there'd be a coach load going down. It was good. There was a fantastic atmosphere on those trips. We loved the fact that we were all going to be together and just have a really good time.

So Elite was the first ever mainstream MMA organisation in England?
Yes. When we started off we were street-style self-defence because, as well as the street techniques that we were taught and knew, there was also the kickboxing, the grappling and then the open combat. When we first used to compete it was just grappling, and we were trained in that so we went along and won. That was when I would compete. The grappling was just brilliant because it's so technical. We were cool unless we were up against some really tough black belt in jiu-jitsu. After about three years, David wanted to introduce the open combat to Elite. It was weird, because not a lot of people were trained in open combat and Elite just used to kick ass really. We'd just win and take home all the trophies.

So you started the first club in 1997, but when did it really become the Elite that we all know?
I think it was from our first demo in February 1998. It was a small demo at Peckham Square. Dave put out flyers and posters all over.

THE BEGINNING

You'd walk round south London – through Camberwell, Walworth, the Elephant and Peckham – and see all these posters. It was out in the open anyway, but gradually, as we started to perform, you could see the crowds that were coming in. The interest was just enormous. We knew, we were just buzzing from that moment on. It wasn't the only martial-arts demo, but when people heard about Elite they wanted to know more. We were loud and aggressive, we were tough and we were all in black. They wanted to know what was going on. When I think back to those things, it was brilliant. Then we started doing other demos, even school events, and it just went up and up and up to the point that we were getting double bookings.

When did the media start to take you seriously?
Back in 2001 there was an audition for *Masters of Combat*; David put Elite in for it. He used to read everything and anything to look for opportunities. Mel was pregnant then, so I went up as team leader with Chris, Rob, Richard and Manny. We put on this demo and I guess we could see they were pretty much impressed, but you don't get cocky. We felt good, we buzzed, whatever we did, we just thoroughly enjoyed it. So they got this brilliant feeling from us all as well. When we knew that we'd got through, *wow*, we were ecstatic, we were just jumping up and screaming – it was brilliant. After that there was this TV show each week, it was a knockout thing where two teams would compete against each other in a lot of endurance games. There were different things as well as just fighting. We were runners-up. After *Masters of Combat* they kept our contact number, because I work with children as well. The TV used me quite a bit actually for kids' stuff.

Eventually you had the *Richard and Judy* interviews.
Yeah, just as the Cage was starting to get some publicity. There was also that girl who's a top boxer, she was talking about her style and I was talking about the Elite. There was also an actress called Josie who had a role as a fighter. Without a doubt, Richard and Judy were interested in women fighting and doing martial arts for self-defence. At the time though, MMA was just seen as this big violent thing. There were two *Richard and Judy* shows actually. I remember Dave and me doing a demo on the second one. When they watched us they were impressed, because I kind of battered David. It was just so realistic, they thought I must have been really hurt and David must have been really hurt. But there

was a lot of controversy too. With David they were talking about the violence and they were just trying to twist whatever David was saying, going, "No, no, it's violent!" They weren't really interested. They got hold of an idea about this violent sport that had come to the UK. David was defending it with all his might.

Can you tell me a bit more about the women's side of things?
Years ago, Mel and I were interviewed for articles about women in the martial-art world. We've trained hard as well with men and our style is realistic, okay? The chances are that if a woman's out there, she's going to be attacked by a man or someone bigger than her, or whatever. Since doing this art I've become aware of where I am and what I'm doing. I don't feel like I'm invincible, but I always feel that I have a chance if anything happens. I have a lot of knowledge, and it gives me a kind of protection. I walk with confidence and I know I can look at a person and it doesn't matter how big he is, I can take that person to the floor or do something to that person. I've been training for ten years and I've learnt that it's about technique, not strength. From the beginning I knew that it didn't matter what size you were, that you could always have a chance.

What about the Millennium Sword?
Well, we'd gone in for this competition against all the top martial-art clubs. We were a bit concerned, but confident. It was the old team again, me, Dave, Steve, Aubrey and little Tom. We did this display and started with our marching – which is really powerful, *boof!* – to get everybody to stop and pay attention. We also used a lot of music. It was a lot of fun, it was just real-life situations made entertaining, we'd sort of compete against other teams. There was a team up there, the Black Belt something or other, who'd won this competition for the last however many years, and so we were a bit dubious about them. At the end of the day we were listening to the results, everybody was nervous because it was a big competition. We were all waiting and waiting and I remember it being really hard to hear, because the mic was a bit distorted. All I remember is hearing them say, "Elite Fighting System," and we just screamed and all ran out to these mats. I remember us all rolling breaks to the middle and just jumping up and down. We were on another planet, it was brilliant, such a buzz. That was the first time, in February 2001, that we were on the front of *Martial Arts Illustrated*, with Van Damme. It's still as fresh in everybody's

mind and still as exciting as it was then. Every time we meet we go over it, it's like an old record replaying.

So was the Millennium Sword the highlight for Elite?

Oh, what? Yeah, it was the highlight for Elite. It was the recognition as well. From that moment, although we were already growing, we just kept getting bigger. People wanted to come down and train with us, and invited us up to train with them. So yeah, it was brilliant.

So how did Cage Rage begin? Everyone knows about Cage Rage, but whose idea was it? Why that name?

It was David O'Donnell's idea. We were sitting up at David's place and we were racking our brains. Then he just said it: "I've got it, Cage Rage!" From that moment on, it just seemed perfect.

Did you ever think that Cage Rage would get as big as it did?

No, but David's really determined and knows what he wants, he wants to get somewhere. Whatever he loves he just puts his whole heart into it. He also moves with the changes and, although we were really big and people wanted to see us, the UFC was getting bigger in America too. Everybody was recognising that and paying attention to UFC. Then David just started thinking and putting things together, and that's where he was lucky because Andrew Geer was his boss. Andy sponsored us and really got into it, he wanted to support David and the club. He had a genuine interest in it. With Andy financing things, the first Cage Rage was planned for 7 September 2001. It started to change then. Prior to that, when we were with Elite, everything was sort of a family. [My husband] Mark would start introducing, "Ladies and gentlemen and families," and whatever, and he'd be the MC basically. And then, as the plans for Cage Rage went on, Dave was like, "Mark, you could be the commentator, the announcer." And Mark was like, "No, no, I can't." Eventually Mark went in there on the first day, 7 September, and he just did brilliantly.

Were other fighting combat schools around the country there to support Dave?

When we started we met people who were soft martial artists. The Elite style of self-defence on its own, oh my God, it looked violent, and so did Cage Rage! But some clubs understood. At first they were a little bit unsure, but as the years have gone on and the changes have been happening, more of the people from soft-style martial arts now incorporate mixed martial arts our way. It's hard. If anyone asked me if it's violent, I'd go, "Yeah, I suppose it is violent." No, I *know* it's violent. Full stop.

It's controlled though?

Yeah, it's a controlled violence, if you're trained. If you've got Billy No Mates coming out of the street, that's a different matter. When you're trained for it and you know what you're doing, it takes all that awful violence away. The thing is, every guy that goes in there knows what he's going in there for. It's just like boxing. There's a lot of respect. That's the nice thing as well. You know that in this hotel you've got fighters from across the world, fighters that have fought each other and torn each other, but you can guarantee that we'll have that opportunity at the end of the night where everybody can socialise and shake hands and talk about it. It is just amazing. All those people who are judgmental about the violence and whatever, they need to see a little bit more behind the scenes before they can judge. They need to know the people.

Are there other Elite clubs?

Since the original Elite, Chris Cummins has gone on to start another Elite club on the Old Kent Road in south London. So he teaches people for Elite, and even when he goes over to Barbados he teaches for Elite over there. Chris and I have both come out as instructors and so has little Paul. Paul 'Psycho' Griffiths was running a club out of west London, Chiswick way.

Did you keep what you were doing to yourselves, in the family?

No, whatever we did was never hidden. We wanted to share it with the whole world, because we were all really show-offs. What we were doing wasn't just a martial art, it was a real style. The way we live, you need to be prepared, and we showed how people *could be* prepared. Our attacks – whether they came from behind, whether they came with weapons – came from the whole street style. The original street style is so realistic and there's not another realistic club out there. If there is, it would be brilliant to see. Street-style self-defence is the realistic style that we need.

THE BEGINNING

Do you think more women should get involved?

I would really love to open women-only classes. There's nothing to stop me except time. I train twice a week, at Aubrey's class and at my original class with David at the Elephant. I teach children, too. I had to cut that down from twice a week to once a week, because my children do activities themselves – there's dancing, there's football. The Elite style is the best in the world. No one can tell me different, street-style self-defence is the best for women without a doubt. You haven't just got to tell me, you've got to prove to me that's there's better out there, because I've seen nothing. That's not being a shithead, that's me being realistic and that's me being here for ten years.

You don't fight these days?

I don't fight now because I know I can fight. I train cage-style. Also I've got family, I have children. Let's be realistic, we go in there and we're going to get bruised. I get that enough in training, let alone going in there for real fighting. I love Elite, it's one of the most important things in my life, but my family are more important. I don't want to look like a battered wife; if I walked down the street with a black eye, I wouldn't want people to think Mark had beaten me up. So you've got to think of that. If I didn't have children, then it would be totally different. My family's really suffered. My dad was having his 60th when we went to Portugal and had to change the date of his party, my sister changed her 18th, her 21st. Everybody knows about me when it comes to martial arts, *because* Elite is so important to me, it really is. It's in my blood and it's in my children's blood and Mark's blood, and the whole family's blood. I have the support of my whole family.

Dave O'Donnell has become a Cage Rage legend. I've been to one of his sessions and I can see the energy that comes from him.

Oh, without a doubt. It doesn't matter what money did or didn't come into this place, David's dream would have got there in the end because he's determined. Elite, Cage Rage, would never have been successful without David, his character, his personality, the person he is. There's no one out there like him. I'd never want David to be shut in the background, because he was the birth of Elite and he was the birth of Cage Rage.

WARRIORS OF THE CAGE

I see you have a tattoo of Elite.

Oh yeah, but I'm not the only person who's had an Elite tattoo. Many people have Elite – and the Elite eyes – tattooed on them. And that's fine. David's obviously got one, but I'm scared to say some names in case I forget others. That will be there forever and I know I'll never, ever regret that, it's in my blood.

When we all get together, away from Elite, where does the conversation lead? Elite and Cage Rage, without a doubt. Even though Joe O'Donnell's passed away, we get together to remember him. At Christmas we always go up to Bletchley Gardens [where Joe was cremated], the kids have helium balloons to let off for Joe, we sing 'Merry Christmas' and we make the most noise, because we're the loudest family on earth. Even when we try to talk about Christmas, we actually end up going on about Cage Rage and Elite and martial arts.

How did Cage Rage affect Elite?

Changes have to happen, but sometimes they cause a lot of sadness. When the first Cage Rage started it was the Elite guys that ran everything. As things got bigger obviously people had to come in, but the guys felt left out with regards to being part of Cage Rage. If you ask any of the originals now they'll all tell you they're not part of Cage Rage. We had an Elite tenth birthday last year that I organised. It was nothing to do with Cage Rage because that's become something different as well now. Elite was the old people, the old times, the old memories. It was important for me as well, that party – it doesn't matter who you are, it's about Elite and it always was. The changes came for a lot of people and we all talk about how we feel. In a way they do feel kind of gutted that the changes have affected them. Those guys don't come to train anymore and the only place that we do the original thing is at Aubrey's on a Monday, but those guys are north London guys. Aubrey's still there with the old style, and that's why I hang onto Aubrey as well. Then again, you never know what the future will be.

But the Elite Fighting System style is still in Cage Rage?

We've still got Elite guys fighting in Cage Rage. New fighters that come in and fight from Elite still get support from the old fighters, even if they fight in Cage Rage.

As we were about to go to press, the authors were informed by Lorraine that her husband, Mark Aplin, had sadly departed this life on Friday 4 September 2009. See Acknowledgements for our dedication to him.

STEPHEN QUADROS

Stephen Quadros is wearing a black suit and purple shirt. We find space to sit in a corridor between the various rooms where preparations for the fights are in progress. Despite the rising noise and excitement, 'the Professor' strikes a relaxed pose, one hand on his knee, sometimes swinging back and balancing the chair on its back legs.

Fighters are passing by on their way to and from medical checks and making their last-minute preparations. Individual voices can be heard rising above the background noise, shouts of "Legend!" and "James!" as fighters greet one another.

In the midst of this is a centre of controlled energy, a man in total possession of himself at all times. A man of passion. A hero with heroes of his own. A man still excited by his own achievements, who's delighted with the opportunities he's taken up. It's clear that he's glad to tell his story from the way he breaks into a smile, leans forward and warms to the interview.

You've been in this industry for a very long time now, long enough to become the Professor. How did this come about?
How did I start? Well, I started training in martial arts back in the 1970s and then I started with taekwondo and then into shotokan karate, more punchy than taekwondo. Then I trained in wing chun kung fu for a bit, and then I really wanted to kickbox. I joined a gym called the Jet Centre which was run by Benny 'the Jet' Urquidez, who was the world champion in kickboxing. Pete 'Sugarfoot' Cunningham was another world champion there and he was my primary instructor for five years.

I saw a videotape in the early 90s called *Gracie Jiu-Jitsu in Action*, where they would take the person down, punch them and then submit them with an arm-bar or a choke of some kind. I was fascinated and frightened by this particular tape, so I realised I had to add ground fighting and wrestling to my regimen. That's why I started to open up and train with different style fighters, wrestlers, jiu-jitsu people. Then I started to train fighters. One was Giovanni Lamb, who became a lightweight fighter in Southern California.

Were you already writing by this time?
No, it was after that I started to write articles for a lot of the magazines, like *Inside Kung-Fu*, *Grappling* and *Full Contact Fighter*. *Black Belt* magazine made me an offer, because I'd been the editor-in-chief of a magazine called *The Kick Boxing Ring Report* from 1993-1998. In 1998 I became a columnist and contributing editor at *Black Belt*, and I came up with the title of my column: 'Fightsport'. Of course, that name has been used by so many other people since then, but I guess I was the first person to use those two words put together. In 2001 the publisher of *Black Belt* offered me the chance to be the editor-in-chief of my own magazine, called *Black Belt Presents Fightsport with Stephen Quadros* .

You've also had a successful acting career.
In 1998, I got a part in a show called *Walker, Texas Ranger*, which starred Chuck Norris. This was the fourth or fifth season, and originally it was going to be the third or fourth episode of that season, but they liked it so much that they made my episode, 'The Fighting McLains', the season premiere! I was the guest lead and I was in almost every scene. I wore a cowboy hat! I played a Marine from Texas who came back to avenge the death of his sister caused by a drug dealer. I wasn't a bad guy. I was going to do it with my bare hands in hand-to-hand combat. I ended up fighting Chuck Norris in the very opening segment of that episode. I was so excited to work on that role because I fought the man who fought The Man, because Chuck Norris had fought Bruce Lee in *Enter the Dragon* in 1973. I was just ecstatic, I couldn't believe it. I got a lot of play on that, and it re-ran so many times that it was on almost every station at some point.

So, while I was starting *Black Belt Presents Fightsport with Stephen Quadros*, I was already doing fight choreography for movies. I did two movies for Warner Brothers Pictures, the first was *Exit Wounds* starring Steven Seagal. I trained Rapper DMX for that movie, up in Canada. In 2003 I trained DMX again for *From the Cradle to the Grave*, and had a very small part myself as a correctional officer in a prison. It was a movie with Jet Li, and I was really, really excited about working with him.

And then you became a commentator.
When I moved to *Black Belt* my stock rose a little bit. I was approached because I'd been a trainer, a fight choreographer and an

actor, and a lot of people felt that I should become a commentator.

My first show for K-1 [the Japanese kickboxing association] was in 1998 at Yokohama Arena. It was K-1 Kings and the main event was Peter Arts v Ernesto Hoos. This was just kickboxing, but that was the top of the line. Those two guys had fought three times and this was their fourth meeting. It was just the greatest thing! There was a lot of pressure on me, and I was just *so* nervous you wouldn't believe it, because I'd never commentated before although I was ready to start. I thought, "I'm in Japan, I'm in the world's biggest MA promotion!" This was before MMA had really taken off. So that was how I got started commentating. Then K-1 had a show in Las Vegas in August 1998 and I was the roving reporter. The other commentators were Don 'the Dragon' Wilson, Bruce Back (the former play-by-play commentator for the old UFC) and also Roy Jones Junior, so we had a really good broadcast team for the K-1 USA Inaugural Show. Then K-1 suspended their operation in the US, so I was without a job for a while, but Pride had started to contact me over the internet and, the next thing you know, I went to Pride.

Tell me about your time with Pride.
I went to cover an event at the end of 1999 – Pride 8, I think – for *Black Belt* magazine, and after that Pride hired me as commentator for the new American pay-per-view broadcasts. So at the opening round of the Pride Grand Prix 2000, I became play-by-play commentator for Pride Fighting Championships. I worked with Ken Shamrock and Bas Rutten. The finals of the Pride Grand Prix were in May 2000, and it was me, Bas Rutten and Maurie Smith. We had three great years working for Pride Fighting Championships. I was able to call the fights of Royce Gracie v Sakuraba, Wanderlei Silva, Mark 'the Hammer' Coleman winning the Pride Grand Prix. I was there at the beginning of Antonio Roderigo Minotauro Nogueira coming to Pride, him winning the title and then, later on, Fedor Emelianenko coming and taking the title from him. So I participated in what may have been the golden era of Pride.

Do you have other interests?
When I'm not commentating on fighting, apart from teaching kickboxing three times a week in Southern California, I pretty much try to relax. I also play drums in several different rock and roll bands. The funny thing was that, before I came to my first Cage Rage in February 2005, I'd just finished a book called *Moon: The Life and*

Death of a Rock Star about Keith Moon. I was always a big fan of his because he was a crazy showman and a wild drummer; he had a big influence on me. I finished this book and I sent an email to Dave and Andy and said, "Where are we gonna be staying?" and they said, "At Wembley Plaza." I said, "Wembley? That's where Keith Moon grew up!" I was freaking out! I was walking down the street in Wembley thinking, "I'm walking the streets in the same place where this legendary drummer, this madman, this comedian extra-ordinaire, one of the world's greatest drummers, walked. I was also influenced by the drummer for Cream, Ginger Baker, and Mitch Mitchell, John Bonham, Ian Paice of Deep Purple, along with great drummers from the US like Tony Williams, Buddy Rich and Billy Cobham, when he was with the Mahavishnu Orchestra. My goal was always to be the world's greatest rock and roll drummer. Some people might actually think that I am, but sometimes I get out of practice so I'm just another bum like everybody else! But I do love playing drums.

Currently I'm in four bands. My primary band right now is Modern Life Crisis (MLC). I also have Whipped Cream, which is a Cream tribute band. I'm also in Sacred Cowboys, and an offshoot of MLC, the Becky Cruise Band, which is me, the bass player from MLC, the guitar player from Whipped Cream and the guitar player's mother, who's a really good soul and R&B singer who sings like Aretha Franklin meets Tina Turner. I play drums to relax, and it's a great cardiovascular workout, especially when you're kicking double bass! I really work up a sweat! They say the drummer usually gets all the girls; I don't know if that's entirely true in my case, but I try and make a statement: I try to twirl my sticks, throw them up in the air and catch 'em. I try and draw as much attention to myself as possible, so that the women in miniskirts with really, really beautiful bodies will approach me and strike up an innocent conversation after the gig.

What's your personal philosophy?
We're not dogs, we're different from dogs. In our minds we may think like dogs, I know I do sometimes. My philosophy is very simple: if it feels right inside, well, then it is right – as long as it's within the law. Of course, if we see a beautiful woman and we're very attracted to her she could be with somebody else, or she might not be into you, or not interested in you, so you have to take that into consideration. Also, in dealing with people in business and in

relationships, there's the golden rule – I think it's from the Bible – "Do unto others as you would have them do unto you." I think that's a really good rule and a good starting point for a philosophy, because all of us have interactions. When we get into a taxicab we have interaction with the cab driver, when we buy food in a restaurant, pay for a service, meet people and become friends they're all relationships, whether they're deep or shallow.

I also believe in a few of the Ten Commandments from the Bible: "Thou shalt not kill," "Thou shalt not covet thy neighbour's wife," and "Honour thy mother and thy father" are important. I'm not the most religious person in the world. In some ways, some interpretations of religion have caused people to be more separate than together, so I really like and respect people from pretty much all walks of life and all religions. I try to be in harmony with people. I do a lot of travelling. Even though I'm from the United States, I consider myself a citizen of the world.

What else do you believe in?
I believe in being sensitive to other people. Sometimes humour and morals can seem to be diametrically opposed. If a person says, "I'm gonna make a joke about white people," then the white people are gonna get offended, or some people might get offended by a joke about women, or a joke about a certain religion. Then jokes go into moral ground. Morals are, I think, respect for other people, so if a joke would offend the people I'm with I wouldn't tell it.

When it comes to the opposite sex, we all wanna get together with women, we all wanna have sex. We all do. Women even wanna have sex, I hear. I've heard a rumour that women like to have sex. I've been investigating this rumour for the last 25 years, and my studies have been varied because different women like different sexual positions. I've tried many of these sexual positions, but morally speaking – and I'm not gonna get too technical here on the sexual angle, because that'll come in *my* book later on – I think that if it's two consenting adults and everyone is above the legal age and there's no one who's cheating on someone else, then it's all good.

WARRIORS OF THE CAGE
DAN SEVERN

Dan Severn has been involved in UFC since 'no holds barred' first hit the American scene. A former amateur wrestler, Dan exploded onto the scene when he beat Royce Gracie. His reputation was made and his career moved from strength to strength. Over the years he has won just about every title going, so it's not surprising that he now runs one of the most acclaimed training camps in the USA. His energy and commitment are infectious and his motivational skills are unparalleled.

Why do you fight?
Well, I can't sing or dance, so I had to express my inner child in a different way. The truth of the matter is that when I was first exposed to the Ultimate Fighting Champions, when it was known as no-holds-barred, I looked upon it as a test of skills. Do I possess the skills as an amateur wrestler to get to them before they get to me? Mixed Martial Arts has 37 rules. No-holds-barred had two: that you could not bite your opponent, nor could you poke them in the eyes. Those were the rules. As long as you didn't bite him or stick a finger in his eye, you were good to go. There were no weight classes, there were no time periods. And it was bare-knuckled action, no gloves.

How do you react emotionally to a fight?
I don't get too worked up hearing what an audience feels, or become emotional if I'm being shaken up by an opponent.

How do you go into a fight?
I've had doctors check my blood pressure and heart rates and they think that I should be asleep! They can't believe how calm and reserved I remain. It's because I've been a competitor for so long, I've done so many matches. I've done as many as 17 matches in one day. Most people only know Dan Severn through his Mixed Martial Arts and no-holds-barred career, but that is a very small segment of my life. I started in 1994 at 37 years of age, an age when most people would have retired.

Is there money to be made in MMA?
When I first began it was pretty small. My guarantee for walking out there was $1,000. And for that I was willing to sign a contract that stated in black and white that we were each worth $1,000 in the

event of accidental death. So although I didn't stick my thumb in people's eyes or bite them, I could have taken someone's life out there. We all signed that contract willingly, but again I don't see myself really as a fighter but as a competitor. It's a whole different mindset.

What else do you do, away from fighting?
I convert my hobbies into businesses. I work a long day, but I like what I do and not too many people can say that.

Are you spiritual?
I believe everyone has their own spirituality.

And yours is?
I'm a conservative man.

How do you see MMA developing over the next ten years?
I think we'll have more corporate sponsors jumping on board. I think the purses will be moving much more in line with those for other athletes. Fighters should be getting paid like other athletes and not what a company is willing to pay them. So, as a few more companies emerge, it will be a good thing for the athletes and they will have more opportunities.

If your children wanted to be fighters, what would you say?
I would want them first to pursue their normal sports through their junior highs, their high schools and in college. After graduation, if they wanted to pursue something like this, I would probably just be supportive – but only if they end up having the right training. I do have a current crop of young athletes who I train, both professional and amateur, and I watch over them as an extension of my family.

MALCOLM MARTIN

Malcolm was born in Bradford-on-Avon, Wiltshire in 1960. As a boy he trained in karate, taekwondo and kickboxing, in which he also competed. As a competitor, trainer and renowned kickboxing commentator, Malcolm – together with his colleague Steve Holdsworth – was the natural choice when Dave O'Donnell was seeking a commentator for the first Cage Rage coverage on Sky. Although he claims that those early commentaries were 'dire', there's no doubt that he helped to create the style that fans expect to hear today.

Malcolm claims that his main contribution to the sport has been his written (rather than spoken) commentary, but he was there at the beginning of UK MMA and is there still. He has worked as a journalist, as the editor of *Combat* and *Fighters* magazines and in television. His latest ventures have included writing and directing a full-length feature film, *Sucker Punch*.

Can anyone be a fighter?
It's the great equaliser. It doesn't matter about your background. All that matters is that 15 minutes in there against the other person. You start with an even playing field. It's just the two of you. That's why, although people complain about the brutality, to me it's the purest sport because it's two men pitting themselves against each other.

It's like one language?
Exactly, it is. It's a universal language.

You mean it's you and them and there's nothing else? There are no barriers, no limitations?
That's the purity. There's no going back in the changing room and saying, "The goalie let us down." There's no going back in the changing room and saying, "The centre forward missed a sitter." It's two men, one objective. When you look at the history of man you know that we're hunter-gatherers. Throughout history, hunting's been the purest form of men proving themselves. It's not about your opponent, it's about yourself. The thing you mentioned earlier that I loved is you can have been to jail, you can have come from anything, but you can become something different in the cage. No one sets limitations on you in that cage except yourself. That's the purity of it, that's the great thing about it. You can become what you want within those confines.

What do you think inspires people to continue being fighters?
Different things for different people. I've known fighters my whole adult life, and some people just love fighting and inflicting pain. It's horrible to say, I know. The reasons are as diverse as people

themselves. If you look at people on the street, how would you imagine that any one of those people could mug an old woman? You and me wouldn't dream of doing that. How can someone else do that? They can though, because we're all different, and it's the same in the cage. I've known fighters that have got in there because they like to hurt people and they can do it legally. By the same token, a large percentage of fighters go in there for one reason alone – to conquer their own fears and prove their own ability. The other person is not the opponent, the other person is the test.

Do you think that only a certain type of person would take up MMA?

We accept that certain young men want ultimate challenges. I mean, I know it's called Ultimate Fighting and I agree with that. When you look at the confines of boxing, you've got strict parameters: above the waist, just your hands. These young men have got a certain mindset: to be the best they can be, to prove themselves, to conquer and to say, "I am a man." The bottom line is, where do you get a purer test of that and a purer proof of that? The money and the getting away from problems is a side effect of that. When they ask why people do it, I don't think some people choose to do it. Some people with that warrior nature *have to* do it. Let's be blunt – throughout history fighting has been the norm: sides, countries, territories, it's always been that way. I think that is genetic. I think that gene remains left over in us. In some men, it's not about wanting to fight, it's not about, "I want to do this or that," it's that it's primeval, they can't explain it but they have to do it. And if you have to, where's purer than the cage?

Do you think that MMA could be a diversion for criminals?

I think it's similar to boxing in the early days. It's showing frustrated young men, who might think they've got no prospects, a reason not to turn to crime. I'm not saying it's converting criminals, I'm saying it's stopping young men becoming criminals. Now we could talk politics, but at the end of the day those young men look in the mirror and say, "What's out there for me, where are the outlets?" I'm saying MMA can stop young men becoming criminals by giving them another outlet. There's now genuine money for fighters if they want it. There's an alternative. When people try to ban the sport, they need to look beyond their narrow ideas and see the greater good that MMA can do for these young men. It serves just as purposeful a function and we know – we *know* – that it's actually safer than boxing.

What do you think that the future of MMA will be?
The heavyweight boxing champion of the world used to be thought of as 'The World's Hardest Man'. Trust me, within ten years or less that idea won't be associated with boxing anymore. The biggest test of who is the world's hardest man will be in the cage. I think the type of hard man that wants to fight, that needs to test himself and prove himself, will be in an octagon.

ANDY GEER

Andy Geer is a long-time associate of Dave O'Donnell, and has always been a fan of MMA. He is a successful businessman, who helped to take the original British MMA to the heights. At the peak of Cage Rage, Andy and Dave went into partnership with an American company, but this venture was less successful than everybody hoped. It's been difficult for Andy to tear himself away from MMA, though. He's still on the scene, sharing his experience and knowledge with promoters and fighters.

You're a successful businessman. Why do you use your energies in MMA?
Well, MMA was my sport. I used to train. Dave O'Donnell was my instructor and it was just a passion of ours really. I was training in MMA before most people in the martial-art world knew what MMA was. When shows started to crop up over here, Dave was putting lads into these fights and the shows were really poorly organised. There were bad match-ups. We honestly thought we could do better than that. For Cage Rage 1 there was no business plan, there was no nothing, we just wanted to raise some money for our club. That was the one and only reason for Cage Rage 1. Just money on the night.

Tell me about the rise and fall of one of the UK and Europe's biggest MMA organisations.
After Cage Rage 1 we got some media interest and did another one. I decided to look on it as a business more than just a hobby and my sport. I was too old to compete, too unfit. I'm an office

boy now and carry a bit too much around the middle. I decided that, with Dave's enthusiasm and my planning skills and finances, I could see a business here. So we went on and brought in another partner around about Cage Rage 6. We just stuck to the business plan. We got the Sky deal, then the other TV deals and the live television deal at Sky. At the height of Cage Rage we were Sky Sports' highest viewed show outside of soccer. We sold on to over 50 countries all over Europe. We were live on CBS in the USA on time delay. It was massive. We were live in New Zealand, Australia, United Arab Emirates and Dubai. Our DVD sales were huge. We sold out Wembley Arena, we did Earls Court and the NEC. It was massive, really good. And then we sold it to the Americans. They're absolutely incompetent. I'm always a straight talker, but the guys we sold it to just absolutely drained the cash out of it. They cut the advertising and marketing. Despite me flying to LA regularly and telling them that you can't increase sales without them. That's suicide. They bust it, they broke it.

What people don't realise when they're at a show is that, when it runs right, it's great for a promoter and is the best night you'll ever have. But it's three months of shit and stress leading up to it, and weeks afterwards on the debriefs and the financial aspects. It's really hard work, particularly at the level that Cage Rage was at. We used to produce the television shows as well, as a separate deal. Dave and I were the only people that Sky television let produce our own shows. Dave and I used to write every minute of that two-hour show. Then we had to control all these lorries that used to come with technical people, camera crews and directors. It was real hard work and we're really proud of what we did. But I wouldn't recommend it.

What about the rebirth?
I'm not involved. Dave O'Donnell decided that it's the only business for him and he's got the rebirth. He'll build it up again. I have absolute 100 percent faith in him. There'll be another show as big as Cage Rage. I decided to focus on my other businesses that have been steady all my life. I lived the dream for a few years and it was a great ride. Very stressful, but it was a great ride

Does MMA pay fighters as well over here as it does in the USA?
When Cage Rage was at its height we were paying more money than the UFC was, except for their superstar. The big UFC fighters were

earning hundreds of thousands of dollars a fight with big sponsorship deals as well. Our under-card fighters were earning more than their mid-card fighters. But we didn't have the pay-per-view money, which we're never going to get in Europe. That's the secret of the UFC's success. Well, that and the Ultimate Fighter TV show that I wrote, and they stole that idea from me because I didn't copyright it. It was very early in my television career then and I didn't realise, so shit happens. UFC was always going to win the fighter thing.

How well do UK promoters take care of fighters after fights?
At MMA we did have a lot of medical staff and the medics were backstage as well, in the dressing rooms. There were post-fight checks. I've been to some smaller shows and it's absolutely appalling how fighters get treated, sometimes there's been no doctors, no proper medical. On the whole I think there still needs to be some improvement. I think people are just looking at the money on the night. In the early days of Cage Rage we invested the money to make bigger bucks. It's too tempting for promoters to cut that extra £1,000 medical expense off their nightly costs, they're cutting it in the wrong areas. One serious injury or one person reportedly not being looked after properly will finish the sport in this country overnight.

Why do you think that the UK media were strongly against MMA but are now slowly coming to terms with it?
I think it was always lack of understanding. Because there's been a few movies around in the past, and a few shady books about cage fighting. In the old bare-knuckle days, what used to happen around the back of kitchen camps, to save the fights going from one side of the field to another, was that they actually used to make a cage out of that arris rail fencing you see outside building sites. They used to block and mesh this little area so the fights could stay contained. That got known as 'cage fighting'. It was, of course, completely illegal, completely unregulated. They still wore boots and all sorts. So when the name cage fighting was associated with MMA, people thought it was unregulated, bare-knuckle fighting. Some of these people in the media are so close-minded, they wouldn't even listen. I did the rounds on the news, on the radio, in the newspapers, trying to convince people that it's a relatively safe sport. It's a contact sport, but it's still safe. Each

time we got someone there, they came round a bit. We got the *News of the World* sitting ringside and they became fans. We took people down the gym and showed them the training. We used to roll with them and show them how skilful all these guys are that are fighting. Once you get someone to that stage where they're willing to open their mind, 99 percent of them are convinced.

Do you think MMA can be a good outlet for young people?
Hell, yeah. We get these kids in the gym all the time. I still train even though I'm a fat, wheezy old man in the corner. I've seen so many people, from bouncers to rugby players to boxers, come in the gym. You get it all out of your system. We've found generally that people who can fight properly don't fight on the streets. They've got nothing to prove.

DAVE O'DONNELL

I'm near Sidcup, Foots Cray High Street, Dave O'Donnell's head office. I've arranged to meet him at 2:00 and arrived around 12:40pm. I'm well early, outside a Tudor cottage, facing a number of doors. I hear a voice through one of them saying, "Don't worry about it," followed by a cackle of laughter. I must have guessed the right door.

Facing me are Dave and his associate, Tony Colasanto. The walls are covered with fight posters and bills featuring everyone in the game, including Royce Gracie. What grabs my attention is a picture of Dave and his boy, and their obvious love and affection. Dave is not just a businessman; he's a truly adoring family man.

While Dave is busy with telephone calls and emails, Tony rubs some cream on the tattoo on his right arm. Really, he's just trying to show off his 18-inch biceps as we talk. I pick up *Fighters Only* magazine: Mark Weir, Ian Freeman, Michael Bisping, Dave O'Donnell and Lee Murray are all on the front cover – good ol' British beef.

I'm no match for this guy Dave. He's been around a long time, trained with some of the best guys in the world and still teaches classes. I guess you're wondering about how old he is, but he doesn't have a single grey hair. But hey, I haven't come here to fight. I'd lose anyway; even though I know that pain is temporary and victories last forever, I'm not up for it.

Dave and Andy are the major promoters in MMA. In my terms they're the puppet masters – they've got all the right puppets, in a world full of muppets.

Does MMA training need to be started early? What could the government and local authorities do to support this?

Local authorities have always been behind boxing. It's time to open up their eyes and go. MMA is the sport that all the kids are starting to go to; not wrestling – MMA. Three weeks ago we opened a gym in Eltham, south London, and last night we had 16 kids there. We've got a tot there, four years old. The oldest is 14. A lot of the parents say that the kids have got too much energy, they want energy taken out of them. It's alright sending the kids to karate classes, marching up and down, but they're getting no contact. A lot of the kids like putting on a pair of gloves, hitting pads, grappling with each other. If you look at kids together, you'll see that they grapple with each other, they wrestle. They don't know what they're doing though. If you can teach them that as a sport, like judo, it's better for them. Kids like judo because it's a very combative sport. You teach them early that it's alright to lose in the gym, and that they don't have to start crying. You've got to try and build up the discipline; I've always taught that when I say "stop" that means stop, and that teaches them discipline. "Stop," "start," "you can't do," "you must do." It starts building in them from early. That's why I believe that they can do anything as long as they're taught the right way. Kids can do all sorts of stuff.

Do you think that MMA training could help to keep young people away from street crime?

I believe that it could take street crime right the way down. There are so many centres all around Tottenham, Peckham, everywhere. If you put kids into this kind of fighting, they see a goal and think, "You know what? I could be a star, I could be like Mike Bisping or Wanderlei Silva." The worst thing about kids and testosterone and drinking and all that is the aggression. Everybody's built up with aggression inside them. Whether you like it or not, most people have got it. You need to find an outlet for it, like a pressure-release valve. What MMA or a good combat sport does is makes you tired. You're exhausted, you're hitting pads. You get this surge of release.

I was an angry person when I was younger, very angry. If I didn't have my two hours of fighting every other night, I would be full of aggression, all of a sudden glaring at people while driving, not very happy. When I'm driving home from training I have butterflies around my little head, I'm singing to myself. That's because I've released it all. For those two hours all the worries go away and I feel like a new person. It's like recharging my batteries. Yes, the worries come back the next day. It's not like going to the gym. If you go to a gym and pump weights, all you're doing is pumping more aggression into you. People don't realise that. When you're exhausted on a mat and you've let out the aggression by hitting and getting hit, you don't want to go out and start more fights. You want to shake people by the hand, give them a cuddle. Trust me – that's why a lot of fighters ain't going out and starting fights, they're walking away from it because they do all their fighting in the gym. If half the kids on the street were doing that, the world would be a much safer and better place to be.

You've been to the top and fallen. What inspires you to continue?

I've been to the top? I wouldn't even say I've been to the top. I do my job and I really enjoy it. I promote. I never intended to be a promoter, I was always a trainer, but I've always looked after fighters. I've put people in big places, and I've never taken a penny off them. As a promoter, I could get a guy and then go, "Right, I'm going to sell him to XYZ." Have a look at my record: I haven't sold one fighter. I've made fighters, but there's no way I've taken a tanner off one fighter. What I've done is push our brand, Cage Rage, so it went to the top. Great promotions, that's what we aimed to do, push it to a certain level and then sell it on to a big American organisation. Unfortunately for us, we got hoodwinked. I was a millionaire for a day and then it all went Pete Tong. But that's the way things go. You learn at the same time. With promotion now I keep my feet thoroughly on the ground, but we're enjoying it more. We're working – I think we're working a lot smarter. It may become such a big promotional operation that UFC will be saying, "Gee, I didn't realise how high you were going to rise." We've got our good deals with TV stations, so hopefully this time we'll make no mistakes, or only very little ones!

Fans sometimes think that promoters arrange fights just to sell tickets knowing that it's an unfair match. Why do some fighters get a show and others don't?

The better fighters don't always get on the shows. Sometimes, some of the more rubbish fighters who sell a load of tickets do get on. The reason for this is to keep the sport alive. I've sat in arenas where the so-called promoters have said, "We'll promote country versus country." And I say to the guy, "Yeah, but you've got eight fighters from Germany fighting eight of the best British fighters from all around the country, but they're not from the town where the venue is. How do you expect to sell tickets?"

Our sport is still in a minority. When you've sat down and you've got 120 people in a 2,000-seat arena, you're looking around going, "Mate, it doesn't work!" What we've learned to do is look for fighters who are ticket sellers. If I'm promoting in London and a fighter says to me, "Dave, I think I can shift 100 tickets," and another guy who's a better fighter but from Birmingham is saying he can't sell any tickets but he's a great fighter, my advice to that fighter is find a show in Birmingham where you can *be* a great fighter. When the show sells out itself without any help from the fighters, then I can pick the best fighters from around the country. Until that point, I've still got to have ticket sellers locally to build a show up, there's no other way of doing it. All good promoters will tell you that.

And all that FX3: perfect promotion; UWC: perfect promotion. You go to their events, banged out all the time. You go to Ultimate Challenge, banged out all the time. There are some promoters around the country who've got no idea of what they're promoting. They're still living in the dream of, "We've got the best fighters, it will attract thousands." No, it doesn't. For the ticket sales we've had See Tickets, we've had Ticketmaster, and you look at the way the tickets go up and down. The fighters still sell the bulk of the tickets. Until the point when you're on TV every time and people go, "Oh, Ultimate Challenge is coming to town," it's, "I've got these fighters . . ." "I don't care, we're just going to see the show." We knew from Cage Rage: you could have Butterbean coming over, or Wanderlei Silva, and you'd still struggle to sell tickets.

Is there anything you would change in the MMA rules and regulations?

It's not like America, where sometimes you hear that a lot of places go right over the top. For us, we sit down here, we do risk assessment, make sure the ambulance crews, doctors and medics have got the right qualifications. We try to put the best in and make sure that the rules are implemented. We don't want any serious accidents inside or outside the show. That means we have to keep an eye out for hooligans and that sort. If I saw one guy selling 400 tickets, I'd think, "Whoa, there could be a problem here." We've got to limit the amount of tickets sold to one person, because if you don't know that guy he could be a football hooligan. So we limit what could go wrong inside the arena, or stadium. As for the rules on fighters' safety checks, in England we have been at the forefront all the time. Our team is always trying to lead the way. Yet people don't like it if they're on the juice. At the end of the day, let's make the fights fair. Get the fighters steroid-tested, get them blood-tested. We need to have good doctors and good medics on site.

As a promoter, what do you feel would improve the UK MMA industry?

We need a sports council or an MMA management council, which at the moment I'm still trying hard to establish. My idea is still to create BAMMA, the British Association of Mixed Martial Arts. It was tried about five years ago, but failed. We've re-bought all the domain names. Trying to get everybody under an umbrella. People say, "Oh yeah, but you want different rules." No, I don't, I want safety for the fighters. Dana White [president of the USA's Ultimate Fighting Championships, or UFC] is a miracle worker. What he's done for the sport is amazing. People say, "I don't like him" – mate, to me he's another guy who took the sport to a different level because he had the money to do it. I took the sport to a different level too. I haven't got the money, but maybe it's coming. I don't use elbows on the ground because we don't pay the fighters enough to be cut open from an eyebrow, or a nose cut, and for that fighter to be unable to fight for months. Fighters want to keep active. It's not because I don't like elbows; I love elbows, but we don't pay the fighters enough to take elbows on the ground. Why don't I put five-by-five-minute rounds in my fights for our champions? Are our champions getting the same money as the UFC champions? Have a look at the pay packets. No, they're not. So why take a fighter who's probably a chippie or a bricklayer and make him train for five-by-five-minute rounds? He's getting one or two thousand pounds, compared to a top champion in the UFC who's getting half a million. You tell me, am I being fair or am I not being fair? I'm looking after the fighters. Maybe they can see it, maybe they can't, but that's what I'm doing.

Why do you think the UK organisations haven't collaborated, like in other sports, to achieve recognition for MMA?
Like what other sports? Do you know how many associations there are for some sports? Boxing is the biggest sport in the world. You couldn't even name the boxing associations on one hand. MMA would be the same. Even with the UFC, you've got Affliction, you've got Dream. You'll always get different associations and they will each believe that their way is the best and that they're going to be the next multi-billion WWE. It's good rivalry to a certain extent. People need to be able to choose. I like UFC, Pride, Cage Rage, Cage Warriors, Ultimate Challenge. Normally the better one will win, or the guy with the most money will win. Everybody working together? I don't think so! I'm just a realist, that's what I've always been. I do work with a lot of promoters. I don't go in and sabotage and badmouth people, but some people do that to me. What am I expected to do? I'll try with BAMMA to bring people together. But If I start saying, "Guys, look, this is good, don't have elbows in there, protect the fighters," they go, "No, we want to be like UFC." Straight away you've got a controversy. What do you do? Do you stick to your guns or do you invite them in and have more arguments? The trouble is too many chiefs, not enough Indians, and it all goes to pot. And that will always be the way. That's why I want to be a fight manager, it's where a lot of the money is

2

The Fighters

In the old days, when there were no doctors, no ring girls and just fields, streets and backyards, a fight only needed competitors and sometimes a few people to cheer them on. As the years have passed, despite the fact that we now have the doctors, paramedics, glamour girls, prestigious venues and big business, it still boils down to two men: the fighters.

These days, it's all very well purchasing a ticket to see a number of bouts governed by rules and with a referee who ensures the safe ending of the contests – be it by submission or TKO. But there's a danger that the fighters themselves will be forgotten amid the excitement of the event.

I travelled across Britain to meet, question and listen to the fighters. The warriors whom I'd interviewed are from all walks of life. None of them are barbarians – in fact, they are committed sportspeople and athletes. I wanted to know where they came from, what their backgrounds, education and upbringing had been like. I heard the most unexpected stories – tales of difficult childhoods, prison, drug deals and war. Some still carry psychological scars from their childhoods. Some have had their self-confidence shattered and have had it rebuilt through their involvement with MMA. Others have witnessed terrible things, have suffered disappointments and loss. Most have made sacrifices for the sport, and have caused their loved ones to make sacrifices too.

One thing that all the fighters have in common is that they each have aspirations. Some do MMA as a part-time activity and are pursuing their ambitions via education or through businesses. The rest are seeking to fulfil their dreams through MMA itself – they want championships, belts and long careers as fighters and trainers. All the fighters, regardless of their backgrounds or beliefs, want to be happy and to do their best by their family, friends and other fighters.

I learnt a lot on this journey, including to never underestimate the power of MMA.

ROBERT 'BUZZ' BERRY

King's Cross station, London, 7.45 am, January. It's just starting to get light, and I'm on my way north, so I'll be in the twilight for a while yet. Final check: ticket, phone, wallet, address, directions, Ribena, tape recorder and copy of the last Cage Rage programme in case the scenery gets dull over the next three hours. I'm on my way to what used to be the industrial north-east of England. Nowadays it's more famous for Durham Cathedral than anything else. The coalmines in Ferryhill closed at just about the time that Buzz was born – a lucky turn, some might think, but not those communities who relied on mining for their living. Ferryhill has produced few famous sportsmen since the work disappeared – former England and Ipswich Town footballer Eric Gates, Phil Nixon, the 2007 Lakeside darts finalist, and most recently Robert 'Buzz' Berry, whose profile just keeps growing.

Buzz was born and bred in the village of Ferryhill, just outside Durham, long before they moved the A1 to the east and it became a motorway. I'm looking forward to what he has to say about how the place has changed since he was a boy, and how growing up there led him into the cage. He's offered to meet me at the station, which I'm glad of, because this place is a long way from north London and I'm not sure I'd understand their accents if I had to ask directions. Wherever we go to talk, I'm hoping it's going to involve food. I wonder if they eat much rice and peas around here?

Buzz is waiting at the top of the platform, the light behind him, and I recognise him from his outline 50 yards before I'm anywhere near his face. Standing 6'3" without his boots, and weighing in at 114 kg, he's a noticeable presence. Apart from his size and obvious fitness, he looks like a regular punter: black combats and t-shirt, trainers, rolled-up newspaper and a gold band. This is clearly a man who makes commitments and sticks to them, in his home life as well as in his fighting career. He raises the paper to me, two people near him duck, and before I'm even close enough his right hand shoots out to shake mine. What a vice of a grip!

We leave the station and heave to in a café a few turnings away. It's traditional – more bacon sarnie than rocket salad – but then, it gets cold up north.

How did your association with MMA begin?

I used to work on the doors. I've worked on the doors since I was 18 years old. One of the lads who worked for me was very good pals with Ian Freeman. We found out from Ian he was going to be fighting down at Milton Keynes. So we bought tickets and booked a hotel. We were going down to watch him. Then Ian got invited to fight in the USA at the same time. We thought, well, we've got the tickets, we'll go down and watch the show. So we went down and enjoyed it. Peter McQueen taught Ian how to fight at that time, so when he started teaching in my village I thought I'll go along and learn jiu-jitsu as I'm working the doors.

You wanted to be tougher than the bloke who comes up to you on the door?

No, no, no, I've never been like that. From 18 years old I've always known I can fight. I've always known I'll go outside with anybody. That's never bothered me that way. I went along to McQueen's classes and he'd show a technique and then we'd pair up and you'd have to try and put the lock on. Then two minutes' grapple. Then he'd say, "Right, change partners." I used to think, "Hold on, I'll get my breath back." So I thought I'd drop weight and come down to just under 19 stone. I'd been learning jiu-jitsu for about three months, and a lot of the time then it was my strength that was getting me out of trouble. We had a grappling tournament down in Colburn and I won the heavyweight division – even though I'd only been doing it three months and it was only my strength that helped me through. So after the win I wanted to go on and on.

What do you think about fighters who have that thing about being macho?

One of my friends now teaches in a gym near where I live and the young 17-18 year olds are all up and coming, but they're all for this macho thing. So I've said to my mate, "You're teaching them, but don't teach young people that. If they're going to go out on the street and use their knowledge, then I won't be happy and I'll come round and see them." You see, I don't want them abusing the power and knowledge. But they've got to go through that process and if they become sportsmen, that's good.

Do they have to go through it? Can you direct them in a way where they don't have to?
I include myself in that, we all go through it. I changed 100 per cent while learning jiu-jitsu. It changes how you cope with people. Once, if someone would come over to me when I was a doorman and say, "Get round the back," I would have gone. Now that I'm a trained fighter, I'd rather say, "Go and have a drink." If somebody was going to take a punch at me I would probably step back and say, "Don't do that." If he carried on doing it, I'd probably take them to the floor and hold them and say, "Look, you, I'm giving you your last chance. You get up again and take a punch, you're going to get hurt, so go home." But once upon a time, I'd just go outside. Now, because I know what I can do with people, what would I be proving? I'd be proving myself a bully, that's what I'd be doing.

Were you bullied at school?
Yeah. Five or six of them used to chase me all the time. Sometimes when I'd be out at night I used to get to my front door, where there was a passageway along the side. I knew if I went in the house I wouldn't be able to come back out, so I'd go in the passageway, shut the door and hide until the boys went and then go back out and play. So yeah, I was bullied at school.

They weren't tough guys, they were bullies.
One to one I could beat every one of them, but they were all a decent size and when there were four, five or six of them, I was getting a hiding.

You must have had macho pride or whatever you want to call it. You don't think that way anymore?
No, because I know what I can do and so now I can choose. So I tend to think, well, it makes me a better man when I choose not to be like that.

THE FIGHTERS

Does thinking that way calm you and change the way people look at life?

It depends how people are brought up. You get some lunatics who've been like dragged up, not brought up, and they get into this macho thing and carry it on. People out there who are doing that, they'll use that in whatever way, shape or form they can. You'll never change those blokes because they want to be hard. Ten per cent of them out there use it in the wrong way.

How do you define a tough guy away from the cage?

I'm from old school, expecting fighters to be like hard men from the village. In the olden days you always used to hear them talking, saying they'd go outside. They'd have their set-to; they'd come back in and have a drink. I've never held a grudge or anything. It's a case of, "Well, it's over now, let's have a drink." There was one time a few years ago when one of my pals had a fight with his missus. There was an England game on and we'd been on the drink. We'd been out all day. He was in the pub and tipped a drink all over his missus. So I grabbed hold of him and I took him outside. I said, "You calm yourself down."

Outside there were two skinheads from near the village – proper bullies – two brothers that all the little village boys looked up to. Anyway, I'm trying to calm my friend down, and they were looking at us and laughing. So he said, "Give up my arms," because he wanted to have a set-to with them. They had a set-to and they beat my friend. One was on top of my friend, banging him in the head. I had to help my mate, he couldn't get up. I pulled one off, but as I did, his brother came up. So they both squared at me and I caught blows left and right. There were two of them, so I banged them. Put one down, the other one took a swing. That's when I took my punch, because I'd been out on the drink. We both connected and it was over in seconds. Straight away I went in the bar, and the police came and what have you. They took my mate to hospital and asked me what happened, and I told them. So they took one of the brothers to the police station, the other one went home. The following day I said to my friend, "Tell them I want no more, let's have a pint, let's forget about it." I don't like to carry things on. But the two brothers, they've never been like that. They've always been bullying, macho types.

What was your ambition before MMA?

I used to play football. I've played football all my life. I always used to say, "I dread the day I ever have to pack this game in." I've been a doorman all my life as well, and when I took this jiu-jitsu up I was still playing football, even when I was fighting. One day I thought, "Well, if it comes to the case now that I get hurt playing football, I can't fight." So then it didn't bother me as much when I had to pack the football in because I was doing something else that I enjoyed.

Have you ever been in trouble with the law?

Just silly driving offences. When I was a kid, drunk once, but there's never been anything major, no.

Are you religious? Do you believe in God or a higher being?

I don't go and pray. I don't go to church or anything like that. I've always left it alone. I didn't want to go to church. I've never ever really spoken about it. In my mind I've never been a one to talk about going to church. No.

Why do you fight?

It's just something I've always put my skills to. When we fight, it's in a cage, it's all legal, it's nothing illegal. We don't say that we're going in there to maliciously clobber or try to cause damage. We're just going in there to win the fight. It's not really the mission to hurt the guy, it's testing our skills really. Yes, you do get hurt, but as a fighter you don't see that hurt, you don't feel the hurt.

How do you prepare for a bout?

When you go in and the cage door shuts, you hear the door click, that's when you say to yourself, "Are you ready to fight?" You can go into the centre of the cage and you look at your opponent, and you're trying to intimidate him. So it starts off with the intimidation before any exchanges go on. You try to psychologically beat him that way. As soon as you crash, that's it. At the end of the day there's no malice in it. You're just testing your skills out to see if your skills are better than his skills.

There was a major scare at one of your fights. You had trouble with your heart. Has that caused you to think about stopping fighting?

No, because I know now it was just a head cold that caused the trouble with my heart. You actually can get hurt, but the majority of the time I find it depends on the shape you're in. You've got the referee in there as well. If it looks as if it's going too far then he's there to stop that, he's there to make sure that there's no real danger. What happened doesn't stop me wanting to fight. My wife, deep down, would love me to stop fighting. My little girl too, I dare say. At the moment, because of what I do and who I am, they just let me get on with what I want to enjoy doing.

What are your ambitions for after you give up MMA?
I would like to think I could train somebody to go on and become big in MMA. I would love to have fighters to train. But I want them to have the right attitude, nice guys. I don't like macho people. I like genuine natural guys. I don't want the macho type. I'd like to think that I'll be able to find the right guy with the right heart, the right commitment, who will put everything into what he wants to do in this game. If I could find the right one and I could dedicate my time to him, I would love to think that I could give any man all my knowledge and get him as high as I could in the fighting game. Or I'd like to be recognised in the country as somebody who arbitrates. I would like to think I could do that.

Where do your influences and your inspiration come from?
It's always been myself. I believe in myself and in what I've done and what I've gone through. It's me that's pushed me to where I'm at now. You've got to believe you can do it. When I first started doing the jiu-jitsu, I just saw it as learning a skill to give myself a bit more confidence. I didn't believe for one second when I started learning that, eight or nine years down the line, I'd be going in a cage with Ken Shamrock.

What was your upbringing like?
I can remember the day my mum and dad first split up; I was hanging onto my dad's suitcases and going down to the bus stop with him. We could see the bus coming. Me and my sister were hanging on, crying our eyes out, not wanting him to go and he gave us 2p each to go into the shop, just to give him enough time to get onto the bus. I can remember those days.

When I was a kid, I was bullied. I'd go out the school gates and run. I was dragged up. I had no shoes – I had wellies cut down into shoes. I had football boots with the studs out for training. I had my sister's cardigan. Now I give my kids anything they want. What I didn't get, my kids get.

WARRIORS OF THE CAGE

I really liked that Lennie McLean book. He was beaten up by his stepfather. I never ever wanted to put the book down, because I always wanted to see if he gave his stepfather a good hiding. He always promised his mum he wouldn't do it, but eventually he did. I couldn't put the book down because I wanted to see how old he was, and what caused him to give the bloke a good hiding. I had a bad upbringing. I've had secondhand toys for Christmas. I look back on my life now for what it was, in one respect you think it was awful, but in another it's made me the person I am today. Who knows what I might have been like? I don't want to see any harm come to anybody at all. All I hope to see is that everybody's happy, one happy family.

JEREMY 'BAD BOY' BAILEY

The Friday afternoon pre-Cage Rage weigh-in at the Wembley Plaza Centre. It's December. While some people are looking forward to a bit of late-night shopping, the cage fighters are looking at a quiet night in, maybe a film and a good night's sleep. As the dusk settles over Wembley, the lights look brighter, the air feels colder, and amid the noise and bustle, I finally find the notorious 'Bad Boy'. His white t-shirt says 'Not guilty' across the chest. 'Bad Boy' had been 'helping with enquiries' just before we met. It's hard to attract his attention because everybody wants a word with him, and for a while I'm at the back of the queue. At last, he turns away from a conversation and spots me. His dreadlocks brush my face. "Ah, the guy with the book!" He calls to his brother, who goes to all his fights. The brother nods, disappears, and re-appears with a chair in each hand. The others make a space for us to sit and talk. People like to make space for 'Bad Boy' when he wants it.

The last time I'd seen 'Bad Boy' was on the night of his memorable bout at Wembley for Cage Rage 16, 'Critical Conditions'. He won that night, as he had on other occasions. But the bout was also memorable for his entrance: an entourage of six of the best-looking girls Wembley had seen for many years, each as tall as 'Bad Boy' himself and each with a letter of his name printed on their scanty clothing. The crowd went wild as the girls got themselves into the right order, turned their backs on the arena and bent over: six arses, spelling out 'B.A.D.B.O.Y.' Now, that's what I call a fan base! The regular Cage Rage crowd is hoping that, next time, the girls will treat us to the full version of his name.

How did you get into MMA?
I started off doing kickboxing. I won all sorts of titles and the World Title and this is like the next stage really, the next thing I wanted to conquer. Everyone said I couldn't do it, but I started in 1999 and I'm still here.

What were you like at school?
I was one of three black kids in my school, there was me and my brother and another kid. So you know, at the end of the day you had to fight whether you wanted to or not. I used to get bullied when I was younger and I can remember my dad saying, "If you ever run away from a fight, I'll beat you. If you ever start a fight, I'll beat you."

Was that in school or out of school?
Not in school. I had two older brothers, so that wasn't going to happen in school.

Did you finish school?
I finished at several schools before time, but I ended up passing my exams. I had to pay for them myself. I wanted to pass them just to prove that I could.

Who introduced you to fighting?
I started off at a judo club when I was five. My dad was helping to teach the local judo club and it just sort of went from there really.

Are you nervous before a fight?
I think everyone gets butterflies. Anyone that tells you they don't get butterflies is a wanker or a liar. We all get nervous before a fight. I'm not scared. The only thing I'm worried about is looking bad. I ain't worried about getting hurt because pain is just weakness leaving the body.

So what are your thoughts and emotions before a fight?
That depends on what type of fight it is. There's been a lot of bad blood around some of my fights and there's been grudge matches. Tonight it's all about business, it's another day at the office. Joe

[Mac]'s in my way so I will probably knock his arse out and then move on to the next person.

What were your goals before you got involved in MMA?
All I wanted to do when I was younger was to be the best in the world at something and I've done that in kickboxing. The MMA is a different thing, but I was a World Champion, I fought all over the world. I fought in all the different associations and I can honestly say, hand on heart, that I've done that, and no-one can ever take that away from me. Now this is the next platform and if I can just achieve just a little bit of what I did in kickboxing, I'll be happy.

You've got your own business, but how important is the money you make at MMA?
At the moment, with my current situation with the local police and stuff, yeah, of course I need the money. Everyone does. I need the money, but I honestly do this for the love of it. Probably the biggest reason I do this, apart from the fact that I do it just because I can, is because I absolutely love to knock motherfuckers out. I love it. There's no court case, no custodial sentence, no fucking compensation, no fines or nothing. I get to iron a man out flat on his back and if he wakes up he wants to buy me a drink, not have me arrested.

So MMA is everything you want to do and you get paid too?
It's the best job in the world. It's better than being a porn star, man. Once you're done, you know, and they tell you, "No, sorry, we didn't get that, can you go again?", sometimes you're struggling to get it up again after a few times. But I will throw punches and kicks all night long, that's not a problem.

What inspires you?
The people around me that put the effort into me. I've got my trainer there, Paul James, and obviously my family and my girl. All the people around me that believe in me and give their time to come and help me train and prepare. Without them, I'm nothing. So I do it all for them.

Cage Rage has been going in England since 2002. How do you see it developing?
Do you know what, I don't think that the two eggheads [Dave and Andy] will be in it that long. They will sell this motherfucker up

for millions of pounds – definitely. The bottom line is that I remember their first shows and everybody laughed at them and I knew that they had something there. I've been supporting these guys since Cage Rage 1 and 2, and they've been supporting me. I wish them every success. Hopefully they'll go on to bigger and better things. They're the best show in Europe at the moment, that's without a doubt. They are really *the* only show at the moment. Other promoters are fearing them and trying to tie them up in all sorts of lawsuits. Obviously, they're a force to be reckoned with.

UFC have been to Manchester and didn't succeed. Can you see UFC gaining ground over here?
This world and this sport is big enough for everybody to survive, but if they all want to start playing silly games, then that's up to them. I'm not the one pulling the purse strings so I can't really answer that. As far as anyone stopping them growing, I can't see it.

You've trained with London Shoot Fighters?
Yeah, I trained with London Shoot Fighters, Alexis and Marios Demetriades, Paul Ivens, all the guys. It doesn't matter how many fights you win, you go down London Shoot and them guys will make you feel like a novice every time you get there. It's the best gym in the country without a shadow of a doubt.

Any great fighters that you've come across in your career who you'd like to mention?
Great fighters in my weight class? I mean you've got Paul 'Semtex' Daley who's an up and coming star; he's already starting to dominate the world. The sport at welterweight is all about Paul at the moment, that's a definite. Anyone else I've beat – fuck you, I beat you, you weren't good enough. Go back to the drawing board, play the game and come back, you never know.

How do you spend your time away from the cage?
I like to just take things easy. I'm not one of those people who sits down and thinks that the world owes them a living. If there's something out there that I want, I'll go and get it.

How has the ongoing issue of you being involved with the police affected you?

I don't think I'm involved with the police. I think the police are trying to get involved with me. And as [the t-shirt] says, you know... you can read it.

Not guilty. It says, in black and white on your t-shirt, 'Not Guilty'.

And that's about all I'm prepared to say about that one.

You've spent time in jail. How was that?

Which time?

Which time do you want to talk about?

I've been in a couple of times. It's nothing to brag about. There's no money to be gained from having been in jail. It's not fine, it's not big. At the end of the day being away is a learning curve and I think I've come out a better person for it. I think if I could go back and do it all again, I would. Like the time I spent in jail, for things I've done, that was down to me. I've also been in jail on remand for a crime that I didn't commit and hasn't been proved that I've committed. I had no control over that, I was put in jail for something I didn't do, and have only recently got out. But I think that without experiences like that in life, you don't learn about life and you can't walk around like I do.

So what did you learn from the experience? How do you feel yourself?

It just confirmed my thoughts about how corrupt the police and the government are in this country, and I felt this especially this time round. I learned a lot of new things about the police and stuff. I'm not saying everybody should go to jail at least once to experience the learning curve, but, if it leads to a better way of life for some people that's good. If you're used to a quality lifestyle then that's where jail is hard. If you're not fussed about how things are outside, then jail will never touch you. It's not a deterrent at all, I don't think. I did have a quality lifestyle before I went in, so yeah, of course it burnt me. But I'm also a strong-willed person and as long as you've got your mind, then no-one can take that from you, and nothing can harm you.

THE FIGHTERS

So what do you think about life now?
You're born, you live, you die. It's that simple.

Obviously there's a journey, though?
There is a journey and unfortunately for some people they don't get to make that journey. Some people's lives get cut short by accident, some people get their lives taken from them, and some people don't choose to live. I live and do what I want to do.

MARVIN 'MARVELLOUS' ARNOLD

Standing at six foot one, with a slender build and weighing around 70 kilos, with a body laden with tattoos, you can't miss him. Marvin 'Marvellous' Arnold is a character of characters, kind of a cocky, showboating Sugar Ray Leonard – but that's the beauty of being marvellous. 'Marvellous' doesn't look like the type of person who likes to be told what to do. He adores attention, especially from women, and is a typical ladies' man. We're in the Wembley Plaza Hotel and his loyal mates signal him that I'm in their presence. He reaches out and shouts, "You're doing that book, when you doing me?"

Relaxed and wearing a cream t-shirt and three-quarter-length trousers, Marvin and his commandos carry me along towards Room 345, as he cheerfully expresses his emotions about his previous fight triumphs, not mentioning the defeats. As we spread ourselves around the room, I'm wondering just how close these guys are, whether they grew up together, attended the same school, or the same college. The unity amongst them is very animated with lots of banter. Bitching, slagging, a blizzard of hand gestures... I decide that these are no guys from Oxford or Eton. Southeast London it is.

Just before I start the interview, 'Marvellous' peels off his t-shirt to reveal his tattoos. He places himself on the bed and says, 'Fire away!'

'Marvin Marvellous', or is it 'Marvellous Marvin'?
Marvin Marvellous.

What were your schooldays like?
I was picked on quite a lot when I was at school, but that was because I had a big mouth, but I couldn't really back it myself, to be

honest. I always had my brother to fight my battles for me. So I never really had to do it for myself.

Where were you brought up?
In Peckham, southeast London.

Quite a notorious area, I believe?
You grow up on the rough streets and you have to learn rough, don't you?

Did you finish school?
I did. I ended up going to the off-site centre because I got kicked out of my secondary school in year ten. I went to this centre instead and I did keep going, I got my GCSEs and everything, yeah.

Have you ever been involved with the law?
Yeah, I've been involved with the law. It's just in the past I was involved.

How did you get involved with MMA?
I've been watching this since I was about ten years old with my whole family. We just watched it with the old bare knuckle stuff, UFC 'no holds barred'. I watched it and I've always loved it from an early age. But when I got older and I used to play football, I went professional at 16. Then I injured myself coming off my brother's moped so I couldn't play football anymore. So I started fighting a lot in the pubs and thought I wanted to get into the MMA scene. I didn't know at the time that you go straight into an MMA deal. I thought you had to do all the different disciplines. I went out one day and saw one of my pals, who was a relation of Dave O'Donnell's, and I told him I wanted to do it. He gave me the number and it went from there. So I think one of the main reasons I wanted to get into it was actually for the fighting.

Has it changed your life?
Yeah, big time, it has changed my life a lot. My whole life is Mixed Martial Arts fighting, training, doing everything I can to be better.

Do you have any role models inside or outside the cage?
Inside the cage, my role models are definitely Anderson Silva, being that he's the same weight as me and the same height as me, and he's

a stand-up fighter predominantly – which is what I like to base my fighting on. Yeah, as role models, Anderson, the Gracie family, Chuck Liddell.

Can you name three people have influenced your career?
It'd have to be Chuck Liddell, Anderson Silva, and the person who really got me interested – this is not to say that I like him utmost or anything, but because where I was living at the time he was the top man and he was world class – it's Lee Murray.

What are your thoughts and emotions just before a fight?
I think I usually channel my nerves well, and I usually just laugh it off. Because the way I look at it is, you're here because you love it. If you don't love it and you're here just to prove to people that "Oh, I'm a fighter," or you just want to get a name for yourself, you put too much pressure on yourself and it can really kill you. I'm usually cheerful and jolly that I'm here and I enjoy the fight.

How do you spend your time away from the cage?
Just going out with my cousins and my friends now and then. Just training constantly and spending as much time as possible watching UFC. I love women, so I usually get my fair share of birds as well.

Why do you keep fighting?
I think to start off with, it was to be good on the street. I was fighting a lot on the street and it's a rough area I grew up in. If I got into a fight, I'm not a troublemaker, but if I got into it, then I was dangerous, you know what I mean? During the early part of my career, I did it because I just wanted to get in there and fight, it was just emotion and aggression and I loved it. But as I've gone on and it's got bigger for me, I know there's so much more skill to learn. I've had top trainers in the country tell me I've got great potential to be a great fighter, so I've put a lot more time and effort into it and I think that's why I made it to Wembley. I just want to show that I deserve to be here.

You're still young at 21. How do you see your career developing?
Well, if God's good to me, then hopefully in five years time I'd like to be a champion. I just want to have a few belts around me and be a very successful fighter.

WARRIORS OF THE CAGE

Which great guys have you trained with?

I've trained with Zelg Galesic and with Ronnie Mann – he's a great fighter – and Jean Silva – he's had a couple of seminars with Paul 'Semtex' Daley. I trained with James Compton at Trojan. Steve Gasso's my trainer, he's got a career record of 60 pro Thai boxing bouts. He went to Malaysia and beat their national champion with a head kick in the third round. These are people I spar with. One other fighter at Trojan is a Commonwealth Champion, European Champion and an Olympic gold medallist boxer. You've got Fahid who's a wrestler in Trojan, he's a World Champion. Just people we're learning new things from, so it's been great.

What are your favourite techniques?

Muay Thai, that's what I base my fighting on. I've always found I had a natural ability for it. In my gym there are people who have been doing it for two and a half years and I've really stepped up my Muay Thai.

Is this a part-time or fulltime career for you?

It was part-time, but when I got the call up for Wembley I just gave up my job as a builder and multi-tradesman. It's been hard trying to pay for training and everything, but it's going big now and you just have to make sacrifices.

Did your friends and family support you when you started MMA?

At first, when I told my family that I was doing cage fighting my mum just brushed it off. Four months later, I turned pro and I called her and said, "I'm fighting," and she couldn't believe it. She was like, "You're serious?" She came to see the first fight and was a bit worried because the geezer I fought was quite big. But the support has been great from my friends and family. It has been great, so I can't really moan at all about that.

How often do you speak to your god? What do you ask for?

I'm not as religious as I should be, but yeah, I believe in God and I try and give Him a lot of thanks for where I am today. I try and speak to Him as much as possible. I make sure I pray every night. But obviously, if there's things that I think I need help in, then I'll just talk to him through the day or whenever. I ask to keep my family well and keep my fighting career going strong and to get over the tough bits in life. Just generally anything that's on my mind. This Saturday, my prayer is to be the best up-and-coming fighter.

How would you define a tough guy, away from the cage?
Somebody that can handle themselves in the right moments, but knows how to defuse a situation. A lot of people have got a perception of these massive people going round just hitting people for the fun of it, but to me it's someone who can handle themselves and will do so if it really calls for it, but can defuse a situation. It's all about being a man and handling yourself and having discipline.

If your career with MMA does end, how do you see your future?
I'd see myself still involved in the sport somehow, maybe teaching. I suppose I'd just try and make as much money as I could out of my building career. God forbid it does end. I can't see my life without MMA at the moment.

How has becoming a professional fighter affected your social life?
I've found it's been good. I've got good publicity from it and stuff, so it's not really changed my attitude or that of other people towards me. People are just intrigued more than anything.

I notice you're a fan of tattoos. Is that an MMA thing?
No, I started getting tattoos when I was 16. Once I had one I just got the buzz for it, and I always had a vision of how my body was going to look. Like I was going to get my top half covered. Then, as soon as I got into the MMA, I was sponsored by a tattoo shop near my house, so I'm getting them for free now. So everything I want I go weekly and get. It's just an easy access thing, so I'm making the most of it.

MARK 'THE BEAST' EPSTEIN

I'm in Nando's, North Greenwich, when Mark Epstein appears at the door with his characteristic walk (too much fruit in that bowl if you ask me) and is greeted by some diners who are already seated. He's wearing a black jacket, black tracksuit bottoms and a t-shirt with a logo saying Muay Thai, with its wasp logo representing Anderson

Silva's training camp. This is a man who has total respect for others, all races at all levels, especially if they're willing to achieve. He respects the doers more than the talkers. As I sit and watch, I can only admire the admiration with which he is greeted.

Mark entered the cage in his mid-30s, fighting in the middleweight class at 90 kg and above. I knew that 'The Beast' had an explosive story to tell. Most of his wins are technical knockouts – so thankfully, most fighters can only imagine the force of his fists. This is a stand up man, no shit taken. Love him or not, you're dealing with 'The Beast'. Associated with London Shoot Fighters, Mark is considered a remarkable person, partly because of his late start in MMA. He gives huge support and inspires determination in those he feels for, both in and outside the MMA scene. His presence is always welcome, wherever he goes.

Born in southeast London, Mark has mass of friends, ranging from people on the music scene like Nicky Blackmarket to David Hayes the boxer and even actors, including TV and silver screen hard man Tamer Hassan. Who knows, Mark may soon appear in a cinema near you. Whatever ambitions he's yet to fulfil, be assured that he will achieve them.

He picks a good restaurant too. As food arrived, the succulent and aromatic smell of chicken was irresistible. I just had to take a few mouthfuls before I started rolling the tape.

Mark, what were your schooldays and childhood like?
I was in foster homes and care homes, so by the time I was nine I'd been to about 15 different schools. From the age of nine I was in a boarding school and I was there 24 hours a day for the whole term. I'd come home in the holidays and play with the local kids, but I was at boarding school.

Did going to boarding school help you?
Not really. It gave me a certain amount of knowledge, so even though I left school with no qualifications, I know I've got a reasonable standard of education. It was good in that it kept me off the streets, but as soon as I came home and there was no male role model to give me any discipline, it all went out the window. My mum was bringing up five kids and she struggled, and I was a naughty child and I got into a lot of trouble with the police. From 14 up until 21 it was non-stop.

THE FIGHTERS

Name three people who have inspired you.

I mean now, as a grownup, I wouldn't say inspiration, but they're heroes to me: Nelson Mandela, Hurricane Carter, and also Lee Murray – who has been a big influence. I wouldn't say he's a hero, but he's a good friend and he helped me out. Lee got me into the game in the first place. There's loads of sporting people that I look up to, like Muhammad Ali, Pele, people like that. I'm not influenced by them, but I do hero-worship these guys

What made you come into the MMA scene? Who involved you in it?

I came out of prison in 2000. I spent a bit of time up in Wayland with Reggie Kray just before he died. I went into prison in '99 and just as I did, Lee Murray started fighting. I didn't know anything about it. When I came home I saw a few guys on a few shows, it was like an all-in tear-up. There were rules to the game, but not many, it was more like a street fight. And I've been street fighting for years, getting nowhere for it. Maybe building up a reputation, but certainly not getting paid, and then going to prison for it. So when I saw that you could earn some money legitimately, and be a sportsman at the same time, it was something that I wanted to do. I saw Lee fighting at his show and then I started training with him seriously from 2001. After about 18 months of solid training with London Shoot, I saw a show advertised on the internet. It was at the Circus Tavern and was one of Lee Johnson's. I put my name forward and I was given a fight eight weeks later against Ryan Robinson. It was my first ever made fight, and I won it in something like 40-50 seconds. I demolished him. I just came out, hit him with everything I had, hit him with a few shots and he didn't really want to know.

Who named you 'The Beast' and why?

I don't know how I got the name, 'The Beast'. I think it's because I'm a hairy motherfucker. I've seen some walking shag piles, and I'm not quite *that* hairy, but I am hairy. People use to call me a caveman because of my appearance, 'Captain Caveman' was a nickname for me. I think it was at my first fight against Ryan Robinson, someone said to me, "Oh you came out like a bull in a china shop, you was an absolute beast," or something like that. And that was it. We nicked the name off Dan Severn. I had it before Bob Sapp anyway, I know that.

Which was your most memorable fight and why?

It was with a guy called Lance King, about my third or fourth fight. I gave away a lot of weight, and a lot of height, and it was a brawl for 13-14 minutes. That was probably the hardest fight I've ever had, and the most memorable. There have been a few others that stick in my mind, but that one was really hard work.

Which are your favourite MMA fights?

Shougun and Nogueira in Pride. I think it was 1986 or '87. That was one of the best fights I've ever seen. That was absolute toe-to-toe war, war of attrition, battle of wills. Definitely one of my favourite fights, yeah. Maybe a couple of Couture's early fights, Randy Couture versus Pedro Rizzo was a great fight, back in the day. I like Matt Hughes's fights as well.

What are your emotions before entering the cage?

I'm usually like a coiled spring. You've done all the pads, you've trained for weeks, and now you're just ready to rock and roll, just let it all hang out and swing for the princes. You go in there to win. It's a competition, it's you versus the opponent, but I personally think I'm a bit more street. It's something I've not been able to quite get rid of. I just look for the looker, I swing for the princes and I don't care if my opponent does too. We'll stand there and we'll swing for the princes.

How do you take your wins or losses afterwards?

Well, the wins are always better than the losses, aren't they? I mean, no-one likes to lose. I hate to lose you know, I'm a bad loser.

So how do you take it when you've lost?

You get a bit depressed and stuff. It's got to come out of you, hasn't it? It's like you know you've got to get back on the bike and ride it. You fall off a bike, you get back on it and you try again. I'm not happy with my MMA record. I've had 14 wins and 11 losses. But I started with all the martial arts roughly at the same time. And I've had a world title in Thai boxing as well, so I've had three British titles and one world title in six years. I'm pretty pleased with that side of things. I think my record as a whole has not been great, but I've taken fights when I've already had injuries, and I've taken fights at very short notice as well, because I needed the money. It takes a lot more than a loss to break my spirit. A loss is a loss. You get over it and you get back on that bike and you try not to fall off again. But shit happens, and that's life and you just crack on.

Are you religious?

I believe in God, but it's no Muslim God, and it's no Christian God. Although I was brought up in the Christian faith, I just believe that I've got my own God and he listens to me. You know those times when you want to go home, then you pray to God to get you out of this situation? But I've got my own version. I think everyone should have their own version. We live in a democracy. No-one should be forcing any religious views down my throat. I won't accept it, I won't have any Muslim or any Christian tell me their religion is right. I've got my view and I think everybody is entitled to their fucking own view of religion – Christian or Muslim or Hindu, Sikh, Jew, fucking whatever you are. No opinions should be forced on people. I think that's how it is.

What do you enjoy away from the cage?

Personal time away from the cage is spent on the beach in a very hot country. You know, laying on the beach with nice company and a big fat one, ready to get lit up for the world.

Have you ever been afraid in a situation?

I've been involved in some shady deals back in the day. Before legal fighting I was a bit of a street thug and I was mixed up in some drugs. I was getting myself mixed up with a lot of gun play, a lot of knife crime. I went to prison for drug dealing in 2000. In 1999 I went to prison for supplying Class A drugs to undercover police. There was a drug deal that went wrong and I ended up getting into a gun battle with some criminals. There were a few hundred kilos of puff involved, which back in 1996 or '97 was about quarter of a mil's worth. The parcel went missing through the Customs & Excise. They'd nicked someone else with the parcel. It all went pear-shaped and I ended up getting into some major gun battle. That was one of the scariest moments of my life. The few days after that incident were quite a worrying time. But it all got sorted out in the end. The people got their paperwork to prove that people had been arrested with this parcel and no-one had ripped anyone off. But that was a very scary moment in my life.

How did you deal with it emotionally?

My emotions were all over the place. I was smoking crack like nobody's business anyway. I was just basically a fucking crackhead that was out there and would have done whatever it took. This was the crazy situation I was in. I was working for a major criminal at the time and he was dealing with other major criminals and I was body-guarding this guy. I was like his minder. And I had to step up, I had to protect my boss, and that's what I did.

Can MMA training help to reduce crime and violence among young men?

I believe that MMA is one of the most positive things that I've ever done in my life. It gave me discipline, it's given me self-respect, it's given me self-worth, it's given me confidence above and beyond my need. I'm not saying I'm super-confident, but I'm very confident in the skills that I have. No-one should have to walk around with a knife, but kids are walking around with knives and I feel that one of the main reasons they're doing it is that it gives them confidence, they feel more powerful. Before I went to prison I was into guns and knives. After coming out of prison I learnt how to use my physical assets in a very good way. A lot of people say violence is a negative emotion, but the training and the discipline that you need to be a fighter is unbelievable. I think the training could be good for children. I'd say maybe start them about 14-15 years of age. There's a lot of children out there with no role model. They look up to the guys who are involved in sports or they look at the drug dealer who's driving the BMW or the Mercedes and wearing all the bling, you know, the bloke on the MTV and the 50 Cent video. No-one says it's never cool to be shot, it's not cool to be shot nine times and survive and then talk about it and rap about it in your songs about the drug dealing. There's a lot of guys with no purpose in their lives. With MMA events, the youth can see. I'm not saying there are people out there that want to be like me, but I'd be glad if I could help a youth come away from the life of crime and do something positive. If they have an anger management problem, or a temper, they need help. I think MMA is a way for youths to channel their aggression into something positive that could build a life and a career. There's nothing better than having a career and making good money from something that you love to do. I don't think there's anything wrong with people that want to fight in a controlled and well-managed situation. I see nothing wrong with it at all. There are children that maybe will be good at this, but at the moment they're getting into a lot of trouble in school. They see a lot of negative role models like the drug dealers and then they want to get into that.

Do you have any advice for your young fans out there?
The only saying or motto that I try to live by, is "live and let live". I don't trouble anyone if they don't trouble me. I'm not interested in other people's business, sexuality, attitudes, opinions or anything. I'm not trying to judge people. I just respect people. The people in my life that I don't really like or get on with are the people who do a lot of talking. They do a lot of talking, but there's no action. If you choose a career, stay with the career and do something with yourself. Have ambition. There's nothing wrong with wanting to be somebody. But it seems like nowadays with the MTV stuff, and the lack of positive role models for the children, and the single parent situation and stuff like that, no-one wants to work, that's the thing. No-one wants to work hard and earn their stuff. With the bling generation everyone wants to be a rap boy and speak lyrics and be an actor and think it's all going to fall in their lap. I wish it was that simple, I really do. Maybe it is for some people, but it definitely hasn't been for me. I've had to give blood, sweat and tears for everything that I've got. The only people that I respect are people that are willing to sacrifice whatever it takes. I'm not saying break the law. You've got to do whatever you've got to do. But I'm saying it's better to have a career where you haven't got to look over your shoulder.

Define a tough guy.
Someone who goes to work, that gets up in the morning, takes care of his family. Not someone who takes a beating and gives up. Maybe it's about the way you take a beating. Because everybody takes a beating at some time in their life. It's just sometimes you see someone that's got a lot of heart and they won't go down. You can't keep them down. No matter how many times you knock them down, they get back up. People like that, I respect because they show an awful lot of heart. They might not have the best skills in the world when it comes to fighting or anything, but I love a person who's a tryer, someone that never quits. That's one thing as well, you never quit, because winners never quit. Quitters never win. That's another motto of mine.

What ambitions do you have?

The only ambition really left for me would be to fight in the UFC. That is like the Mecca of MMA and it's where every fighter in the world, anyone who's involved at any level, wants to be right now. That's where you really get the biggest money, the biggest publicity, the most recognition. UFC is the only organisation out there right now that anyone wants to be a part of.

Where do you see yourself once you retire?

There's other things I'm getting involved with. Property is one of them. I'd like to get involved in some acting work too, just as an extra, you know, I'd like to be in the background of the match and letting it off. I'm not interested in being a star or anything like that, but I do like the movies. I've got a friend who's a stunt man, Maurice Lee, he's been in James Bond and Harry Potter films. I think he's done about the last three or four James Bonds. So my plans are for stunt work, getting into property and becoming a landlord, and opening a gym. That's the future that I want.

Are there any messages you'd like to send to anyone?

I'd like to say thank you to Lee Murray, because he's the guy that started me off in this business. But there's loads of guys I'd like to thank who I've worked with and fought with.

How do you see the future of MMA?

It's a great sport, the greatest sport in the world. Hopefully it will go from strength to strength. With organisations like the UFC, MMA is becoming more mainstream. With the great British fighters we've got fronting the sport and pioneering the sport, I think that Britain has got a very bright future in MMA.

PAUL 'SEMTEX' DALEY

I caught up with Paul 'Semtex' Daley at the after-party for Cage Rage 25 at Wembley Arena. Paul hadn't had a bout that night, he'd come down from his home in Nottingham to suss out some likely opponents for himself, and had his full entourage with him. He's a young man to be in the middle of such a crowd, but then he has a lot of potential and he likes to have people looking after his interests.

Paul's a winner, and everyone likes to be around a winner. He explodes into the room in the same way that he explodes into the cage – all eyes – and most of the girls follow him, drawn to his presence. It's not that he's flash, with designer clothing or draped in gold, just that his power runs through the room when he enters. He makes no noise, treads softly, and I see him work the room with his eyes, looking for me, as we have an appointment. Paul catches my eye, the slightest of nods, and we each move towards an empty table in the corner of the room. The entourage parts to let me pass, then closes again to stop others from invading Paul's privacy. Nobody takes anything from 'Semtex' that he doesn't want to give.

In training for his next bout, Paul has drinks delivered to the table and invites me to share. He's ready to talk about his life in and out of the cage, and the things that brought him there. He's been fighting at welterweight in the cage since 2003.

How are you enjoying the event?
I'm good. Drunk and hungry, but I'm alright. The event was sick, some good fights. The main part of the card was a bit whack, but you know Cage Rage tries some different things. They win sometimes, they lose sometimes. I think the main part of the card was a loss this time.

You're very well known within MMA. What's it like living in the public eye?
The bigger the sport gets, the bigger I get. Right now, the sport's smashing, so my profile's up there. As the sport continues to grow, it gives people an opportunity, another direction to go in to make some money and set up future generations.

I've heard you started martial arts very young. How old were you?
I was seven years old and made the transition to MMA when I was about 18.

Did you finish your schooling?
Yeah, I finished school and went to college and got some A levels. I joined the army for a short spell, two years. It didn't work out for me. I still had a problem with discipline and I was also competing in MMA. The time I wanted from the army to get away to do MMA they wouldn't give me. In the end I had to just go AWOL [Absent Without Leave] and they didn't like it. So, it went down a bad road from there.

Apart from the military police, have you ever had trouble with the police or been drawn into crime?
Yeah. In the past I've been to Young Offenders through doing all sorts of shit. I've been arrested a couple of times.

How did you come to change agent?
It was about money, but we're going to let that rest now. I know he's under a lot of stress from the problems caused by failing to hold an event that he promoted so widely. So we're not on speaking terms at the moment.

You've got new management now. How's that going so far?
Right now, I'm fighting for one of the biggest promotions in the US and the world. I'm still here fighting at Cage Rage. I have all my belts. I have sponsorship. I'm still training full time and MMA is my full income, so I'm doing alright. I was doing alright before the management problem, and now that's sorted, I'm still doing all that. That's the hustler in me, I just keep doing. I just create that money and keep working.

Have you done anything different in your training to prepare for your next bout?
I've been working on my defence a lot and I've been working on my technical skills, especially the takedowns. In the next fight hopefully I'm going to be a lot more aggressive than usual, so I'm going to bring the action to him this time.

How do you spend your time when you're away from MMA and the cage?
I like to go out with my friends I still know from school. I like to have long-term relationships. I go home once in a while, look after Mum, look after the family, and just try to be happy. I like to be around happy people, regardless. Happy people, that's all I want. I don't want any hate, I don't want any people trying to come at me, I just want happy people.

What inspires you to fight?
The fact that I enjoy it. Now that I've reached the top, I'm happy. All I wanted to do was reach the top.

Do you ever suffer from nerves before a bout?

Never. I'm never nervous. Nervousness I would define as no belief. I believe this is my destiny. I've dreamt about it, I've seen it, and I'm just going to keep following the same path.

Are you religious?

I believe in God and I have a tendency to lean towards Buddhism because it's simple and makes a lot of sense if you can understand the way they're trying to get people to approach life. It's not even a religion, it's a way of looking at life. They don't call Buddha a God. I believe in a greater power, and believe that there is something that guides everybody in their lives. To this day I've never had an event in my life which has led me to believe different. I believe that everything I've done has shown me that there is something guiding me. Good or bad. Even when shit goes wrong, in the end it turns out right and that's not luck. Luck doesn't exist. You have to have a belief in a thing and be able to see opportunities, take those opportunities and when they don't pan out the way you want them to, realise the lesson that's in them. That's life, that's religion for me.

Can you name three people who have influenced who you are today?

My mother first and foremost. The Buddhist leader, the Dalai Lama through his books, I've read a lot of them. Other than that, every-body I meet in life has a lesson to teach me regardless, good or bad. Every trial in life makes me who I am today, so props to all those people that tried to cheat me, props to all those people that tried to do me wrong and all that shit, and props to all the people who have done me good. All love.

What are your emotions and thoughts before and after a fight?

There are no thoughts. I've won the fight before I've even gone in there. In my head, I've won it. Every time. I had a guy come up to me the other day and say, "What makes you so confident?" Because I've seen the fight a million times in my head. I've judged it and I feel it. There's no other option for me in life. This is my path. I can't fail. I'm a victor. Even in losses I'm a victor and that's been proven. I've lost six times but I'm still on the second biggest promotion in the USA. I'm still a fulltime fighter. I am still beating top names. This is my life, this is my chosen path, this is why I'm here.

Do you still have your childhood ambitions?

Yes, I have the same ambitions. I've been brought up around people who have got good personalities, genuine spiritual personalities, who, no matter what their struggles in life, just want to help other people, whether it be family or not. That's me, I just want to help people. MMA is my opportunity. That's why I started fighting. It's my opportunity to help other people, and that's what I want to do once I've made it, once I'm at the top. And even now I'm helping other people. Right now I'm just trying to help myself and the people around me.

Since this interview took place, Paul Daley has been contracted to UFC as a fighter. His first professional bout takes place in Texas on Saturday 19 September 2009.

RODNEY GLUNDER – 'THE SILENT ASSASSIN'

Spring in Birmingham. Early summer, really. I took my overcoat and scarf, not realising that waders and a waterproof would have been a useful addition to my outfit. The National Exhibition Centre is a little way out of town. It's hardly near Birmingham at all, but the train does go straight there. It's just as well, or the thousands of fans going there to see Rodney Glunder strut his stuff would have had to swim the last bit. Coming from Holland, Rodney's no stranger to water. However, he's long since rejected the more traditional Dutch career of life on the waterways, choosing instead to become a fighter.

It's 2pm and I'm on the lookout for Rodney (a.k.a. the Silent Assassin) amid the steam generated by thousands of drying overcoats. I should recognise him from his funky multi-hued hair colours. Finally, I spot him with James McSweeney and their coach. Standing around six foot and with a fighting weight of 92 kg, he's an imposing figure even in jeans, trainers and a Transformers t-shirt – Megatron, if you're interested. He's dark and covered in tattoos. I'd like a closer look, but hesitate to get too close, I've seen his rear-naked choke! The Assassin has a record of competing in Japanese Hybrid, Professional MMA and K-1. Make no mistake, this man has fought some very tough opponents and has beaten both Melvin Manhoef and Cheick Kongo.

THE FIGHTERS

Rodney glances around the venue as if he's never seen such a sight before. Maybe he's just disappointed, wondering if this is the best that Britain has to offer. We manage to find a quiet spot and I let the tape roll.

This is your debut in the UK cage. You must be ecstatic.
I feel very excited. I am very glad they called me up to come and fight and I think I can give them a good show.

What were your schooldays like? Were you ever bullied?
No, I was an average guy. I made it a little bit busy for the teachers, but then I had normal school years. Nothing easy or nothing strange about it. I did all my classes till the age of 17 or 18, then I dropped out of school. I was a little bit on the streets, doing my thing. Then after that I started to do some lessons. I don't know how you say it in English, I just do some lessons to educate myself. I sell clothes and sell stuff on the market and I got a diploma in two years. After that I started fighting.

What did you want to be when you left school?
When I was at school I didn't exactly know what I wanted to be, because I was too busy with the boys in the street and doing things. Like I said, I was an average kid. I didn't have dreams like I wanted to be a policeman or a fireman. I always knew that I wanted to work with people because I like to work with people, I like to be with people, I like people around me. But I didn't have anything that I wanted to do especially.

How did you get involved with MMA?
I first started with Thai boxing. Many years ago there was the free-fight. That was very popular in Japan. It came to our country, Holland. Then I also started free fighting and from there it just went on.

How do you spend your time away from MMA?
I have three sons. I have a beautiful wife. So I'm busy with the family.

What are your emotions before your enter a cage?
I got some tension. Some tension is normal when a fighter's going to have a fight. I feel pretty good when I enter in the cage or a ring or something, because a fight's a fight.

Are you religious? Do you believe in God?

I believe in God, but it isn't that I'm going to the church or that I'm praying every day or something. It is with me, it is in me and I do want it.

Define a tough guy.

The only person who is tough in this sport is my trainer. He's like 56 years old and he's still beating us up in the gym. He's the only tough guy that I know.

The reason I ask is because people think of tough as being big and bold.

But it's not tough. I don't see tough as somebody who is very big or muscular. 'Tough' is something that you show, I think, because I know small guys, little guys, who are very tough when they are meeting and fighting with the big guys. So if you mean that, that's my explanation.

Do you believe that MMA is a sport where young people can learn to be more controlled?

I think that every sport is good for the youth to do. I think that there are lots of people who can start in MMA now or start to train. I think if they explore it that's good, because then more people will come and do this type of sport.

What was your most memorable fight?

I have a few, not only in MMA but also in kickboxing. And not only in the A Class, also in the C Class and B Class. Every fight is something you work for. Every trophy is a great story, I think, because you train for every fight. It is good to know that now I am fighting in the cage I have knocked out two champions.

Who are they?

Melvin Manhoef, who was a Cage Rage champion, and now Paul Cahoon, who I stopped also. For me it is a good feeling to be here and to have knocked out two guys who are champions.

How do you feel when you've lost?

A fight's a fight, and of course you are disappointed, but it isn't like my whole world is turning around and you can't speak with me for a week, you know. If I've had a fight and lost, maybe the next day I am a little bit grumpy, but after that I'm just normal again, I start to train again. This is the life, you have ups and downs. I don't especially want to send a message to anyone, I just want to say that if you start this sport, if you decide to fight, of course you will lose someday. If you lose, just pick yourself up and you can go further. If you really decide to do MMA, it's going to control your life. You have to do everything for it to reach your goals. And not everybody has the same goals. What you have to do is respect everybody.

Your name is 'Silent Assassin'. Who gave you that?
I get the name a few years ago from one of the promoters in our country, Holland. He said that I was rising to the top, but very quietly. I wasn't making a lot of noise and knocking people out, but I was winning my fights. One day I was with the top five guys in our country, so he called me the 'Silent Assassin', because I'm silently climbing to the top. So it has nothing to do with my fighting style or something, he just called me like that because I was very quiet.

I see you're covered in tattoos. Do you have a favourite?
All my tattoos are my favourites because it's a way of life now, it is not like I'm putting a tattoo and after a year I think, what the fuck I am doing? I love all my tattoos, because all my tattoos have a story. I can't explain all of them, but some tattoos are like my dark side. They express my dark side, so that means I also have a positive side. Some I just like.

MELVIN MANHOEF – 'THE RHINO/NO MERCY'

Reading, Berkshire. FX3, an event promoted by Jeremy 'Bad Boy' Bailey. The night will become memorable for Popek Rak's first defeat, beaten by a fighter from Mike's Gym. I'm in the front entrance hall of the sports centre watching Melvin Manhoef. He stands at five foot ten, with a well-defined frame, muscles bulging out of his t-shirt and wearing blue jeans. All I can say is that when God made man he paid considerable attention to the details in Manhoef's case. His peers cluster round him, unable to eclipse his brilliance. His girlfriend stands beside him, holding on tight. Melvin Manhoef, a.k.a. 'Rhino' – a machine has been created.

'Rhino' is an exceptional K-1 fighter who holds many belts in his division, has beaten the best and successfully defended his titles against such contenders as the Brazilian Chute Boxe Academy fighter Cyborg. That fight finished just short of mortal combat. Just as 'Rhino' dominates in the cage, so he dominates his surroundings outside of it. He sees me and tilts his head, raises an eyebrow, and turns towards the dressing room.

As I sit in the dressing room and watch Melvin prepare his fighters with Mike the coach, I see him dictating to his warriors with his body movements. He shows them the manipulative moves and ambushes and it's like watching a game of chess. His up-and-coming soldiers respond to his actions with flares of determination as if they are already in the cage.

While the gladiators from other camps train, I take a wander around the venue and notice some punters trying to argue their way in but not succeeding. Bad Boy's security men won't concede. Like they say, 'be polite and everything will be alright.'

After the bouts, Rhino salutes me and we find a quieter environment so he can answer my questions.

What were your schooldays in Surinam like?
Yeah, okay. I could learn a little bit, not so good. I had a hard time at school, but it was okay you know. I was a little bit of a bad boy, so...

'A bad boy' – fighting all the time, or was it girls or something else?
Yeah, fighting, girls, a lot of things in my younger days. But this was a learning experience. You learn from your faults.

You're a soccer fan?
I like football. I was playing soccer since I was eight years old and I played at a pretty high level because I played with a football academy. I almost turned pro, but I broke my ankle so I couldn't play anymore. Then I went with my brother to the gym and afterwards it was like I was hooked on the sport. Then I saw the kickboxing and then once I did my first fight, I kept on going.

Do you ever worry about breaking something again? It takes some courage to continue with your ankle.
This thing that happened couldn't happen again, so I just trust myself and I go on, keep on fighting because the fighting was in

me already I think. But it came out late, so I started very late with fighting. But I'm never scared to break something and this is the risk that we take. If you do something, you have to understand the consequences and you don't have to worry about what can happen, you have to be positive. And that's what I did. I started and now I'm concentrating on becoming a great champion.

I believe your uncle Djenko inspired you to fight?
When I was 11 or 12 years old he would always be fighting and I always went to watch. He was my favourite uncle because he was strong and big, like a champion to me. At that time I was still playing soccer, so I wouldn't go fighting you know. Afterwards, I tried it and I liked it. He was the real inspiration for my fighting in the early days. He helped me a lot, because when I was ten or 11 years old I was always fighting in the schoolyard. I was a small boy.

You said you got into trouble. Have you ever been involved with the law?
Yes, I spent a lot of time in prison, this is later on. I spent like six years in jail. But this is behind me now, because I changed my life from the negative to something positive. I am not proud of what I did, but this was my past and I cannot change it. Everything that happened, happened for a reason, I think. I spent time in jail in Holland, in Greece. I think now I'm at a certain level that kids can believe in, so that's why I try now to say to all the kids, "If you can do something, try to be somebody. Learn for yourself because I've been there so I know what can happen." And I started late, but now everything is going well. So I'm a very blessed person now. Fighting with K-1, I've got a good contract, earn a lot of money. My mother's proud of me that I've made it so far.

Were there any inmates in jail who inspired you?
No. I was a little bit lonely because I didn't know anybody, I was fighting and that's something serious. I stayed in jail a few years. Came out, trained hard again, fought again, went to jail again. It was off and on. And at a certain moment I thought, "This is not the life that I want." My trainer and my manager and my sponsors, they talked to me, they said, "Listen, you're going to get a salary every month. Stay off the streets and away from crime." And they said, "If you don't become somebody in two years, you can stay and be a

criminal if you want to." But I didn't want to, so they inspired me. I trained every day for maybe 360 days, and in one year I had almost 50 fights. It was fighting, fighting, fighting. Then everything started to pay off, the hard work and the training. So that's why it's very important to keep on believing in yourself and try to be a real sportsman, so when things go a little bit wrong you have to go with the flow. Not to think that everything is against you, and that you've got to stop and rest. No, no, no, you have to go on.

Who are your role models from outside MMA?
My kids, because I have a son I'm very proud of and my daughters. They are my role models. For me, it's very important how their lives are going to be because my life wasn't so perfect and I did a lot of stupid things and I want to prevent them doing that. So I'm glad that I made this journey with a lot of troubles, a lot of things that I could teach my kids, show them the right way.

What are your thoughts before a fight?
I'm not so emotional. I just want to win. I want to win and I want to put everything into the fight. This is how I am, this is my character, I cannot stop. When I'm in the cage, I want to destroy everything that's in front of me because this is what I have to do, because it's my sport and I like it. I see it as a sport. But even though I see it as a sport, I'm still a fighter inside, so don't misunderstand me, because when I'm in the ring I want to fight and I want to win, no matter what.

Are you spiritual, do you believe in God?
Yeah, of course I believe. Of course I believe there is a god. I think he put me in jail – it's my own fault, but if I hadn't had this experience, I couldn't fight with guys. You know now there are kids at my home – "I want to be just like you" – and everybody's coming to exhibitions for the autograph. We have a little guy at the gym, we call him Danny. He always fights. Now I can talk to him and say, "I was the same as you." We ground him. He has to be all the time at the gym. He cannot go out, because he's going to start a fight. We search for sponsorship for him so he can fight properly, so that he can become somebody. If I hadn't had my experiences, then I couldn't pass on what I have learned, so that's why I think there is a god. He doesn't just do things for no reason.

THE FIGHTERS

What are your goals?
I've got a lot of goals because before I wanted to become World Champion, and I have. I now want to become World Champion in K-1, so this is my goal now, because when I'm finished with fighting I want to be remembered as a fighter who a lot of people respect and I want to be a legend. This is what I want to be first, this is my main goal, because I like fighting. Afterwards, I have another goal: Some people have talent and cannot develop it. I want to help them. Just like I want to have my own gym and help guys who are on the street all the time, making trouble, I want to help those guys to build something up. And the other goal is I want my kids to have a very good life and be happy.

You say you fight because it's in you, what is in you?
The drive, the drive to be the best. I'm a perfectionist, so I started with fighting, and now I want to be the best fighter. Everything that I do, I want to be the best at and make something out of it. So this is very important.

How have your thoughts about raw power, confidence and the powerful lifestyle influenced your life?
I compare fighting with living. Fighting is living. In life you have to be strong. In fighting you have to be strong. In life, you get a lot of trouble. In fighting you can get a punch and you have to go over it. Everything that happens in fighting, you have in normal life. Sometimes when you have a fight you can go hard into it or you can step back and watch. Sometimes in life there is something that's going to happen. You're going to go berserk or you go crazy, but sometimes it's better to step back and judge what's happening. And then you go again. So fighting is just as life for me. I compare it with life, so that's why I like fighting. And now the fighting has given me peace in my life.

How do you teach others in your fighting camp to control their anger away from the cage? Do they sometimes want to carry on outside? How can you stop that?
You get all these faults with them. I cannot decide what they have to do because they have their own lives and they make their own mistakes. But if I say something and from ten guys, four listen, then I'm glad, then I've already helped four, you understand? I have to be perfect also because then they can believe in me, because if they're

67

watching me and I do well, they're going to follow me. If I do bad things, they're going to follow the bad things. So that's how I stimulate my students. My trainer does the same with me. And that's what I want to do with the other guys at our gym. Talk and give a good example, these are the things that I think I can do.

Do you read books?
I don't read books a lot. Sometimes when I have time I read, but, my life is very busy. I give shows, I organise shows for kids, I have to teach kids' league for small kids from six to seven years old to 15. I have a big league for the kids. The kids can win 3500 Euros for their savings account for later on for school, for everything that they want – their driver's licence or something, because the money's going to stay in the account till they are 16-17 years old. They can use it for their study if they want to go to college and everything. I did that. I organise a lot of shows. I do so many things, so the reading I do is mostly around work and training.

Well, that's a good scheme. You're putting back what you've been given.
I like to give. And I'm in a position now to give. It's a lot easier for me now. People are willing to help me because I am fighting well and putting also something back. Now people want to help me so when they help me, they also help other people.

Where do you see yourself in ten years?
I want to keep fighting for four or five years still and then I'm going to be having a school, a gym, do teaching. I'm going to be a trainer, mentoring a few guys. Also I'll be enjoying my kids and my grandkids.

Away from the cage, define a tough guy.
A tough guy can do everything. In life you have certain problems. You can walk away or you can go in. You know you can do everything that you want. If you are a tough guy you can do everything. This is what I mean – it doesn't matter what happens, you're always going to come up and be better. What doesn't kill you, makes you stronger.

Are you Rhino or No Mercy?
I kept 'No Mercy', but 'Rhino' is also nice, I like it. I never choose my own name. I find you cannot pick a nickname yourself because you have to deserve it. People have to think you deserve it, people have

to give you something out of appreciation, that's why they give you a nickname.

WES MURCH – 'THE IMMORTAL'

I met Wes Murch in the busy dressing room at the art deco Troxy venue on Commercial Road, in the East End of London. It was the evening of his fight against Francis Heagney from London Shoot Fighters at Cage Rage Contenders 5. Wes usually weighs in at between 73 and 77 kg, which means that he loses at least five kg from his walking weight in his final training and dehydration for each fight. Around us in the shared dressing room, Team Titan, Elite and Trojan Free Fighters are wrapping each others' hands. In the deeper reaches of the room, fighters for the next bouts are gently warming up, sparring with their training mates.

Wes Murch is sitting, having his hands wrapped by Ronnie Mann, who was the youngest ever Cage Rage fighter when he had his first professional bout. Ronnie patiently binds Wes' fingers with tape to add a little protection to that offered by the regulation lightweight gloves. 'The Immortal' is taking advantage of a few minutes peace amid the movement and noise of the dressing room, to mentally prepare for his bout. The image of the more experienced fighter talking quietly to the man still learning, sharing his knowledge, will stay with me for a long time.

As the cheering which greets the announcement of the last result dies down, Wes beckons me over with a bandaged fist. He's ready to answer my questions. We exchange greetings, a smile and a laugh. He's got a really big smile for a bloke who's just about to go five rounds in a cage.

You grew up in Bristol, what were your schooldays like?
I went to a comprehensive school. It was a predominantly white school, but there were three black kids in my year and they were my sort of group. I hung out with them. I grew up listening to drum and bass music and garage music, going back to their houses for Caribbean yard food and jerk chicken. I grew up with those guys. Those guys suffered a bit of bullying because of what it was like in our area, and they were the sort of guys who I stuck with, and that's how I grew up really.

How did you get into MMA?

I was doing some bailiff work with a friend of mine, James Thompson, who you might know as James 'the Colossus' Thompson. Anyway, I was doing bailiff work with him when had his first fight. I was competing at quite a high level at judo and he said, "You should get into this cage fighting, come training for a bit," so I did. Then James said, "I can get you a fight," and I had my first fight at Ultimate Combat 9. I fought there and won. I beat Phil McCall. That was 2003 or 2004. Things sort of snowballed from there really.

Are you religious?

I don't study a religion or practice a religion. I see religion as one of the biggest causes of racism. What I like to believe is that everybody's got the right to their own beliefs. Nobody's got the right to push a religion or their thoughts about religion onto somebody else. I like to think there's a higher being or a higher force, but I'm not gonna tell you that you're wrong for believing in, say, Allah, and I'm right for believing in my god. Everyone's got a right to their own religion. I don't have one myself, I just believe there's a higher being and a better place to go to after this life.

What inspires you to fight?

My training. I train really hard and I work really hard, and it really matters. People say, "Oh, it must be hard getting in the cage and fighting," but it's just 15 minutes of your life. When you're training six hours a day six days a week, the fight's the easy bit, all the hard work's done in training. The fight's where the fighter puts the training into practice. The hardest bit for me is finding the motivation to train. But when you're doing something that you really love and you really enjoy it's easy to get out of bed even at the hardest of times, you just pull yourself up and get on with it.

Who do you train with at Trojan Free Fighters?

James Thompson, Ronnie Mann – who's up-and-coming and gonna win a title, Zelg Galesic – who's just fought in Pride and beat Mark Weir in the last Cage Rage. There are a few other guys coming up, like John Phillips. It's a really fast-growing team.

THE FIGHTERS

Are there any fighters you look up to?

James Thompson, because I've trained with him from the beginning. I've seen that he's made it to the highest level, he's come over big obstacles, and he's still there. He fights obstacles every time he fights, and he's up there with the big guys. Along with him, you've got people like Mike Tyson who came from having absolutely nothing at all, fighting someone like Trevor Berbick and getting to be World Heavyweight Champion. For someone like me, it's a great inspiration that someone can come from that and achieve the world.

Are you intending to stay in MMA, or might you go back to fulltime work?

Fulltime work's not really an option for me anymore. I love what I do. This *is* fulltime work for me. I want to carry on doing this, and I want to get to the highest level. I want to continue with this, and then, when I'm done, I want to move on to teaching or training a team maybe or working with Trojan full-time and we can progress further from there.

How do you feel before a fight? How are you feeling now?

Now I feel good. I mean, I don't really suffer from nerves. The things that get me nervous are: Am I gonna make the weight? Am I gonna pass the doctor's medical? As soon as all that's done I think, "Ah, that's great, now it's time to fight." I don't see the point in taking nerves into the cage with me, because what's the point in training hard for three months and then throwing it all away with nerves? So I just think, "It's time to get your head down." Now I'm ready for tonight's fight. I'm focussed and I'll get on with the job.

How do you take losing?

I lost my last fight. I got caught with an arm bar. It was the best thing that happened to me. It was the loss of my record, but after all my wins I'd gone away and I'd thought, "Yeah, great fight! I'll go out and do that again." So in all other my fights, I fought very much as I had the last time. After losing, I had to study what I'd done wrong and had to work on my weaknesses, work on my mistakes. I know now that every single fight that I fight I need to take away and analyse what's been going on. It really does put me in a good frame of mind for my next fight.

How does the publicity from fighting affect your life?

That's part and parcel of the game. I like it. I like people coming up and talking to me. I don't like the drunk guys in bars who think that you're a thug and just want to say, "Oh, you think you're hard because you're a cage fighter." That's not the kind of thing I'm trying to project. I'm an athlete. I'd like people to consider me the same way they consider Sebastian Coe, or someone like that. Someone who they look up to and think, "He's trained hard." Well, fuck me, that's me, I'm an athlete, and I work hard for what I do. So, yeah, I don't mind publicity, as long as it's good publicity.

Are you married with family?

I've got a daughter. She's six years old. Married...? Well, I'm kind of seeing a girl now. I'm really close to my family actually. My dad's getting re-married today, but I'm missing the wedding because I'm here fighting. My mum's out in the crowd though, she comes to all my fights. I've got quite a good following out there today.

How long have you been with your girlfriend?

Probably about ten months now. It's one of those things that I didn't think was gonna last because there's a big age difference, as she's only 18. She fits in really well with what I do for a living, she understands. My ex-girlfriend couldn't handle the fact that I give up everything to fight. She didn't understand the passion that goes into what I do, so me and her sort of drifted apart when I fought. But this girl's really close, really understands. I think that the fact that she does understand my passion for fighting and how important it is to me has brought us closer. She doesn't really like to watch, it's not the sort of thing she enjoys, but she doesn't mind me fighting. She's very supportive.

What would you say to youngsters starting out?

Anybody can do anything. If you get bullied, don't allow yourself to get bullied. We're all human. You're just as good, no, actually you're better than anybody who picks on you or bullies you. You can overcome everything. It's just takes mind, heart and thought and you've got them as much as I have. I'm no different to you.

THE FIGHTERS

BRAD 'ONE PUNCH' PICKETT

Brad 'One Punch' Pickett was born for sport. Before he went anywhere near a cage he played cricket, rugby, basketball, semi-professional football, and had a career as a boxer like his dad and granddad. These days, he fights in a cage – the most exciting thing he's ever done, he told me. I was lucky enough to meet Brad during a training session at Team Titan. Lucky, because he isn't a man who likes to be interrupted. He takes his training seriously. Very seriously. Six days a week, five hours a day, in the gym and road training whatever the weather. He's chasing the featherweight belt, which he won at Cage Rage 13 when he beat Ozzy Haluk, before sustaining a serious injury. 'One Punch' knows about injuries, having fought back from (among other things) a torn cruciate ligament and hand damage. His health and fitness regime has been designed to maintain top condition, and it shows. No fast-food, lots of protein and a 24-hour fast before bouts have all contributed to 'One Punch's' current winning form.

At five foot six, Brad originally took up boxing to build weight, yet still fights as a featherweight at 66 kg. He looks every inch the east London boy he is, down to the accent and trilby hat. Brad likes nothing better then to fight at the Troxy in front of a home crowd. He's proud of his roots and his family, and not too upset that his nickname was awarded by fans who thought he looked like Brad Pitt in the movie *Snatch*. He's single-handedly responsible for the rise in the sale of trilbies in that part of London, as fans, friends and family all attend his bouts wearing them! Brad's a man of style, and very much in demand, as evidenced by his modelling and film career.

When Brad took a breather from his cardiovascular workout with Dynamite Dean, he was happy to sit down with me in the gym and share his thoughts and his jacket potato! He didn't take long to recover his breath (opponents beware!) and was soon telling me about his move from Elite to Team Titan in December 2004, his training trips to Florida with American Top Team and Ricardo Liborio, and a great deal more.

Tell me about yourself. You were a footballer at one stage?
How I got into the fighting game is I used to play football when I was younger and football has always been my number one love – big up the Spurs. When I was playing football, I was playing at quite a good level and I wanted to get myself fit. So between training and

football I decided to take up boxing, because the fitness training there is real good, intensive training, and it gives you good cardio. So I trained at boxing for about three to four months and after a couple of months, and they said to me, "Do you fancy having a fight?" And because I've got short man syndrome I was kind of like, "Yeah, I'll give it a go." I didn't want to sound like a sissy and say, no, I don't want to fight. So, I basically had one boxing fight and knocked the guy out, and didn't look back from there. I carried on training and boxing, having fights, and I was doing well at boxing. Doing really well at football. And I got to a stage in my life where I was thinking, "Do I follow football or do I follow boxing?" And then at that moment where I was at a crossroads I had a real bad knee injury and it put a hold to all my sport. I was told I'd never be able to do any sports again. After the surgery, the first thing I did was buy a pair of football boots because I wanted to get back playing football. Beside boxing, I wanted to play football. I started playing again against the doctor's wishes. Not at a high level, at a lower level with my mates. Where I was a defender before, I turned into a striker, so I didn't have to tackle as much, to protect my knee. It didn't work because I got the shit kicked out me of up front. Then I moved back to London. Went to the Peacock Gym to try and start up boxing again. I didn't really have the same sort of buzz and feel for it and then a mate of mine called Del Edwards said to me, "Why don't you try this cage fighting? I'm going to go up to Elite at Elephant & Castle – why don't you give that a shot?" I was a bit dubious at the start, thinking it was all rolling around with men and that, but I'm quite competitive. So I went up there and rolled around with Dave O'Donnell and I had a first session and fell in love with it.

Did you finish school?

Yeah. I wasn't really good at the intellectual side of things. I was dyslexic, so I found school very hard in terms of concentration. All I was thinking about was playtime; to play football, or when the next sport lesson was. It was all a physical thing for me, I loved all sports. I represented my school in basketball, cricket, rugby, hockey, everything. I was active in most things. I played a good level of football, I played for county at football and cricket.

Which county?

Northamptonshire. Then I boxed for East Midlands. I had county basketball trials, despite my size. I didn't actually get in the team but

I was quite good. Every sport, you name it, I've played it. I loved it, and I played at not a bad level for most sports. So after school I went to college and wanted to do Leisure and Tourism. I did my courses and all that, passed them all.

How much of a disadvantage was your dyslexia when you were at school?

I found it hard to concentrate. So it's definitely a disadvantage, so all I really did was concentrate on my sports. When I was younger I had it in my heart that I was going to be a professional footballer. Most kids dream that. I believed that I was going to really do it. Obviously, at 21 when I had a bad injury it kind of stopped it. I knew I wasn't going to get to a high level and get to be paid and live off it, but I loved football. I was always small and it made me the person I am today because I've got a lot of heart, I never give up, I'm a fighter, I'm competitive. When you're small in the playground, when you're playing football or playing rugby, you've got to fight. Kids were twice the size of me at school, so I had to fight to keep staking my claim in the football teams and stuff like that. So I had to put myself about, I had to put my life on the line. I found myself being really good in the air playing basketball and football, heading and stuff. I'm so small I had to jump all the time, so I got really good at jumping. So I had a good spring.

You became British champion?

Yeah, I'm the former featherweight champion at Cage Rage. I've fought internationally now, in Costa Rica. The highlight of my career was when I fought in the Los Angeles Coliseum in the USA in front of 45,000 people, in K-1. I fought that. Holding the belt at Cage Rage was another highlight of my career. Hopefully, it's not the end of my career, I'm still going forward.

What inspires you in fighting?

The will to win. I know that I'm very strong for my weight and I'm just very competitive, so I know that anyone who I fight my weight would always be in a fight. I would never make it easy for them. So it's not losing, I hate losing, I'm a bad loser, I never give up. I might even get my arm broken or end up on crutches.

How do you spend your time away from MMA?

At the moment fighting takes up a lot of my life. I'm trying to be a fulltime professional. Training takes up pretty much all my time. When I rest, I play a lot of computer games, I chill out on my laptop. Chill out, eat in, spend a lot of time with my girlfriend. I've got to look after myself. I'm no spring chicken anymore, I'm 29. I can't afford to go out and then train the next day.

Do you have a role model in MMA?
George St. Pierre. I think he's an astonishing fighter. If you could have one name that could stand for an ultimate fighter, all aspects of the game, it would be George St. Pierre. He's got great wrestling, great stand-up, he's the complete fighter to me. That inspires me and I look up to him. Before that I was a big fan of Bruce Lee when I was younger. I loved Bruce Lee. I related to him because he was small and strong and he had to fight to get anywhere in his life, and he did really well.

Who are the three people who have had the most influence in your life?
My brother is a big influence on me. He helps me out a lot and supports me. I'd say mainly my family, my mum and dad. They've always supported me and they've made me the person I am today. I've been brought up very well. My parents are old. My dad's 83 and my mum passed away the other year. She was 11 years younger. I was brought up the old fashioned way, and it gave me the morals I have today.

Everyone sees when you're entering into the cage. What's the outfit?
My trilby and braces and my white vest and my shorts.

That's very traditional. Why is that?
I'm from the East End. My mum was big into Chas & Dave and they were family friends. So it's an East End sort of thing. My granddad, my mum's dad, was a bare-knuckle boxer and he used to wear a trilby. It's a family thing. I used to wear it quite a bit outside, then when I started fighting I thought I'll wear it in. I thought I'd do something different you know, because everyone just comes in normally to the hip-hop music and 'I'm going to kill you' and 'you're dead' kind of music. I just wanted to bring a different sort of flavour to the whole MMA thing. You've got to sell yourself. You've got to see yourself as a product. And so I decided to stand out and be different to everyone else. I quite like the get-up. It's more

enjoyable rather than coming out, focussing, 'I'm going to kill you.' I forget about the fight as I'm coming out. When the music goes off and I'm in the cage, then I'm back in my fight mode rather than wasting all that nervous tension coming out, pumping yourself up. I just get in there and relax and then get ready to fight.

What are your emotions before and after a fight?
Well, before the fight my thought is don't get beat. As I say, I'm a bad loser. I never want to get beaten. If I get beat, it happens, but when I go into a fight, all I care is about winning. I'm not scared of my opponent, I'm just worried about getting beat in front of the people who have come and paid to watch me. That brings me on a lot. Like I say, I'm a bad loser, I'm more worried about getting beaten than anything else.

How do you feel after a win?
Thrilled to bits. No matter how easy or hard the fight is, I'm always emotionally drained and tired. I don't really go out on the drink after. I think if I have two beers I fall asleep. Even if I go in and knock the guy out in ten seconds, because the adrenalin's pumping all day, you're exhausted.

And if you lose?
Gutted. You reflect on where you went wrong. It depends on how the defeat came about. Did you perform well or just get outclassed? It has different aspects, you know. You feel like you've let yourself down, you feel like you let your family down. I remember a time when I got beat, when I went in there thinking I was going to win – thought the fight was going to be easy. I didn't train hard and I thought I was going to win, a walkover. I got beaten. It was my first loss. It had me in tears.

You actually cried?
Yeah, yeah. It's an emotional thing as well. I'm a man, I ain't too proud to cry. Emotions are emotions. They're there to be shown. You don't bottle things up. I feel everyone should show their emotions: angry, happy, sad, whatever. You should let your emotions out. So I cried, I was upset. I was upset with myself. As you say, there's a lot of tension, and yeah, I welled up. Then I promised myself I'd never let myself look like that again because I was a bit beaten up. So I try and protect myself a bit more now. But I do get hit a lot when I fight.

Are you religious?

I'm not religious, no, but I have very strong beliefs and I've got very good morals. I think I'm better than being religious. I'm good, I've got a very kind heart, I'm very friendly to people, I'm generous. All the good aspects that people go to religion to try and get, I already have them, because I've been brought up well by my parents. Do I believe in God? Honestly, no. If someone else believes in God, it's their own belief. I'm all ears. I listen to people. I've been preached at a lot by so many people about religion and all that sort of stuff. I don't mind. I take in what I want to hear and will decide what I don't take in.

How has MMA changed your life?

It's made me a lot more confident with myself, handling myself outside the cage. I don't really get into many street fights. I don't have to because you earn a lot of respect for what you do and a lot of people get to know you, they know not to screw around with you, so you don't really get into trouble like that. I feel good about myself a lot of the time. When you're training, you're fit and in shape. You always feel good about yourself if you're doing MMA or not. If you just like to run every day, you feel your body's in good shape and you naturally feel good about yourself. It's a good thing, any sort of exercise is good for you.

What's your favourite technique?

Striking. I'm a striker. I'm just trying to bang, knock someone out. It's me, it's what the crowd wants. It's what I want. It's fair combat, you know. The guy can't say, "Oh, you got lucky with a triangle, or submission." No, if you knock someone out they've got no comeback, they're out. You're standing above them.

Is there a fighter out there that you'd like to challenge?

Not really. I'll fight anyone my weight who you book! That's my game; I'm at a level now where I could fight anyone at my weight at any level. So I'm just ready to fight anyone. There's loads of good fighters I'd love to fight at my weight. Uriah Faber in America, he's a great fighter, Jeff Curran, there's a lot of American fighters who are really good and I'd like to fight them. There are a lot of Japanese fighters as well, like Kid Yamamato. They're all good fighters. Win, lose, draw, whatever, it would be good to fight them.

Do you still see yourself as an MMA fighter in five years?

No way, no way. I'm going to give myself a few more years, though. I want to do as much as I can in my career – two more years. Get enough of a name for myself and then go into training, teaching, become a personal instructor. Stay in the game definitely, but I don't want to be hanging around and making someone else's career: "Oh, he used to be quite good." I don't want to be someone's stepladder for them to get to the top. As soon as I'm not as good as I should be, I'll retire. Like you say, when you get older, you lose speed. The heavyweights last longer owing to their size. It's four years in boxing, you know. In MMA, when you're a smaller weight you rely on your speed and reaction times. As you get older you lose that. So that's why small people don't really last as long in the game as the heavyweights.

If you could influence or inspire someone, what would you say to them?

Basically, just train hard. In everything you do, anything you want to do, if you train hard, you can be the best. All you can do is be the best that you possibly can be and no-one else can take anything from you. If you push yourself, you push yourself. You know that.

Away from the cage, define a tough guy.

Someone who could stop trouble without raising his fist, with respect. If you're a tough guy, you don't have to be throwing punches and knocking 20 people out to prove yourself. A tough guy is the kind of guy that people love to look up to, respect, and they don't want to cause trouble around him because he's got a reputation.

POPEK RAK

I met Popek Rak at the Troxy. It's a major London venue for Cage Rage, and regularly draws crowds of 2000 people. Popek was making his UK debut in legal cage fighting that night, and while not overwhelmed by the setting he certainly respected the fact that he'd been given the chance to fight at such a prestigious venue. That night's fights were promoted by Dave O'Donnell and Andy Geer, who had spotted Popek at his regular training venue at Team Titan.

At 26, Popek brings a lot of fight experience to British Cage Rage, none of it from a cage or a ring. He grew up in Poland where he learned to defend himself on the streets. The night we met, Popek was wearing a black hoodie emblazoned with the words 'MMA Fighter', black tracksuit bottoms, and a black hat embroidered with several small white skulls and crossbones. Had he come, like a pirate, to raid the prize money, I wondered? But I didn't ask. Popek's fierce eyes, broad shoulders, and heavy build for his height of five foot eleven made me think twice!

This is your debut in the cage in England. How are you feeling about that?
I'm feeling a little nervous, but that's normal when you do something new, yeah? I'm nervous because I'm waiting... I just want to go to the cage and do my job. I want to do this tonight, I made an attempt to do this last year. I have been training pretty hard for this night, I'm ready for it now.

What were you doing before you took up MMA?
Before MMA, I just had a few illegal fights. No rules, no judges. Street fighting, you know. That's it. After that, I knew I had to do something more professional, so I'm here in England to try myself at cage fighting. I thought I'd try fighting with rules!

How was school for you?
What do you mean, school?

Your schooldays, what were they like?
School? I didn't go to school [laughs].

What did you do instead?
In the school time I was doing crazy things like robbery. Stupid things. I was in prison for seven years. Now I just want to do MMA. For the next ten years I think that will be my mission.

Why did you become a fighter?
I've been fighting since I was 15, on the street with no rules, no judges, no ambulances. I think it's just something deep inside me saying, "Popek, go fight," and I'm here. I can't tell you any better than that, because I don't know or understand this thing inside which makes me, drives me to be a fighter. I'm just myself. I don't know any more than that.

THE FIGHTERS

Where did you fight in Poland?

In my country, when you've got a problem with somebody, you will fight with him, like MMA fight – no guns, no knives, no nothing. Poland is simpler. It was always like somebody borrowed money and was never going to give you back the money, so you're going to fight him. In Poland everybody is looking for money.

Now that you are a professional fighter, if someone approached you in the street, would you fight them?

Yes, of course. If somebody asks me to fight in the next 30 minutes, I will do it. It's no problem to me. I would not fight in a cage in two days time because I have not prepared, my cardio would be no good. If you ask me to fight on the street, I have to do it.

What are your emotions before a fight?

It's like adrenalin. I feel like a junkie when I go to the cage. It's like a different world, different planet. Like a small world.

How did you feel after your first MMA win?

After my fight I was extremely tired. I was on the floor in the changing room for 25 minutes. I couldn't stand up. I couldn't even stand up on my fucking legs.

Do you prepare better now?

Every time I fight I want to go in the cage with 100 per cent cardio – bam, bam, bam, and that's it won. I know how to finish my opponent. I feel more confident because now I know how it is in the cage. I was thinking it is similar to a hip-hop concert. I play a lot of concerts with 1000 people, so when I see the crowd I'm not nervous.

Do you want to be a champion?

No, no. I just want to do a good effort. I want to fight, to go to a cage and fight for my fans, my hip-hop fans and for me. There are a lot of better fighters than me. I don't do it to be a champion.

What's your favourite technique?

It's 'ground and pound'. I feel like a fish in water on the floor, yeah? My opponent tonight is a kick boxer and I don't want to fight stand-up with a kick boxer. I want to take him down and get a submission or something with a knee lock, or an arm bar or something like that.

WARRIORS OF THE CAGE

Do you have a favourite fighter?
I've got a few. Tito Ortiz, Chuck Liddell, Ken Shamrock ... I could talk about fighters forever.

You have a phenomenal fan base.
They're just my fans from the clubs, from music. A lot of fans, fans, fans. 350 people have come to see me today, so there is big pressure on me you know. I am rapper, a professional rapper as well. I have made two albums. I have a tattoo of Tupac Shakur here on my chest. I play Victoria in UK, I play my second solo album, so I have a lot of jobs to do.

So has fighting legally in the cage changed you?
Yes. Legal fighting is very good because you've got ambulances if you suffer something. Ambulances, they give you a hand, they help you, you're not left in a corner like the last time I fought on the street. This is very important for all the fighters and for myself as well. Sometimes people are hurt and it's good to have help when that happens. There are 2,000 people in there tonight, and 350 of them have come to see me, so after that fight, when I've won I think there are gonna be more people coming to see me. More people are gonna see me in the cage than used to see me on the street.

Do you believe in God?
Yeah, of course I believe in God. I'm from a Catholic family. But God doesn't change things. I'm not such a good person, but I used to be worse. Five years ago I used drugs, a lot of drugs; cocaine, amphetamines, marijuana, everything. I stopped one year ago, and I just wanna train, train hard and be good. I just believe in myself now. Nobody's gonna help me if I don't help myself. So I have to do my best. That's it.

Is cage fighting a good direction for people like yourself to take?
Yes, of course. I think every sport is good. Mixed Martial Arts, cage fighting, K-1, anything like this. This one is tough, though. Cage fighting is a tough sport. There could be a lot of injuries from fighting. You could even break your leg ... it's really a tough sport, so not a lot of people do it, just a few hard people meet in cages and fight. It's not like boxing. For me, boxing is a very light system of fighting. MMA is what I want to do.

THE FIGHTERS

What do you see yourself doing in five years time?

I'm gonna do the same thing. I'm gonna fight, because the fighting thing is with me, in myself. I'm here, with my mentality. I know I'm going to do something proper now, not do drugs or drink alcohol and become a nothing. I wanna do something in my life and maybe I'm gonna do it as a fighter. I've got a girlfriend. It's no time for a family at this moment, because first you have to get money. You need money to have a family and to keep them, a job or something like that, and I'm not ready for it, not now anyway.

Can you see yourself opening a training school?

I don't know. I'm not thinking about a fight school any time soon. In my opinion, I need ten years training to learn, and then after that, maybe I could open a school and think about teaching others. I would tell them to train hard to be better fighters and to show their skills to everybody.

HENRIQUE 'THE LIZARD' SANTANA

Henrique and I meet in a Brazilian restaurant in Hackney, he's invited me to his birthday party. It looks warm and comfortable, and I've heard good things about the food. So have his family and close friends, it seems, as dozens of them have showed up for the celebration meal. As we go in, the steam, the aromas and the music in the background tell me we're in for a good, relaxed hour or so to talk. It's clear no strangers will bother us – they tend to give people a lot of room when 'The Lizard' is in the party. He just looks like a man who doesn't like to be interrupted by strangers.

As we settle at a corner table, away from the speakers, we exchange pleasantries while we wait for the food. Henrique speaks a kind of South American/north London, full of the soft sounds of his first language, overlaid with the glottal sounds of the London idiom. No wonder he loves the sounds in this place, and when I see his broad smile at the waitress, and her friendly grin at Henrique's daughter who's sitting on his lap, I know I'm experiencing the warmth of a culture I haven't encountered before. The cake was good too, and we all helped to blow out the candles.

Henrique came to England as a teenager – originally to study – and decided to stay. He had trouble persuading me that London has more to offer than Brasilia, but each to his own. He has been involved in MMA since 2003.

I believe your nickname is 'La Patisia', 'The Lizard'.
That's right. It comes from Brazil where I used to fight.

What were you like at school?
I always got bullied with other kids, so that's why I came to do martial arts.

Did you finish school?
Yeah, I finished school.

After school, did you get a job or did you go straight to fighting?
After finishing school I came straight to England, studied English and then started work. So I tried to learn the new culture. That was February 1996 when I first got here.

Where was your first ever fighting camp?
My first fight happened in 2003. My friend did martial arts and a little boxing. My teacher, he used to enjoy a cage fight, so he invited me once. He said I had a lot of talent and that was in Cage Rage 2003, when I first started enjoying it.

Who do you look up to or want to be like?
Anderson Silva, that's one guy who I appreciate. We come from the same city and his story is incredible and I like his style, the same as mine, and that's why I really like the guy.

What's your favourite way of spending your time away from the cage?
I love time with my family, especially. That's the main thing, enjoy my kids and my wife.

Would you show your kids the way to be a fighter like yourself if they wanted to?
I would like them to have choice in what they want to do in the future, but definitely they could enjoy the martial arts. I am going to make them learn jiu-jitsu, capoeira, whatever they need, for themselves. First of all, for self defence. Then once they've got that, it's up to them. If they really want to become a fighter like me, I

would definitely support them. If you get the support, that's a lot. I won't just say that because I did it, they can't do it. If they really want to, I will support them.

Who are the people who have influenced you in your career?
I have two people; my coach and my father. He really loves me to do it and he encourages me a lot.

Are you close to your family?
Yeah, 100 per cent. Without them, I'm nothing. I talk with them every day. My parents live in Brazil. I have two brothers and one sister who live in England and we're always together. My father comes over from Brazil every six months. So we are very close.

What are your emotions and thoughts before a fight?
I think about glory and winning. That's what I've got on my mind all the time. Never any weak feelings. Strong feelings are what I've got on my mind. Winning. That's what I want.

Once your fight is over, whether you win or lose, how do you feel afterwards?
Well, I just like to make it my job. That's what I think like, I've got a mission to do and once I do it I feel very, very relaxed. I take it very seriously when I've got a fight. It's something I have to do, and I will try to do my best to make this right. So once I finish that I am very relaxed. I just feel like I've finished my mission.

What made you start MMA?
Well, it just came day by day. Once I started enjoying the Mixed Martial Arts with a lot of people joining in, it is something I wanted to do in life. That's what made me become a fighter. It's something that I really love to do.

What do your friends and your family think of you fighting?
It's very hard, especially for my wife, and my parents, and my mum. They really wish for me to stop soon because they think it is a very, very dangerous thing to do to put yourself at risk. But, at the end of the day, it's what I like to do and I know they will support me.

I notice you're wearing a cross. Are you Christian?
I'm Christian, yeah. I've been born again.

Did you change your path to become a Christian?

No, no, this has come from my parents. My father is Christian so that's why I follow him for the religion. I am very open minded and I believe in God, that's the main thing. Every Sunday I go to church. I try my best to be as good as possible, if I work, if I'm training, fighting, I will hold the cross. It's something I believe and He will protect us. That's it.

Do you pray for your opponents as well?

Yeah, I always pray to keep them safe. I had a big fight before and I have been knocking people out. Before I free up my hands, I watch my opponent to see if he's alright. When we're there it's harder to think I don't want to hurt anyone. You have to hurt to win. But you hurt the way that he's going to be able to wake up, stand up and carry on his life. So I believe that if you hurt someone badly, I hope God is with them. God be with them and keep them well.

What are your challenges and goals within MMA?

I'm not really sure. I just let it happen, that's in my mind. I don't think about tomorrow. I mean, I think about today. What they give to me today is what I'm going to hold and I leave tomorrow for God to decide what is going to happen

What's your philosophy of life?

The main thing is that life is not easy for anyone, especially when you have a mission and my mission is to look after my family and the kids. For that I work really hard, I start at five in the morning. I train hard, I work as much as I can to keep the family and help friends, help family, everybody who is on my side. People that are not on my side, I still try to help them out. I do whatever it takes to get where I want and I know it's not going to be easy. I have a very hard life. I try to give the family what I believe is right. I believe my mission in the world is going to be fulfilled. I know it's going to take some time and that the hard work, it's not going to finish so soon. You have to believe yourself and you have to believe that you can do it, and just to keep going for every victory in life. Live one more day eating, drinking, and it's one more victory you get in your life. Once you know that, you will be happy. So that's the main thing. That's what I think.

Away from the cage, define a tough guy.

Probably my father. He's a very hard worker and he has always been good at heart to keep the family. I think he is a strong guy.

You mention your father many times. What does he give you?

I think that he was the man that tried to give me the best. He's the man that gave me support whatever happened, whether I was on the up or on the down. You know we go up, we go down. I see that same thing a lot in my trainer too. It's what I'm going to give to my kids. So my father is really important for me. If you don't have a father, you must have someone that can be like your father, to listen and to do what you believe is right.

IVAN 'THE TERRIBLE' SERATI

Ivan Serati was born and grew up in the north of Milan, the style capital of Italy, and it shows. Although he mostly trains and fights in England, he has fought all over Europe. He still spends a lot of time at home in Italy, where he is a taxi-driver. I don't imagine many try to run away without paying their fare.

When I'd rung him up, Ivan the Terrible had invited me to his hotel room on the fifth floor of the Wembley Plaza Hotel. I knocked on the brown door of room 512, only slightly nervous, despite the fact that Ivan's reputation had preceded him to UK MMA. I was about to meet one of the most feared men from Cage Rage, I didn't speak his language or he mine, and I had no idea who else might be waiting behind the door. Maybe I've seen too many movies, but I began to wonder what I might have let myself in for. I didn't have time to wonder for long, because the door was flung open and I found myself face-to-face with Matteo, Ivan's trainer and translator. He was clearly going to make sure that I would say and do nothing which might put his boy off the next day's bout.

Ivan was relaxing, lying on the bed wearing shorts, a t-shirt and listening to an iPod. I wondered how such a big bloke, with a fighting weight of 103 kilos, could actually get any rest on such a small piece of furniture. He sat up, flexed his tattoos, and smiled at me. It reminded me of the way he'd smiled when he'd knocked out his last opponent. Eight wins from ten fights in the cage, and the other two only lost on technical knockouts.

We talked through Matteo, whose English is certainly better than mine, and he had me beat on Italian, too!

How were your school years?
I only liked the practical subjects and the sports. I did finish school with some qualifications. In Italian it's called 'perito meccanico' – it's like a specialist qualification in mechanical projects with some other aspects. I've always been good with my hands.

What made you decide to become an MMA fighter?
Since I was young I've always liked boxing and every kind of fighting sport. I started with boxing in Italy and it was only in 1995 or '96 when I first saw Ultimate Fighting Championships – the third one – that I started to want to learn about MMA. I had to come to England in the end, because fighting in cages is illegal in Italy, so the gyms don't have all the equipment we need for training. I had to be very determined to do this.

So MMA must have changed your whole life?
Yes. I changed my job to taxi-driving so that I can train morning, evening and night and do my work around the training sessions. Now I live for this sport, and the rest of my life fits round it. I don't earn as much, but this is the choice I have made. If you have something you want to achieve, then you must change your life and do everything you can to make it happen.

Do you have a role model inside and outside the cage?
I look up to Anderson Silva for his high level of skill as a technical fighter.

Can you name anyone else who has influenced you in your career?
I can, but she's not a fighter – she's my partner. She knew me when I started to fight and she always is behind me in my training and practice schedules, and makes my ordinary daily life run smoothly too. She encourages me in my career and keeps worries away so that I can concentrate. She's a strong influence because she believes in me.

THE FIGHTERS

Why do you fight? There are many things you can do, so why fight?

It's my nature. I believe I was born to fight, I'm a natural. It's the thing I do best. I like to fight and beat other people and I like to use my skills in the cage.

What are your emotions before a fight?

I'm very, very nervous but I'm not nervous of fighting. I'm excited and nervous because of the event itself, the noise, supporters, music all make me excited. We do not have this in Italy – cage fighting is not encouraged, and we have few Italian fighters. So, to come to England to fight at Cage Rage, that is a big event for me. I don't care or think about what's in my opponent's head, because when the bell rings everything but the bout goes away and I want only to kill my opponent.

What about afterwards, what are your emotions? What if you were to lose?

I have only lost twice. I was more angry than anything. The first time was against Vitor Belfort and I was angry with myself because I made some big mistakes that I normally don't make when I practice in the gym. I've been working on doing the same things during the bout as I do in practice, keeping in control of my moves, as I don't want this to become a big problem.

Are you religious?

No, I don't believe in any of your gods. This is difficult in Italy, where religion is so important to almost everybody. If you don't believe in God, they treat you as if you've got three sixes on your back, like you are the devil or something. I cannot be religious because I don't believe in God, but I don't worship the devil or other things like that either. But in Italy, you know, not to believe is to be treated like an underdog. So, because they treat me like that, I do it all the more! Now I have had the three sixes tattooed on my back! People ask, why have I done this? I tell them, it is my pleasure. I like this, and all my other tattoos, they are part of who I am, who I have become.

What might you do when your MMA career comes to an end?

I think that my career is finishing because I am 37 years old. I don't care about winning titles, belts, or other things like that. I do care about getting good matches and opponents, and would like to fight for UFC. Other than that, I only want to add something good to the MMA story. I want people to remember me as someone who left good memories and experiences for the fans – big matches, big shows and some good victories. After retiring I'd like to stay in the fight world and use my knowledge to train guys that want to start practising MMA. I can help new fighters to get to the right places with the right people, I could guide them in the way that I was guided when I started out. I can be a role model for fighters who have to change the way their lives are so that they can get to train and fight.

Do you act the same in the cage as you do out of it?
I don't fight outside the cage. When I'm not in the cage I'm a normal person. I'm a quiet person. I work with the public when I'm driving my taxi, so I have to be quiet, be calm. When I'm not working, I sometimes let my passions loose, but when I choose to.

What if you bumped into a guy who thought he was a bit tough when you are out?
Sometimes, when I'm out, if I've gone to a club, I might have to show my machismo if I meet a guy that has a big head, or one who thinks he is a tough guy. I don't do this often. I'm a straight person and I'm focussed on my career. I want to finish the things I've started to achieve. I usually walk away from any fights that aren't in a cage. I keep myself to fight the real struggles of life.

JEAN 'THE WHITE BEAR' SILVA

I first met Jean Silva close to the merchandise area at Cage Rage. The t-shirts bore the slogan 'the White Bear' with a picture of Jean on them. It took me a second or two to realise that it was Jean himself pinning them to the railings. I knew at once that this guy was a hard-worker, determined to get where he was going and do what he was doing. In fight terms, I was looking at a winner. I wandered over to him, and said that even though I wasn't in the purchase market, I could assist him on his mission by interviewing him and publishing his story. It must have seemed like a good deal, because I soon found myself arranging to meet 'the White Bear' the next time he fought at Wembley. I never did buy a t-shirt, and Jean's not likely to give one away.

Some weeks later, at the weigh-in at the Wembley Plaza Hotel, we sat down over a pre-fight high-protein snack of sea bass and lightly steamed vegetables and juice. A lightly chilled Chablis would have gone well with it, but both being in training that wasn't on the cards!

Jean was wearing a t-shirt from his red range, and I was surprised at how good a likeness the graphic was of the face which sat above it. 'The Bear' fights at 71 kg, welterweight, which means that his narrow frame and haunting good looks sit as well with casual clothing as they do with his cage kit. They do say that he cuts a cool picture in his leathers on the 850cc bike, and that he doesn't really need a mean machine, because he *is* one already. Many of his opponents would agree, since he has won by submission on many occasions.

How are you today?
Yeah, I'm fine. I'm very happy about the next fight.

I see your hair's grown, it's getting as long as mine.
Yeah, yeah, I think it looks more nice, the girls enjoy it!

You've been with Cage Rage for a very long time. How did it start?
It was about five to six years ago when I met Andy Geer and Dave O'Donnell, and they just asked about the cage fighting. I didn't know then that this kind of style had become very famous in Brazil. They were looking to do something here, they organised the first show and invited me to fight at the York Hall in Bethnal Green. They made a great show there and I carried on.

What changes have you seen since you started MMA?
I think the most important thing is the rule changes. The role of the fighter is much broader now, it's improved. When I fought in Japan I didn't like their rules. Now MMA looks like a sport, not like a street fight. When there are no rules and when you can use your head, you can use everything, it's so horrible. But now MMA looks great and I hope it's going to be improved more.

What were your schooldays like? Did you finish school?
In Brazil I got to seventh grade, but I stopped school for fighting because it's my love. It's very bad, but I stopped studying and just

trained a lot, because I had a dream when I was a little boy and I used to tell my friends that one day I'd be a good fighter. All the friends just laughed at me, but here I am now.

So you would fight a lot at school?
Yes, lots and lots. When I was a little boy I was in a lot of fights, I realised that a good fight is just great. But I'm not a little boy anymore. Now I don't fight in the street anymore.

You're not exactly the biggest guy, so even in school you must have been small. Were you ever picked upon, or were you the bully?
Yeah, yeah, I was small. The problem was just because of the girls – all the girls. It's the same today: I meet some girl and the guy goes, "Come on, man, that's my girlfriend!" I don't care, man, what can I do? So I say, "Okay, let's go fight."

So you always dreamed of being a fighter?
Yeah, yeah, yeah. Nothing else.

What is your background?
I was born in a very, very poor place and there were a lot of really bad guys. My dad was forming a team, teaching Vale Tudo from his house so that people could train together. They just enjoyed training and I thought to myself, "One day I'll be out of this place and I'll carry all my family together. One day I'm going to buy a proper car and a house to put my family in," because when I lived in this very small place a lot of people had to sleep there together, my brothers, my dad, everybody. They sold plastic bags in the market to survive. Always I thought the same thing: "I'll be a big fighter one day." Sometimes people laughed at me.

You were selling bags to make ends meet?
Yeah, I sold plastic bags because in the markets in Brazil it's normal. People buy something but they have no bags. So I sold the bags to survive and I sold other stuff, like ice cream, that they sell in the football places.

What persuaded you to continue until you got to where you are now?
I think everybody has got this in themselves, everybody has to take chances in life if you're a man. If you've got something, not just an

ability to fight, if you've got a dream you have to believe in yourself, that's it, and never, never give up. In this life everybody has to be a warrior.

What advice would you give to children today?

Firstly, don't do the same as me. Young people have to carry on at their studies and they have to keep training, to improve and learn and think for yourself. Whatever you do, you have to put your mind first. It might take a time to be successful, but one day it will happen.

So are you saying that education is more important than MMA? A lot of guys are getting more involved in MMA and giving up education.

Yeah, I think of course people should have their education.

How do you like to relax outside the cage?

Man, I've got some music. I like to dance. I like the girls. I go to clubs sometimes. I don't drink a lot, but I enjoy a couple of drinks and dance. I love to dance. If I don't keep fighting then one day I suppose I'll start dancing.

What are your ambitions for five to ten years time?

Firstly I want a good team in Brazil, and to teach a couple of guys. One day maybe I'll manage a team, and maybe in ten years I want to see my boy here carrying on my job. He was four last Saturday. My boy in Brazil has started fighting, he's a committed fighter.

You train very hard. How much time do you get to see your children?

That's so difficult now, it's so difficult to see my boy. Sometimes when I ring him, he says, "Dad, why don't you live with me all the time?" But I have to spend a couple of years here, that's why. It's quite difficult to explain to him, but one day he's going to understand better.

Can society benefit from MMA?

I can't explain it very well: out of the cage I respect everybody, but I don't respect anybody when they stand *in* a cage. Some people see me fight for the first time and think that I don't respect anybody. But a fight is a fight and everybody has to understand this. You have to explain a lot about respect to people.

WARRIORS OF THE CAGE
MARK 'THE WIZARD' WEIR

I'm pissed off. I'm at Paddington train station and I've just missed the 9.46 to Gloucester. I find an alternative via Swindon and eventually arrive at Gloucester station four trains and six phone calls later, where 'the Wizard' awaits in his Land Rover. He welcomes me as he scrolls through his phone preparing his future appointments. What a calm environment – but then again, coming from London, most towns are. As we drive to his home, I take in the surroundings, contemplating if this could be an area for me to live in. Observing other drivers while discussing appointments on his headset, you get the feeling that this is a man who is serious and organised about his business. Mark has been there and done it. He's beaten the rest to be the best in Mixed Martial Arts and kickboxing and has even featured on UFC. He still fights, and also organises and runs training for adults and children in Gloucester. This is the wizard of wizards, a man who has truly earned respect, not just in the MMA scene but also in his county.

When we arrive at his home, Mark greets me with two full boxes of nutrition bars and has a bowl of tuna and pasta for himself. He's already wearing a tracksuit, ready for his evening training session. This is a man who is strict in his diet and his discipline day and night. As I take a seat I meet the eyes of his dog, a ridgeback, which stands around four foot high with a brown coat. He's inspecting this new intruder. Having owned two rottweilers, I was in no fear as there was only one general in this house and when the Wizard waved his wand the dog responded to the command. Mark explained that Leon the referee and Che 'Assassin' Mills both live within a ten-minute journey and that Matt 'the Hardest' Ewin lives seconds away. How amazing is that? We drink our fruit juices while he tells his story.

What were your schooldays like?
I didn't have a very good reputation. I was always getting into trouble fighting, usually. I relied very much on my survival instincts in junior school. A lot of it was to do with keeping to yourself, keeping away from people who had racist tendencies, and basically just looking after myself and my sisters who were in the same year.

Were you ever bullied at school?
No, I had a sort of madman perspective. What I did was I created a

persona where if someone said anything racist to me, I'd leave it for a bit and when their back was turned, I'd jump them. They just thought I was mad. I didn't care if I got beaten up, but the main thing was getting that guy who racially assaulted me. I don't know why they did that.

What inspired you to become who you are now?
Muhammad Ali inspired me. To me the guy is amazing. The other person who inspired me to be the person I am is my father. The reason for that is because I tried to do so much to please him. In doing that, I realised I can't please anyone else but myself. My father was such a hard person. Even when I won the world championships in taekwondo, which was a big sport at the time, one of the biggest, he just said, "Is there money in it?" So I thought, "Right, don't try to please him anymore. I'm going to please myself." I progressed to a higher level for myself.

You're using your own training to teach others. How did that come about?
As soon as I could kick and punch, I learned the basics of martial arts. A few friends were impressed and they came round to my house and I started teaching them indoors. Then the word got about and more people wanted to come. I was winning everything I went in for, every competition in all of the traditional arts, taekwondo, you name it, I was winning. I was doing about five to eight competitions a year and more and more people came round. And then my reputation grew and grew. So coaching was just a natural progression. Also it allowed me to analyse everything I was learning because I had to pass it on, which is harder to do.

Were there difficulties growing up black in Gloucester?
In Gloucester I watched a lot of opportunities pass me by. I've been to London for a few interviews and things that have been arranged, but a lot of times they've grabbed someone closer for that work rather than to get someone to travel. It's only since Sky went up that they travel out of their way and leave London to do an interview with someone like myself.

You have children, do you want to pass a love of MMA on to them?
I don't really. I've always just passed on the experiences I've had in my life. MMA is just an extension of what I want to have in my life.

I try to tell them I will support them 100 per cent whatever they want to be, but I say to them don't try and live my life instead of your own. Don't chase martial arts down. If you find you like music, dancing, singing, follow that. Whatever your heart's in, you follow that the best you can and I'll help you.

What made you decide to fight MMA?
It was just a natural progression from single martial arts to lead me to MMA. Taekwondo is traditional karate. 1996 was the first organised MMA event I ever came across. It was the first in the country, and I fought in it. They had good men on there like Lee Hasdell. I think the under-card kickboxing was Alex Reid, but I was the main event, fighting Buster Reeves. Ever since that, I had a taste for Mixed Martial Arts and then I always kept looking out for it because it meant I only had a fight once or twice a year.

What do you do in your spare time?
I love my family outright. I just love sports. My main things are having a pleasurable time, I like watching movies when we're together. We play a lot when we go on holiday, any time we spend together, that's great to me.

Are you religious?
Yeah, I'm very religious, so religious I keep it to myself. I don't really talk to my wife too much about it, or my kids. I teach them to be grateful and pray before a meal. I don't talk to my friends too much about it, even the ones who are religious. I sit down and talk to them about their religion, but I'm very personal on my side because of my beliefs. I try to analyse religion as such, and my views on it are very strong, in a way that I tend to keep to myself.

What are your beliefs?
That there are powers we don't understand. I do believe in God as such. Jesus ... I've got a perspective on that sometimes. I've been told lots of different things about religion. I believe that some people are gifted and some people can be led easily. I believe there's an almighty power. I don't believe anything ceases to exist so I believe in reincarnation, because science has proven that. But, where science tries to take religion away, I don't like it. I do believe there are things even science can't prove. I do believe I'm blessed and that God only helps those who help themselves.

So I know I must help myself, because God will only help me if I try first.

You come across as very spiritual and philosophical. What nurtured that?

Survival really. I had a very hard upbringing. Me and my sister had it the worst. We're an Afro-Caribbean family, so it was either make or break. I was very aggressive when I was younger and I believe I'm a better person than what some like to think. So I decided to look within myself and try and correct myself. We will all always react, respond, talk and laugh, or show characteristics that we picked up when younger. So my main goal is to better myself and slowly strip away the imperfections, strip away the bad and try and recreate good. In other words, reading, studying, trying to become a better person.

What book are you reading now?

I'm not reading anything special at present. I tend to come across a book once in a while which captures me, and which I think is unbelievable. And then I'll read those books over and over again after underlining certain areas or paragraphs. *Thick Face, Black Heart* has always been my outright favourite. *Book of Five Rings* is another one I like and also *Rich Dad, Poor Dad*, which is very good for business ideas. Those are the ones that come to mind at the moment.

Have you achieved your childhood ambitions?

Yeah. I've always wanted to be a great fighter, but I didn't have a sport as a framework, and now it's my life. I wanted to go into engineering and I've already accomplished that and gone as far as I can go. Engineering has got me to where I am, got me a nice house. Career-wise I wanted to get money behind me to be able to start my gym, and I did that as well. So whatever I dreamt of as a child, believe it or not, I kept it, followed it through and I completed it.

What are your emotions before and after a fight?

Before a fight I get excited because I just can't wait. I love fighting. You know there's no way I'll be fighting for 20-odd years. Right now I'm 41 and I'm finding there's so many people fighting now, in so many clubs with lots of members, that I've got to concentrate on the upcoming talent. I've had my time, so I find it harder to jump in the cage and fight. But in the early days I used to fight anything up to ten times a year. When I changed to Mixed Martial Arts, I was still fighting about six times a year. There's no way you can be doing that amount of fights unless you really enjoy it. So by now I should have slowed down, but I've been forced to slow down anyway, due to focussing in other directions.

Would you recommend MMA as a form of self discipline?

Yes. You can understand how to control your aggression. It allows you to hit and be hit without malice, without retaliating. The first thing people do when they spar – I see it in a lot of people – they just want to hit someone and if they get hit they just want to hit the person harder. But you don't take it any further. You laugh, you get hit, you laugh about it, "Oh, you just caught me," and you just take it lightly. The other thing is I've studied knife fighting for two years. Actually seen video footage of what a knife can do. I realised that just in the arm along from the wrist, the inside of your elbow, up by your armpit, how many different areas you can get caught and your life could be over. Within about a minute and a half you pass out and you're dead soon after that. I wouldn't even consider tackling a knife, even though I've been taught to fight a knife. So I think training helps in that way. It cuts down your tendency to want to be violent and it also makes you understand that when you get hit, you don't really have to retaliate. You get used to not reacting, because you've learnt that you don't have to prove anything. Unless, obviously, you get hit seriously hard or badly.

Define a tough guy.

There's two sorts of tough guys. There's mentally tough – that's a person that never quits and never gets put down and seems to keep driving himself until the end, until they literally die. A physically tough guy is a person whose pain threshold is high – he's determined, he doesn't like to be defeated. I've got a lot of that in me because I always like to push and see how far I can go before I pass out or get dizzy spells. Anybody can inflict pain on someone lesser than you, but not everybody can take physical pain.

Would you ever take your fighting team to Europe?

Not really. I've got about six or seven gyms at the moment. The main one's Gloucester. I've got another one in Stroud, which has just done well. It was on this television programme, *Fighting Fit*. I've got two in Stroud and another two in Nailsworth. There's one at the government camp, GCHQ. I'm running a club there. What I want to do is start spreading and having a recognised system of training. The thing I bring, which is different to most martial arts, is a system of training. You can go to any of my clubs and we have the same warm-up principles, training principles, programmes to get yourself ready – it's called the Rage Fighting Programme. It teaches you how to better yourself from start to finish. The way it's supposed to work, if you like to fight, you fight, you study, you improve. But you're constantly improving because you're studying, upgrading yourself and your knowledge and experience. It covers fighting, self defence, martial arts, the mental approach. Whether you've got a belt or not, you've got to be able to defend yourself if someone's coming after you. There's more open knowledge, not just the skills for straight-forward fighting in a cage.

Has MMA changed your life?
Martial arts changed my life in 2002 because of television. The first time I was on a pay per view event, I won. After that, I must have had hundreds and hundreds of people storming me on the day just to get my autograph, which was unreal. I felt recognised for all the years I've been training. Even travelling to America, people still recognise me. It means that I can go to practically any part of the world and people will recognise my face, which to me is a high. At the same time, I know that everything is short term. You know nothing lasts forever, so I enjoyed the moment, but the main thing I had to do was strive for the next 'high', the next point of where I can impress myself on the world.

What was your greatest turning point?
1988, winning the World Championship at taekwondo. I proved to myself that no matter how small, how little, how minor you think you are, you can do great things. 2002 was probably the biggest thing that happened after that, there was the recognition. I finally got rewarded financially, but also world recognition. But self recognition with my friends around me – that happened in '88.

Have you ever had a moment of fear?
I think fear probably came when I was a teenager, early teens. I lost a best friend. He had an asthma attack. I kept on thinking I was going to die soon. I didn't realise you had to die really, you don't consider things like that. His brother is still one of my best friends.

He's a few years older than me. I remember he was in a worse place than me. So I went round and we're close friends now. I think what I feared was that any of us can die at any time.

JAMES 'THE MESSENGER' ZIKIC

This man is no ordinary man. When you think you're close, you're not close enough. When you have hit him, it's not hard enough. It's like knowing the unknown. Who would ever believe that he would beat the likes of Cyborg to claim the Cage Rage light heavyweight title belt? Who's next, Melvin Manhoef?

James Zikic is not your average six foot two, 93 kg muscular guy with bulging biceps, visible laterals or a tree trunk of a neck. But you should never let the definition, or lack of it, deceive you. To me, this man is a gem with hidden facets. A diamond in the rough.

Having trained with top MMA fighters and even in Cyprus with boxer David Hayes in late 2008, 'the Messenger' is a uniquely spiritual figure within the MMA scene.

It's a Saturday, Greco-wrestling at London Shoot Fighters, the class has already started and Zikic appears wearing London Shoot Fighters hoodie, blue jeans and a pair of Timberland boots. I notice his untied laces and realise he's made his entire journey like this, head full of training and time and nothing else. It's as if to say, "Let's get this going." He greets me with a thumbs up, then gets involved with the rest of the warriors. He didn't even warm up, another sign of a true soldier, always ready for war without bearing in mind the possible after effects. London Shoot Fighters have gained a lot of respect within the MMA scene through their many victories with fighters such as Mark 'the Beast' Epstein, Mustapha Al-Turk, Francis Heagney and many other quality fighters. London Shoot Fighters is regarded as one of the best camps in the UK for Brazilian jiu-jitsu.

After the session Michael Johnson, an MMA fighter himself, congratulates his trainees. 'The Messenger' directs me into the gym so that we can talk. He's a surprisingly thoughtful and private man. They call him 'the Messenger' because he's a committed Christian, one of God's disciples, but also because he spreads the word about the benefits of MMA, especially its discipline and philosophy.

THE FIGHTERS

'The Messenger', how did that name come about?
[Extreme Brawl founder] Andy Jardine came up with the idea of calling me 'the Messiah'. But I wasn't really happy about that, so eventually I got it changed to 'the Messenger', because I believe I'm here to give a message to the public through my fighting. I'm an ambassador for the Lord, so that's why I'm 'the Messenger'. I'm not the Messiah.

Were you ever bullied at school, or were you a bully?
I had a little bit of trouble at school. I wouldn't fit in with everybody. I had my fair share of fights at school and outside of school. Sometimes fights would be arranged with other schools. I had my own sort of group of people that I hung around with. We had differences with other pupils.

Did you take school seriously?
I was just going through the motions. I was attending all the classes. I would never try and skip school, but my heart wasn't really in any of the subjects, you know what I mean? I was cut from a different cloth. There was always something deep down that I was searching for that I couldn't find in any of the subjects at school.

Do you still have the same ambitions that you had as a child?
I've always wanted to be some sort of great warrior, that's always been a kind of dream in me. I don't know if it's from watching a lot of fighting films when I was young, but I always had that passion in me.

Did you go to college after school?
Yes, I did go to college and studied various subjects, but again, there was no real passion behind me for any of those things. I was also training in traditional martial arts from my teenage years.

You seem very focussed and determined. What inspired you to become who you are today?
It's an internal thing really. I believe it's God-given. All my talents have been given to me by God and it's something within me.

You've mentioned God more than once. Are you religious?
I'm a born-again Christian. I believe that Jesus died for my sins and there's redemption through His blood. So He's always first in my life. There aren't any limits when it comes to God. The closer I've been to God, the more I've done the right thing, the more success I've had

in my fighting. The times when I haven't done great were when my spiritual walk had been quite poor, so the two go hand in hand. It doesn't hinder but enhances. Some may come to the wrong judgement that Christianity can hinder, but it enhances. I mean when my spirit is strong then the body follows. When I'm weak in myself, then the body is weaker.

Do you have a role model from the cage?

Randy Couture is a most inspirational figure in Mixed Martial Arts. You know, at his age (45), to carry on beating these young guys coming up is phenomenal. He is the single most inspirational figure for me. He's set a new standard. Forget all the preconceived ideas about age and everything. He's set a new bar and it's good to have guys that you can reach up and try and emulate.

Away from the cage, who else is a role model for you?

Well, I'm so fixed on fighting that most of my role models will actually come within fighting itself and not from everyday life.

How do you have fun apart from in the cage?

I like to travel a lot. Going to a new country is good. I like to go to places like Brazil. Lying on the beach, doing a bit of surfing, or hang gliding, or going into the rain forest or something like that. So travelling is my thing. I like to see different cultures and new places. And reading great books, I have an interest in books that give you an insight into what's really going on in the world.

Could you name three people who have influenced you in your career?

Three people that influenced me most are probably my very first karate instructor, Andrew Watson. He instilled in me a lot of discipline and self control through my teenage years. Not necessarily the technical aspect of the martial art, but the mental and psychological aspects. He was a great influence. And also Shamrock, who I trained with in my early twenties and he took me to the Super Bowl in Hawaii where I won a four-man tournament back in 1999. He was very innovative at that stage, and was the first guy to show the importance of cardiovascular conditioning in the UFC when he outlasted Tito Ortiz. Sham showed what conditioning was all about and paved the way for other fighters to emulate that. And the third person is Randy Couture because he's set the bar and he set the standard. Game lad.

THE FIGHTERS

What emotions do you have before and after a fight?
Before a fight I like a calm environment. I like tranquillity. Some fighters like people to gee them up and shout in their ear. But I like the calm before the storm. I like to be pretty focussed. I like my mind to be clear as I'm entering the cage for what I'm about to do. And then after, the sensation of winning is a great feeling. Also realise that I've beaten another human being and I have respect for my opponent. If they're injured in any way I don't lord it over them.

And losing?
Then I'm very critical of myself. You know it's not pleasant, but you have to become more determined to get back in there and erase the loss and work on the things that put you in that position. After a fight, I work on the mistakes I've made.

Your fight against Cyborg was phenomenal. Did it affect your life after that fight?
I got a lot more respect after that fight because it was a war. I didn't give up, I just kept holding on, I kept believing that I was going to win. I went after the victory, and I had a lot more respect from people after that fight.

What are your future MMA plans?
I'm entering into a phase where I'm bringing together all the things I've learned over the years to become the most well-rounded fighter I can be. I still have big dreams of entering the most prestigious organisations in MMA and becoming a world champion, becoming the Number One ranked fighter in the world.

Do you have plans for once your MMA career has ended?
I'd like to share my knowledge that I've learned over the years in the striking arts, in the grappling arts. I'd like to do that with willing fighters that want to achieve. I could become a good teacher.

Would you teach just in the UK or would you take it overseas?
I enjoy travelling, so I wouldn't mind teaching wherever the market is. Wherever's available, I can go.

Do you believe that MMA is a good thing for young people?
MMA separates the men from the boys. It develops character in

people. You find that most fighters are usually decent people, they all have decent hearts. Those with less moral fibre can't usually handle the training. So it is good for developing character in youngsters and keeping them out of trouble. It's a good outlet.

You mentioned reading before, what kind of books do you read, and do you have any recommendations?
I read a lot of books, religious books, books relating to the Bible. I read books about world events, conspiracies. I read a lot of auto-biographies of people that have achieved great things in life. As for recommending, well obviously I'd say the most important book to me is the Bible itself and also other books on strategies. Strategies of the Samurai and mental strategies that very few fighters use today.

Define a tough guy.
A person who is confident within themselves and doesn't have to show the world how tough they are. The toughness is present in the action, in doing the deed. It's produced in the ring. Somebody who has true toughness is not a coward. Also, a tough guy has to have morality – you have to be fearless to be moral. A coward can never be moral. A person who has integrity and virtue has real strength, and that is real toughness.

You're a national and international icon in MMA. How does that affect your life?
It's not like I feel I've become some kind of icon – I just get a lot of respect from people within the MMA community. They look up to me, and some people who start training see me as a role model. It's not like I've become some kind of big-time celebrity outside the MMA community. You never know though, that might happen one day! I might get that sort of recognition, but I've just become a kind of an icon within the British MMA.

What's your philosophy on MMA?
To the fighter MMA has to be the be all and end all, because the struggle in the cage or in the ring can represent the struggle of everyday life. How you deal with stuff inside the cage can also reflect how you deal with stuff outside, in life. You find out if you're the person that gives up under pressure, that folds at the first punch, or the one who keeps striving forward, keeps persevering until you've conquered your goals and achieved things that you really dream

about. The way people's characters show in the cage, the truth comes out, and people can see what you're made of. Life and fighting go hand in hand because life is a fight and the most important thing is to never give up. You should always persevere and hold on to your dream.

Is there a message that 'The Messenger' would like to send out?
I'd just like to say to any aspiring fighters that posterity is the greatest judge of all. When you look back at a period in history, then you can judge, then you can say whether this fighter was great or whether this fighter was not great. Never give up when people tell you that you can't make it. Go out and prove them wrong. Go out there, train hard, train like a champion, train consistently. Consistency is the key to all success. Always be disciplined. What you do outside the ring has a habit of turning up inside the ring, so live a clean life and do what's right, be committed and never let go of your dream and you can do it.

SAMI 'THE HUN' BERIK

Sami Berik was born into the Turkish community not far from Wood Green. He stands five foot ten, usually weighs in at 75 kg and trains at the Bloodline Academy in north London.

Sami's extensive knowledge of wing chun, tai chi, Brazilian jiu-jitsu, wrestling and kickboxing means that his style is constantly evolving. He has been Armageddon Welterweight Champion, and also held the British san shou title. He now fights pro MMA at lightweight. Sami is a fighter who taps into his intuition to improve upon his natural abilities. His unpredictability in a fight, and the heart of a lion, mean that he is always going for the kill, and his awesome striking is usually treated with considerable respect.

What did you train in before MMA?
I always did traditional martial arts as a hobby for self development, from the age of 14 until I was about twenty, when I started to go to tai chi. We did lots of pad work, stand up clich work and used the concepts and drills of tai chi. Through that I entered Chinese boxing, chen xiao. We introduced Chinese boxing competitions which were full contact fighting at the end of tai chi competitions.

There was a promoter who saw me and she offered me a fight on the pro chen xiao circuit. Chen xiao is basically a ring with no ropes, it's really just a platform off the ground, it's like kickboxing rules, and when you get in a clinch you've go three seconds to do a throw. You can throw them out of the ring, so it's fun. That was in 2000. It's a leap from Chinese boxing to MMA and I needed to learn about grappling. So I was checking the internet and I found a thing called open mat, it's a grappling competition with no head shots.

So was that the real beginning of MMA for you?
Yes, it was really. I entered the competition for experience. I won one and lost two and it was good experience to see how I could measure myself. After that I emailed Ultimate Combat to see if I could fight there. They refused me three times because they didn't know who I was, and I had no experience in the cage. They understood that I could fight, but felt that they couldn't just put me as an unknown into a big show, though eventually they gave me my chance in MMA. I didn't have a manager.

You're a full-time fighter now. How did you earn your living before that?
I worked in Woolworths. We all start off somewhere small.

Has your past made you the man you are now?
What's important is a person's perspective on good or bad. Every loss I've had, I hold high. It's what's made me who I am. If I had ten losses and 20 wins, I wouldn't be able to sleep at night until I'd beaten people, if you see what I mean. That's the sort of person I am.

What are your emotions when getting into the cage?
Keep cool. Keep my head clear, and then get ready to go all out, because there are no excuses for screwing up. It's like I'm there to do a job.

How do you feel when you've lost a fight?
Each time I have a fight I'm in a different state of mind. I keep testing myself. I come out angry for one, chilled in another. I have a different game plan for each one, so when I lose it depends on that state of mind, and things like how much time the fight took. I always make it positive after, so it might be that for 30 seconds after

I've lost, I'm going, "Damn, shit, how did this happen?" and then it's like, "It's all easy, don't mind about the little things." I dwell on a loss for 30 seconds, or maybe a few minutes.

That sounds spiritual?
Karma is common ground for everyone. So, intent-wise in a fight, it's not that I want to hurt the person, I just want to finish it. See, if when I go to punch someone and for a split second I'm going to enjoy hitting him, that means I stop thinking about the next move. Emotions in the cage take up time, so I'd say you have to narrow it down. Even when I've blasted someone up, I don't get satisfaction from the fact that I've beaten them and put them down and raised my hand up. When I've blasted the guy so much that when it's that final blow and he stays down and the referee comes over, even if I could do a bit more damage, I don't. Usually the guy is appreciative of it. We can fight each other again and test ourselves again. It's not a case of 'the more blood the better'.

Breaking someone's arm or leg is not a nice thing to happen.
C'est la vie [that's life]. If it happens during the fight and my arm breaks, I won't get angry. But to break an opponent's arm, to break his leg, I don't really care. That's why I go for the kill in my fights. I don't hold back. I'm putting my whole existence in all the movements it takes to make a punch, and when I do it in the cage it's gonna amount to something. In the time it takes for a fight we go all out with one another until it's time to stop. I never punch anybody outside the cage. People don't know what a punch is, it's my whole existence behind each punch. The way I see it, fighting is the extension of a conversation. With fighting, it's what you can get away with. If someone's going for a takedown on me and then I go to grab his head, then I remember and I let go straight away even if it means splatting myself on the floor.

What inspires you to keep fighting?
Fighting's open ended. Anyone from any planet could understand what a fight is, an animal can understand what a fight is. I find it troublesome and tedious to argue, but comfortable to fight. You could bring me someone from another country or another background, but if we end up fighting in MMA we speak the same language and we understand each other. In fights you see how people are, even if I respect someone and I have a fight with them,

I'll hold them as close as a brother after the fight. If they happen to be in the UK in the future I'll help them in any way I can.

MMA has been called brutal, is that fair?
Each person who fights brings their own intent into it. You could have 100 people in a fight all doing neanderthal caveman style, everyone wants to see a knockout. I'm involved in everything, but I go all out. It's like a symphony. Each fight can be different. I could say in my next fight that I'll compose, but I only know the beginning, and I'll know the next bit when he steps into sight, I wanna see what moves he makes. It's just for the fun of it in between.

Do you ever fight outside the cage?
No. The moment you hit someone, you stop. I've done door work at a place where the doorman weighed 100 kilos, and they were smirking when I asked for a job. I've only had two scuffles, one was a choking, he was drunk and I stopped him going in. He was choking himself as he was running forward from me, and I had to punch him while we got the manager. I avoid it, I do it by talking. I'm not gonna fight outside the cage.

What do you do when you're not fighting or training?
I take it as it comes. I enjoy my days, whether I'm gonna help my mother with the shopping or do nothing. When I fight, that five minutes is equal to five years, time is relative and open-ended. Time for me is not like time for most people. I like to read and listen to different types of music, but I'm not musical. I'm going more into teaching now and teaching on the internet too, as another way of proving myself as a fighter. My whole life revolves around fighting and I can't shirk that. My job is to hit people, so there's a counterbalance to that, I will do things like helping people in the community to keep the balance.

How does your family support your fight career?
My close friends and family mostly find it hard to watch the fights. My mum watches all my fights but doesn't like to see me get slammed, she says that it sometimes makes her want to crack the head off my opponent! It's worrying. I always smile when I come home, because I can't look like I'm getting hurt. My mum makes my lasagne. You can't beat your mum's cooking. Some people get this readymade stuff, but you miss all the nutrition if you buy it.

Is it worth it?

If people are doing it only for the money, it's not worth it. If I break my arm or leg, it's not worth it, there's no amount of money would be enough if I broke a limb because I regard myself as priceless. I only get paid what the market pays, it's a matter of supply and demand. I usually get £3-400, sometimes £900, if it's a promotion or at short notice. Money is a by-product of my self-improvement. I might fight for peanuts, for £50 if I want to. I'm 27 this year and it's my year. I feel so comfortable. I'm gonna be a millionare by the end of this year, through teaching. Money from fights is a by-product.

Do you believe in God?

Yeah. I see religion as a tool, it's about what you do for yourself. Common ground and karma. I've a funny way of measuring things – if I were to help an old lady across the road, she's in a bond with karma. I get more karma for helping her.

How long do you plan to fight?

It's about my evolution. I don't bind myself with rules, and I might change my mind. As for retiring, when my body has had enough, I'll hang my gloves up. I know my fights are numbered and won't keep squeezing one more out. It's exciting and I look forward to doing it.

JAMES McSWEENEY – 'THE MACHINE'

James McSweeney fights his MMA in the heavyweight class at 100 kg, which gives a solid covering to his six foot four frame. With a background in Thai boxing and kickboxing going back to before he started school, he is a skilled and experienced exponent of the ancient arts. More recently, James has made the transition from single art to mixed fighting, and has trained hard to develop his ground skills. It's never an easy move from stand-up to grapple, but James made it easily. He competed in several Cage Rage events before signing a contract with UFC to fight in the USA.

I met him at the National Exhibition Centre in Birmingham in the middle of a thunderstorm. It wasn't hard to hear him over the sound of the driving rain – his voice is as big as his heart.

WARRIORS OF THE CAGE

You're a good commodity for Cage Rage. What's your magic?
I don't have a secret, just that I've become a fighter, a high-profile guy and we put on a good performance that the crowd remembered, even to this day they still talk about the fight, so we try and make it as exciting as possible.

What were you like at school?
I was okay. I left early. I left at 15 rather than 16. I had a few problems with discipline. I only did the things I liked doing. My school was more into sports. In reading and writing I wasn't paying too much attention.

Were you messing around?
I was hanging around with a lot of older people and when the teachers were talking to me like a kid, I didn't appreciate it. I wasn't spoken to the way I thought I should be spoken to. When you're young and you think you know it all, you have an attitude. So you soon learn by your mistakes.

Were you ever bullied?
I was in my younger days, yeah. It wasn't until I started getting to 14-15 that I started to learn that either you get an attitude and look after yourself or you're just going to get picked on all your life. So I started to stick up for myself a bit more and I think that's what got me into trouble.

What were your ambitions when you were at school?
I always knew what I wanted to do, I always knew I wanted to be a fighter or do kickboxing, because I'd started when I was young. That's what I wanted to do. Whether I had the capabilities at the time to do it or not is a different thing. I never really had any other dreams apart from that. Some kids want to be football stars. I know it sounds like a pipe dream, but a fighter is all I thought I was ever going to be. It was the only thing I was ever good at, so I tried to put as much into it as I possibly could.

Are you from a big family?
I've got an older brother and sister. They both went through school. They're the complete opposite of what I am. They don't do any sports, anything like that. They're just normal people with nice jobs, nice families. I was a bit more of an erratic person when I was young.

So how did they respond when you took up MMA?
My parents didn't really want me to do it, they didn't like it. They thought that I was going to earn money beating people up. I think they also knew it would be a good release for me because it meant I wasn't getting into trouble on the streets and I wasn't bringing police to the house. I was saying that we're shown a lot of discipline in MMA. When they learnt about what it was that it wasn't just the brutality of a cage fight, and they realised that it took a lot of discipline and heart, then they started to enjoy it and understand that it could actually be something and that it meant something.

Do you believe in God or are you religious?
I'm not religious at all. My family are all Irish, so they come from a Catholic background. I never got pushed to believe in a religion and it was never pressed on me. It was pushed on my parents though. They were really pressed when they were young, so they never pushed it onto us kids. I believe there's something, but I just don't know what. So, I've really had a choice whether I believe in God or heaven or hell. I'd like to think that there's something, but I haven't made a decision.

How do you spend your life away from MMA?
I chill out with my family and I've got three dogs and some pets. My girlfriend and I like to relax and just try to remember that this is a job, this is what I do for a living. When you're in the gym you fight, you come here you fight. If you have that outside as well you're in destruction mode. You need that opposite reaction really, time to relax. You need to try and do something that's going to be calming. I like to go and watch movies and come and talk to my friends and just relax, just chill out.

What are your emotions as you enter a cage?
Like any fighter I try to totally concentrate on what I've got to do. Try and envision what I have to do and what I've been trained to do. So I try and react on that and to get the job done. I try to make sure nobody gets seriously hurt. At the time I want to make sure first and foremost that I don't get hurt, but we're both in there to win the fight.

Which three people have inspired you the most?
One is my coach. He's an inspiration – the way he lives his life and the discipline he's had all his life, and the type of man he is. My father,

he's an inspiration to me. He gets up every day at five o'clock in the morning to provide for his family on a building site. Also, I think one of my close friends inspired me. He passed away a long time ago. He was someone I'll never forget because he brought a whole world to my life. To have someone like that in my life meant a lot to me.

Who do you train with?
I train in Holland. I try to go there as often as possible. I've been going there now for nearly four years. In England I train with several partners that I use from the gym in different types of training. Since going to Holland the level of my fighting, my profile and my understanding of the fight world has improved a great deal. When you're training with people like Tyrone Spong, and even some of the smaller 60 kg guys and see the way they're preparing their head and their heart, it's so big, the way they fight. It gives you strength to see them, because you think someone like that can come at you at 60 kg, 40 kg less than me, and he can give me such a hard time in the gym. They can give you hell in that gym, but they give you strength too. Once you get through these bad situations then you learn to love.

Define a tough guy.
I think a tough guy is someone like my dad. A normal working class guy, not upper class, a working class man. He provides every day for his family just to get by each week. He works six days a week, 12-13 hours a day on a building site, freezing cold weather, just to bring enough in to pay the bills, keep the family out of poverty and nothing for himself. To get up every day and do that, six days a week, that's a tough man. Guys like that, I think they're tough. They live a heavy life and still keep a smile. That defines a tough guy in my eyes.

Why do you fight?
I fight because I enjoy it and it's the only thing I've ever been good at. I like the discipline side of it and the training, the lifestyle, the clean living. You learn to grow and it gives you self-confidence and strength, and you can actually make something of yourself even if you haven't got much intelligence. You can be good at English, maths and science and things like this. Fighting is another form of intelligence that you can't learn in school and it's the only form of intelligence I've ever been quite good at. You can keep learning and improving and every day you learn. It doesn't matter even if you're my coach, he's 56 and he still learns every day after all these years

of training. I've got a world of learning yet. I haven't even begun to open the book of intelligence for fighting.

When you lose a fight, how do you feel?
I lost my last fight, and it still bothers me. I learn more from a loss than I do from a win, so if I didn't lose then I wouldn't grow so much. I look back and I learn from my mistakes, and I think that you always know about what you lost. But yeah, it hits your heart because you train hard, a lot of people have come to see you and you want to win. Then when you lose, it's okay if you lose and the guy's beaten you on the day and it was a good fight, that's no problem. If you lose where it's your fault, where you gave the guy the fight, then it's going to affect you inside, so that means you've got to go back and train harder and make sure it never happens again.

Is there anyone out there you'd like to fight?
No-one in particular. I just want to keep fighting and keep growing and learning every day. I have a five-year goal. It's not my next fight or my next three fights. My goal is to achieve what I need to achieve in five years, and then when I achieve that I'm sure that's not going to be enough. I'll want another five years and I'll keep going until the last day. If I can walk to the ring, then I think I'll still want to fight.

MMA is growing. Is it a direction for young people to take to control themselves and to channel anger into sport?
I think so. MMA is definitely one side of it. But I think any sport can do that if it's handled correctly. I mean it helped me out to channel my anger and stop me getting into trouble, and learn that there's always someone out there bigger and better than you. I also learnt what a violent reaction really does. A lot of the young kids have video games, they watch the fights on the telly. They don't realise what violence is really about. They don't see the real effect of punching somebody in the face. When they come to the gym and they learn that it really does hurt, or what can result from it and how you must do it properly, then I think it can be a saviour. Whether it's MMA, kickboxing or Thai boxing or football, any type of sport can teach discipline where you have to learn from somebody else and show respect. I think it can only bring positive things from children.

Is there a message you'd like to send out to anyone?
Not anyone particularly, just keep training, just do what you're interested in doing or what you're looking to do. Don't judge a book by its cover. Learn, look into the sport before you go into it and talk to the fighters and talk to the trainers at the promotions. Remember, a lot of the guys, they way you see them fight is just an act, they're putting on a show. They're not really animals, or they're not really out there to kill anybody, they're just someone who comes there to sell tickets. So, look into the sport first.

Your fight name's the Machine. So that's two machines that we know.
I'm a good one. The other one's a rusty old machine, he's broken down, he's gone. I asked him to fight for the name and it was refused.

Is that a challenge?
I challenged ages ago. I set up the fight because he was saying the same thing about the name and I said, "Okay, we'll put on a fight in the heavyweight section for the name 'Machine'." And Dave said the fight wouldn't happen and refused to fight.

If your fight career was to end, what would you do?
I don't know. I'd just try and train, I'll still learn. Maybe I couldn't quite compete, but I would still train every day, and try and put it into the gym. Try and help other fighters learn or take them on the pads and teach what I know and help out any way I can. In UFC we're like a family. Everyone helps each other.

WANDERLEI SILVA – 'AXE MURDERER'

Fight Club, Curtain Road, London EC1. 11.30 am. Wanderlei Silva is being mobbed by fans, which he's used to. He greets people coming towards him and I'm following him, escorted by Fighters Inc founder Joe Long. Wanderlei has arrived to run a seminar for around 130 students. Every face there shows pleasure and excitement because their hero has arrived. By noon, each trainee gladiator is prepared to be instructed by their master.

Energy and excitement fill the air, as the students show

determination, dedication and, of course, sweat. The Axe Murderer is working his students hard. He has opened like a flower among the students. He's home. Some take the session very seriously; others are just delighted that they're being taught by the 'Axe Murderer' – UFC star and Pride Champion. Silva shares his techniques and skills, making contact with each person. He evens teaches them a little Portuguese – the phrase 'thank you'. They're delighted. He gathers everyone to sit and listen as he describes the potential that he has seen in the room. He entertains his soldiers by sharing some of his fighting stories. Wearing a black t-shirt and his own Wand Fight Team black tracksuit bottoms, sponsored by XYIENCE, he's as relaxed as if he were at home. He's entirely comfortable amongst his friends, a fish in water at the training camp, surrounded by punch bags, ropes, mats, cage ... the lot.

The session ends and Wanderlei shows his disappointment that it couldn't be extended. But there's another seminar due to be taken by the K-1 Champion Remy Bonjasky. The Axe Murderer happily poses for pictures and gives autographs to his beloved students, who idolise him. Joe Long chauffeurs Darin Mahlke, sales director at XYIENCE, Wanderlei and me to the hotel. In the back of Joe's 4x4 BMW X5 there's silence, and the air seems to stand still as I start to record. Not even the traffic passing by can interfere with the excitement of the moment.

Wanderlei Silva was born in Curitiba, Brazil. He stands at five foot eleven tall, with a fighting weight of 84 kg. His fighting style is Brazilian jiu-jitsu, but you probably knew that!

Did you have a good seminar?
Very, very good. It's a very nice gym. A lot of guys and it's a lot of fun. I love contact with these guys. For me it's a pleasure.

What were your schooldays like?
I was at school for 11 years. And the year I was going to university, at Christmas I started work. Work and training meant I didn't go to university. But after I stop fighting, I want to go to university in United States.

Name three people who have inspired you.
I think everybody has inspired me. Every time I see a guy who is a good businessman or a martial artist, or the guy is a good boxer, I look at his style and I bring this in and I copy what I think is best.

If a guy has good technique, I copy him. I take from everybody what I think they're better at. I copy everybody.

Who's your favourite fighter and what are the best fights you've watched?

I love the MMA. They have many, many good fights. I like all fighters, especially those who have very tough fights and my favourite is the great Sol Ferguson. I love that fighter.

Has this been a turning point in your life?

Yes. I live for the fights. The biggest thing in my life is my fights. After I lost three fights, I moved. I lived my whole life in Sin City [Curitiba]. I trained with the Sin guys and I moved around, I am a nomad. After I lost I came here to train. When I was going to fight I had a lot of pressure. Many guys talking about me so much, saying, "Oh, he's not the same anymore, he needs to stop." It was a very, very tough fight for me and I had to win to go forward. But I kept going. Winning that fight was a turning point. I have lived through the most hard time.

When you're not training, what do you do for fun?

I don't have a hobby, but I love to read books and I love to play with my son. Every time I have a fight I have to focus. I go to train in the morning and come back so tired. I eat, I sleep, I wake up, I eat, I go to training and come back tired again. I have no time for my son or my wife. After I have done a fight I want to stay with him all the time. I love to play with my son. That's the best time in my life.

What did you want to be when you were growing up?

When I started the training I was so bad at technique, even though my friend was a good teacher. I trained every day, and my parents didn't help me because they were working all the time. They didn't give a lot of attention to me and my brother. My daddy has a small bar and I worked in there every day, I started working at seven years old. It was great experience for me because now I have good relationships with all people. I thought I was going to work in the bar for my whole life, I was going to study but I worked instead. I left home. My father came to see my fighting when I was a professional. I fought before 5,000 people.

Above: Murilo 'Ninja' Rua feels the pain, as he defends himself against a kick from Xavier 'Professor X' Foupa-Pokam. *(Frank Mensah – Ringpics)*

Below: Marius Zaromskis kicks out against Ross 'da Boss' Mason.
(Image courtesy of 'Demon' Lee – Demon Photography)

Top left: Promoters Dave O'Donnell (left) and Andy Geer tell the media that MMA is here to stay!

Top right: On a mission that can't be stopped: author Jonathan Buffong (left) meets French heavyweight Cheick Kongo, a recent signing for the Wolfslair gym in Liverpool.

Above: Popular MMA commentator Stephen Quadros, a.k.a. 'the Fight Professor', introduces Lee 'Lightning' Murray (left) and Ian 'the Machine' Freeman.

Left: The world is yours: Alex 'the Reidernater' Reid (left) and Ricco 'Suave' Rodriguez, both of Liverpool's Wolfslair, with Scarface looming in the background.

(All pictures on this page from the personal collection of Jonathan Buffong)

Above: One of the best MMA brawls ever seen: Melvin Manhoef (right) vs. Cyborg.
(Frank Mensah – Ringpics)

Below: Heavyweight behemoths Glen Reid (left) and Popek Rak battle it out at London's Troxy. *('Demon' Lee – Demon Photography)*

Above: UFC star Anderson 'Spider' Silva makes a ferocious knee-to-the-head against Tony 'Freak' Fryklund.

(Frank Mensah – Ringpics)

Right: UFC veteran Ross Pointon gains a submission via heel-lock. Say cheese!

('Demon' Lee – Demon Photography)

Left: The Wolfslair MMA Academy of champion fighters welcomes author Johnny Buffong.

(Author's personal collection)

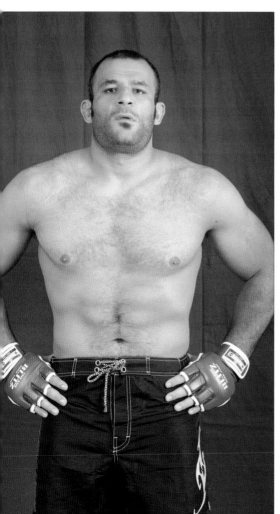

Top left: Ian Freeman demonstrates the rage of 'the Machine' to opponent Paul Cahoon.

('Demon' Lee – Demon Photography)

Top right: Polish rapper and dedicated cage fighter Popek Rak's tattoos combine hip-hop legends Tupac Shakur and Outlaw with his Team Titan training venue.

(Author's personal collection)

Above: Rodney Glunder, 'the Silent Assassin' – Dutch expatriate and Team Hardcore champion.

(Author's personal collection)

Left: Mustapha Al-Turk – former British Cage Rage heavyweight champion, now a UFC combatant.

('Demon' Lee – Demon Photography)

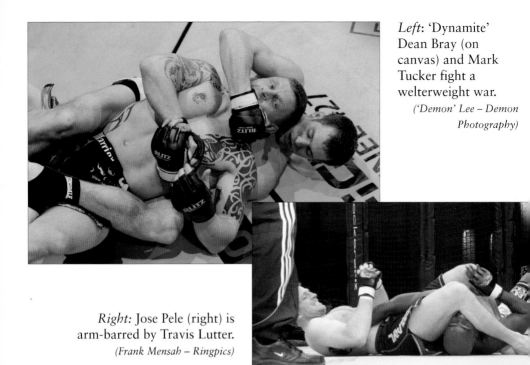

Left: 'Dynamite' Dean Bray (on canvas) and Mark Tucker fight a welterweight war.

('Demon' Lee – Demon Photography)

Right: Jose Pele (right) is arm-barred by Travis Lutter.

(Frank Mensah – Ringpics)

Left: Dean Bray (on canvas) dominates Darren Geisha with a rear naked-choke.

(Frank Mensah – Ringpics)

Right: Masakuzu Imanari (right) and Jean 'the White Bear' Silva grapple for a submission via leg or ankle-lock.

(Frank Mensah – Ringpics)

Sol 'Zero Tolerance' Gilbert lands a kick on John 'the Hitman' Hathaway, at Gilbert's Fight Skool.
(courtesy of David Ellis)

Mixed Martial Arts is a full-contact sport combining a variety of fighting techniques. Professional medical treatment is on hand for fallen warriors, with each and every fighter given a medical check both pre- and post-fight. *(Images courtesy of 'Demon' Lee – Demon Photography)*

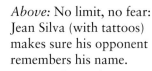

Above: No limit, no fear: Jean Silva (with tattoos) makes sure his opponent remembers his name.

(Frank Mensah – Ringpics)

Left: Robbie 'the Flame' Oliver (right) on the verge of submission due to an arm-bar by Masakuzu Imanari.

(Frank Mensah – Ringpics)

Right: Daisuke Nakamura (top) vs. Vitor 'Shaolin' Ribiero – Nakamura lost, unaware that his elbow was dislocated.

(Frank Mensah – Ringpics)

THE FIGHTERS

Is MMA training a good way for kids to get rid of their energy in a positive way?

Yeah, yeah, yeah. This is a good point because the martial artist is like a Samurai. The discipline, the respect, is a lifestyle. And every time you go for training you need to go into the gym, know who is the master, who is the teacher; talk with him, look at the place, because the guy will explain the energy and understand about the respect.

Have you ever been scared?

A lot of times you have to fight not to be scared. Last week I saw my son, who's five years old. I showered him, and I don't remember my daddy showering me. It's hard to have no good memories. After I finished school in Brazil at 18 years old, I went to high school. I did not have the money to go to private school, I went to a very bad school. Nobody did anything for me, I was scared about my future because I had no money. I do not want that for my son.

Define a tough guy.

I think a tough guy has a good heart. One guy says, "I am not afraid," but this is not true. Everybody is afraid. People are afraid to lose, afraid to be tired, afraid of opponents, afraid of publicity. There's a lot of worry in your mind before the fight. Some guys are very good in the cage, and beat everybody. You need to train so hard, and you need to have good guys with you to give a good direction. You need to have God with you, this is so important, and a guy needs to have motivation. This combination makes a tough guy because this guy has it all. I think he is now a warrior, I respect the guy. He's not afraid to punch, not afraid of blows, not afraid to be your opponent. This is a tough guy.

How did you get involved in MMA and why?

My brother started to do capoeira in Brazil four years ago and he used to show me and give me a few movements. I started to lift weights. I had a big head and no money to have good clothes and I worked so hard. My friend at school wanted to start to talk to the girls and not to me anymore … it was so hard. So I was thinking, "I'm going to start training." I went to my brother's academy to watch him but his academy was expensive, maybe $30. So I went to another gym, it's $15 per month.

What would you like to be remembered for?
I want to have the opportunity to help another fighter through. Now I'm going through transition in my life because I'm going to have a gym and to start work as a coach. I would give good direction for the younger guys, a good example.

What's your philosophy on MMA?
Respect and hard work, these are so important. Respect the other guys.

You believe in God. Why is that?
Because my life is so hard. My mum, my dad, say to me, "No, man, you need to work, you need to stop fighting, you're not making money with this." Why would I stop? I've got no reason to stop. This is my career, I know it and God knows it. I believe in God because He helped me many times in my life. He saved me in a crashed car, crashed motorcycle. I had a hard fight and the guy beat me, but I have no injuries. I'm fine, I'm training. God loves me.

ALEX REID – REIDERNATER

We're sitting at Seni, the biggest martial arts exhibition in the country, me and Alex Reid. They only sell cool, high-nutrition food, so we're eating noodles – not that they taste that good, but at least we know they're healthy. Another sacrifice for sport. Alex Reid knows about giving things up, he's been training since he was a young teenager, and fighting on the UK MMA circuit for ten years. When he's got a bit of time to spare he acts, makes television appearances – *Gladiators* and *Holby City* are among his favourites – and travels abroad to learn new techniques.

We manage to get through the interview, despite repeated interruptions from fans, both male and female. He never turns a fan away when they approach us, even though we're pushed for time. That's why he has fans.

How did you get involved with *Gladiators*?
I was 21, it was going strong for about five years in America. I thought, "I could do this," be a contestant not a gladiator; I was small and the gladiators were like beefcakes on droids. A pal of mine,

Buster Reeves, got into the final two years before I went in for it. I started doing martial arts properly and training heavily when I was 15 years old, to build up my self-esteem, confidence and competitive nature. I started kickboxing and jiu-jitsu tournaments, when it was just another athletic show. Being a Cage Rage fighter now is just like putting on a show. I tried to get into *Gladiators* when I was 20 years old, the following year I tried and got through.

Did you finish school?
Yeah! I wasn't a bad kid, I just was naughty and getting into trouble but I never got expelled. I'm average intelligence, not the most academic. I wanted to be a soldier as a kid, to be a paratrooper or an officer, which motivated me towards completing my exams. I believed in fighting for freedom and democracy.

Did you have a favourite subject at school or college?
I was creative, so I loved acting. I liked the action and physicality. I did drama and theatre studies at college. So what I'm doing now is the perfect combination. I had some success in the acting field. Although Cage Rage is not an act, I'm fighting for real, there's that performance element side to it.

Tell me about *Hollyoaks*.
I joined the TA as a part-time soldier. Did modelling, a few bit parts and got fed up. Went back to acting school and I was Tom Hanks' double in the film *Saving Private Ryan*. You only see my legs and bum. I was also in *Judge Dredd, Sliding Doors, The Saint*. I was on set doing *Saving Private Ryan* in 1997, I remember because we all had a minute's silence for the death of Princess Diana. Tom Hanks and Steven Spielberg went to her funeral, so we stopped filming that day. Then hey presto! I landed a role in *Hollyoaks*.

You were a contender in Tuf 9. Did you feel that the UK selection was good?
Yes, well as far as I'm concerned anyway. Sometimes I think they pick the personalities that are best for TV. I think they could have picked better fighters, better competitors. Obviously, I don't mean myself, but I wonder if they pick up who's going to be the most entertaining for the American team. They've got to put a lot together for the TV. Who can they make a star? Who can they mould? Who will interview well? Who's charismatic? So I think they

did a good job. I was surprised at some of the people they had there. I was expecting to see some other names, and it almost looked like they'd selected some decent people, and then some not so good people to take the fall. I'm not entirely sure, it's just a feeling.

Who do you think deserved to be there but wasn't?
Me and my team buddy both tried out and only I got in. I was so sad for him. Other team buddies of mine got the call and got to the final selections, and at the last minute they said, "Sorry, you're not in." It's just bullshit. It's a shame there's only eight places, because there's so many other fighters I thought should have been on there, like Abdul Mohammed.

How are the fighters selected?
The trials are based on fighting ability, charisma, and whether you can bring that across on camera and perform under pressure. They also consider how the different people are going to perform with each other. People tuning in to watch people fighting want to see the drama and the entertainment, so they want the characters, the clashes, the camaraderie – that's what makes it. Why is *Big Brother* so fascinating? It's because all the different factors make the drama. MMA is a performance.

So would you say there's a lot of bias involved?
I don't think so. You still have to fight. Everyone in there was a fighter. They were competitive. There was no clear certainty that fighter 'A' would totally destroy fighter 'B'. It was all reasonably matched. Some people think that Bisping had too many of his guys in there, which is a bit unfair. That's going to happen. He runs one of the best training camps, Wolfslair. I think they had a fair enough shot. More English guys would have been good, but maybe it's the English barrier, maybe it's politics and all that malarkey. They want a stereotypical English guy, and that would stop them selecting a lot of our fighters.

Has UK MMA reached its peak?
Well, I think it is starting to now. I think in *Ultimate Fighter* we'll see that we are reaching our peak. We used to be bad wrestlers compared to the rest of the world, but not anymore. I've actually seen the first episode. If you take *Ultimate Fighter* as the level of what's going on in the English scene and compare it to the US scene, it looks like

we've caught up. I think we've always had the upper hand in striking. They have some of the best in the USA, but the world is getting smaller and everybody has access to top class training. It's not like, "These guys are shit because they're from such-and-such." Everybody's got the internet and access to cheap travel to go training at different camps. Fighters do that. I'm always in Vegas, Holland, Thailand and different places. It doesn't matter where you come from, everybody can be as good as everybody now.

Do you think the relationships between fighters, promoters and sponsors are different in other parts of the world?
You can compare the relationship between promoters and organisations to the fighters. In America particularly, there's so much paperwork it's ridiculous. I mean, I recently got screwed over by Elite FC wanting to go to the UFC. And I was like a pawn in a big war and I'm the one who suffered. If you look at the English scene, Cage Rage, Ultimate Challenge, they got took over by Elite FC, and they screwed them over and took all the best fighters out. They didn't have the funding to get the better fighters in. Cage Rage was one of the best shows on the planet, and look what it is now, Ultimate Challenge, which is sad. Hopefully it will come back. In England, the promoters seem to be friendlier, smaller. I can phone up the promoters here and have a good chat with them. I've got more influence in getting what I want. I can't see myself doing that with Dana White. I tried to do that with Elite FC and Gary Shaw, but I couldn't get to him – not interested. With big organisations there's too much politics, bureaucracy, too many people in the way. The arrangements change too much, and then they pass the buck. With UFC, they really do call the shots round the world. I can't go up and really negotiate for myself because I'm not a big enough fighter.

How would you motivate a fighter to deal with all the obstacles to getting to the top?
I started this not to just get in and fight to pay the bills, I want to get to the top, to be the best – that's my vision. I enjoy what I do, just for pure competing. We aspire to become the best we can be, the best in the world, champions. We want to make lots of money and to do something we love. I think a lot of fighters can be very disillusioned because promoters will see that and they can capitalise on that. They can throw you in at the deep end against a lot better fighters who are going to destroy you and make mincemeat of you,

just so that they can have a good show. Look at how the famous fighter Matt Lindland was thrown in. He got his chance in the UFC and was expected to lose. He only had a couple of days notice, I believe. Yet he's become one of the top ten fighters in the world. You do get that Cinderella story sometimes, that's what fighting is like. You can be quite unknown and then the next minute catapulted to super-stardom. That's what I dream of. When I was younger, I was manipulated and influenced to do things I wish I hadn't done. When I look back now, at my promoters and organisations, I wonder why I took that route, I was a bit stupid there, I should have been just a bit more patient. But with the arrogance of youth, you think you can do anything. It's great now, because I have hindsight. I'm still young enough to accomplish my goals.

Is it hard to find a good trainer?
The problem with MMA, of course, is because it's a relatively new sport. Although we've been fighting for thousands of years in different guises, wrestling and what-have-you, we don't have very old trainers with experience. Look at boxing, for instance: some of the best trainers are quite old men with experience, they've been round the block. They're not that athletic anymore. Look at Micky in the film *Rocky*, he's a stereotypical trainer. When I become an old man I'm going to be a fantastic trainer all round the world. My coach is younger than me. I mean I still respect him. His knowledge is fantastic. An older trainer can guide you through all the pitfalls. I'm not just talking about training, the promotions, the making money, but also about how to live your life, what decisions to make, what is or isn't a good relationship for you, what is affecting you inside the gym. They can guide you through everything, from business to emotional to spiritual. We're not quite there yet in MMA, but give us another 20-30 years.

You must have had some adventures with MMA?
I train with one of the top teams in the country. When the first Iraq war started, I was training one night. In the gym there's a dojo and it's cut up into two sections by a really thin bit of plasterboard. And we're all doing MMA on one side. We've got crash mats, we're doing drills and all sorts, doing punching and kicks. Next door there's these guys, ex-SAS, and they do sprint jiu-jitsu or something and they sometimes come in and have got funky new weapons, defence and stuff. They bring on all these gadgets and stuff. It's not unusual

to see some guy dressed up in full body armour and there's another guy beating them up. So we can't really see what's going on. Anyway we're all doing our MMA one day and we hear all this dog barking and all this shouting like, "Get on the floor." We think, "Blimey, they're going to for it today." We just carried on thinking the SAS blokes were getting a bit carried away.

The next minute the door's kicked in and we've got SO19 [the Metropolitan Police armed response unit] coming in with dogs, shotguns, and they had us all up against the wall. Then it was, "Everyone get on the floor." I thought, "What the fuck's going on here?" It was a raid. We were held there. I was training for a fight. I was saying, "Oh God. Can I just train? Look, you've got guns, I'm not going to run anywhere, I'll just train." And they refused. They held us there and after about 20 minutes I just sort of got my power and started drilling techniques. I was thinking, "Look, if you're going to shoot me, shoot me." Then it would be, "They're not going to shoot me – I haven't done anything." We didn't know what was going on.

Apparently, they'd made the biggest drug bust ever in the entire country at the gym. It wasn't so big on the news because the Iraq war started the same day. So that kind of saved the gym; it was a good gym, but it was just the guy who ran it. They had shotguns, automatic weapons, hand guns, everything. £60 million worth of drugs all over the place. I know fighting can attract unsavoury characters. We'd heard the guy on the phone, "You fucking owe me 20 grand. If you don't give it to me..." but we'd go, "Yeah, whatever, mate." We thought he was just trying to be big, but that night we realised it was real. Looking back, it was quite funny though.

Which was your most memorable fight?
Another time we went up to watch a show in Manchester Arena and I was in the front row. I've got a VIP seat due to being heavily involved in MMA in the UK scene. I've gone into the VIP lounge; had a bottle of champagne, some canapés or crepes or whatever, stuffing my face and sitting there. I took another bottle with me. I'm drinking this champagne feeling a little bit sort of alive, and it's lovely. Suddenly, somebody's pulled out of the show and my pal went, "Go on, why don't you have a go?"

"Yeah, why don't I have a go?" The champagne talking. "Yeah, I'll have a go." Not really thinking, being the big man. Even though I'm a fighter, I'm all relaxed in a suit. Anyway, the promoter comes over and offers me a few quid. And I thought, "Oh well, maybe." Anyway, after my pals convinced me stupidly to fight, half an hour later I'm fighting, only I know I was a little bit inebriated. But I soon sobered up. I thought, "What the hell have I done here?" The fight went the distance and I lost on a split decision, so in hindsight I was very stupid. It was against a guy called Jason Tang. Good guy. I've seen the fight many times now on the net and I don't know how I lost it. It's ridiculous. At worst it's a draw. Buzz Berry said he thought I was crazy. It was a good opportunity to meet people. I got to meet Mike Tyson. He said, "Man, that was a bad decision. But don't worry, it's a hometown crowd. Take the rough with the smooth. You're a fighter, man, you're a good guy." Even though I lost, I had a great experience.

Can MMA help to reduce crime among young people?
Yeah. MMA is brilliant for reducing crime because it teaches self worth. When people have got self respect, they respect other people more. Athletes get to let out all our aggression in here. Training is like the glue that holds our lives together. It makes you so chilled out, so calm. Obviously, if you're a professional fighter and your career's not going too well, then you can have your moments where you're angry and you're pissed off, and that can carry over to different aspects of your life. But generally, if I get pissed off and angry because my career isn't going well, I'm still not going to go out and start fights in the street and turn to crime. The fact is the skills I'm learning could help me in a criminal activity if it involves fighting, but the thing is I don't think like that. You don't think like that if you're with a good team. That's what it's all about: having a good team, good ethos, good morals. We are martial artists and it teaches you honour, respect, discipline, self respect, and with all of those qualities you want to do the honourable thing. One of our creeds we have here is honour and respect.

What was the most frightening moment in your life and how did you deal with it?
With hindsight they change all the time. You look back on things and you grow as a person. Because you've grown, the event that you're looking back on isn't as fearful anymore and you think, "Well, what was the big deal?" Some of the biggest fearful moments have had nothing to do with fighting. Being caught by

your girlfriend doing something wrong, or being caught by your boss cheating. Where you've let someone down, you've disappointed someone, you've lost something. Those are fearful moments. This fighting game, it's a game. It's not even a fight to me. I don't consider myself a fighter, I'm a sportsman. You know a fight is ugly. We're consenting adults, both getting in there. We're not soldiers. We've got rules. We've got judges. There's honour, discipline. Even these guys who do all the smack and the bad sort, the second the fight's over, generally 99 per cent of the time I see them shaking hands. Before, it's, "I'm going to kill you, arsehole," and then afterwards they're raising the other guy's hand.

Has there been a turning point in your life?
I'm going through turning points all the time. One of the biggest turning points I found is in trusting myself, listening to myself, knowing that I have got the answer. I've stopped looking outside for approval, or for someone else to give me the answer because deep down I know the answer – we all do. You ask yourself what's really right for you and trust it. That's such a big thing in this fighting game. Ultimately it's a lonely sport. You're not in there with your trainers. I always say when I'm coaching, "He's not just fighting you, he's fighting all of us. We're all here together." That's true. I mean you've got your support unit. You're in the cage and your corner is telling you to do something, but I always say to my guys, "If you feel it's not right, don't do it, you're the boss in there." And that's a good analogy for life, as well. I mean, it's you making the choices and we are each responsible for whatever's happened in our life.

How do you deal with the negatives?
We might blame other people if someone's horrible to us, but it's us at the end of the day, it's about how we react. I'm not saying that bad things aren't going to happen. Someone slagged me off on Facebook. They said that I am a disgrace to the sport, and asked what the fuck was I doing. "When was the last time he won a fight?" They said I should give up. I was furious. I went to bed with this. I didn't retaliate with nastiness; I was very intelligent and poetic in how I retaliated. I said, "Look, how dare you attack me, you come across very small." He came back with something again this morning. I thought, "Hang on, I'm getting myself wound up." I wanted to go and find out where this guy lives and smash his face in. I'd never do that but that's my human thought, like road rage. In the end, I wondered why I was

responding like this. And the second I did that, I felt so much better. I said to this guy, "I'm really grateful that you've taken your time to come on here and say all these things about me. It shows you must care. Thank you." Whatever he says, fuck it. Yeah, I wasn't too keen on what he said, but he's talking about me.

Boxing has often been associated with criminal activity. Is this true of MMA?

We all hear stories, but I don't know what goes on. I do know firsthand of some of the shenanigans that go on here, but basically MMA and fighting sports attract that criminal element because it's a tough, masculine, macho thing that tough guys want to be associated with. I know people who have started off by doing some unsavoury things to make a few quid to start gyms to pour into promotions. If you look at any big organisations, they started off bending a few rules or breaking some big ones. It doesn't mean they carry on like that, they change. You see these Hells Angels today with proper legitimate companies, but some of them started off doing some very not very nice things – drugs, prostitution, all that business. Look at Las Vegas, the casinos, some were run by criminals, but they're legitimate businesses now. All I can say first hand is that a few of my friends have opened up gyms with money which wasn't legal, but now they're completely legal. They're good people, just bending rules. It's the nature of this beast.

How do you relax after a fight?

Sportsmen or athletes seem to have addictive personalities, we want to be the best at whatever we do. So you can imagine, we're training all the time. Non-stop thinking about fighting 24-7, it's exhausting. Sometimes the only way we can get out of that mindset is by taking some recreational pharmaceuticals that get you high and get your mind off. Which is great at the time. But, more, it's not conducive for a professional athlete, because if that blow-out becomes more than once in a while then it's not good. Every fighter needs to break the rules completely sometimes, eat some shit, have fun and have a beer, or have a lot of beers. But when you're smoking a joint every night or every weekend, then that's no good. I've never been there. The worst I've done is to have cocaine once too often, say like once every month or after a fight, and that's not good. It's taken vital years off my longevity and my health. And I regret that. But I've grown from that. Before a fight, I'm totally disciplined to the point of insanity. I won't have sex for up to a month before a fight. I watch everything I eat. Then it gets to the point where I think, "Fuck this, I'm going to do whatever I want, break every rule, just rebel." After I've done that I'm disgusted with myself, I don't want to do it again. Then I go through the whole cycle again of two to three months training camp, have a fight, and then it's another blow-out.

How do agents work?
You have agents like in football who manage different fighters. I've just started to come into that now. There's a guy called Ken Pavia, who looks after a large percentage of the UFC fighters and organises fights all around the world. He's like a fight promotions agent and gets different fighters. He organised Mustafa Al-Turk and John Hathaway to get some good sponsored deals. But that's only at the high end.

AISYEN BERIK

Aisyen was born in north London to a family who believe in equal opportunities, despite clichéd stereotypes about the Muslim cultural heritage. She's still in her early twenties and trains close to home at a gym used by other members of her family. When not in the gym, Aisyen is studying for her degree, and funding the study by working too. She is a very determined young woman who has a bright future ahead of her, whether she should choose to fight, to work, or simply to become a homemaker. I spoke to her at the weigh-in for her first MMA bout.

What were your schooldays like?
I enjoyed school. Maths was probably my favourite subject. I had a really good time at school.

Did you finish school?
Finished school, finished college. I've got a year of university left to do but I've got a break. At the moment I'm a repairs officer for the council.

How did you get into fighting?
Basically, doing this in our family, it's sort of always around. I've got

my two older brothers always wrestling and I always had it around as a kid. It was something that we always knew, cage fighting. It wasn't something that we were ignorant of. Eventually, I trained my brother for his fights and I realised that I could compete. My brother and my cousin said, "No, no, you just train first." So I trained and I trained, but I was never in a position to fight before because I was studying at university. Now I am in a position to do it, so I said to my brother, "Listen ... I do want to fight." He waited until he thought I was ready and then he entered me into a competition.

So this is your first professional fight?
My first professional fight. I've fought before. Well, street fights, nothing really.

I did win all of them, though. I'm quite confident in my abilities. If I wasn't then I wouldn't do cage fighting. I know it sounds big headed, but I've always said that any girl that isn't a professional fighter I can take, no ifs or buts about it. A lot of people think in stereotypes when they think about girls punching. I know I've got a good punch on me and I've learned from my brothers that when you punch, make it a good punch. So yeah, I've always said I can take any girl, I've even had a few run-ins with some guys. I've always said unless they're a professional fighter, I can take them. Sometimes, even then I'll try.

You grew up in north London. Which part is that?
Wood Green.

Is that rough?
No. It's near Tottenham. Tottenham's a bit edgy, but it's home, I never think of it any different.

Do you have any role models in fighting?
I've always looked up to my brother Sami. That was the first way I ever saw what fighting is – I've always seen his style. If you watch his fights you see that with Sammy it's not quantity, it's quality. He would rather lose a fight than win a filthy fight. With him it's like, "No, let me show you how to fight," and then you see a good fight. That's something I've always admired, something that I've looked for. I want to fight in a professional way and yet enjoy the sport, which is something that he's always taught me. Yeah, I'd say him fighting-wise.

And morally?

My dad. The way my dad raised us was always never to back away from a fight. If anyone comes for a fight, it's better to take a beating and have your pride than run away. With bullies usually, they don't even want to fight, they just want to scare you. So if you stand up to them, even if you take a beating, next time they can't even be bothered with you. Whereas if you keep running, they keep coming. That's one thing my dad said to us, "Don't run. Respect yourself and respect other people, but if it does come down to it, you have your pride." In our family that's something.

How do you feel about your next fight?

I've had a lot of support from my family. My sister's been wicked. At the moment I feel a bit drained – just physically from training, working. I can't wait for this fight. My sister's been great, my boyfriend's been great. He's my nutritionist, he knows everything there is to know about muscle, what to eat, what not to eat. From the beginning of the fight preparation, he's been helping me cut weight. If it wasn't for him I wouldn't be ready.

Which three people have influenced your career the most?

My brother Sami – like I said, he's been the biggest influence there is. I've seen other female fighters and they have influenced me. There's Gina Carano, she fights. I remember Gina before she got into fighting and I do admire her because she went in there and she did take a bit of flak, but a lot of people now see that she's good. I admire the way she handled it.

What challenges and goals have you set yourself within MMA?

I'm under a trainer and I told my brother that the way we train he never pushes me, like, "Come on, come on, come on." It's always, "As long as you're still enjoying it then we go ahead." And if it becomes so tough, we'll just move onto something else. Later we'll come back to what we were doing so that we've hit that target. As for fighting itself, me and my brother have learnt that it's something to measure your skills against. I'll do this fight and I'll pick up on my own mistakes. No-one has to run through for it me, I'll watch the fight and I'll pick them up. Then that's what I'll work on for my next fight.

Your energy is now focussed on fighting. Has it changed how you are towards others?

No, I've always been the same. I've always been training. All that's different is I'm going to be in an arena with a couple of thousand people doing this fight. I've always been one of the most positive people that you can meet. My mentality has never changed.

Does MMA offer women good opportunities?

I've got a brilliant opportunity, I can't wait. The fact that they've given a female fighter the opportunity to do this is excellent. Hopefully, people watching this will see that women can do anything. Fighting, well, not everyone agrees with fighting, but you can go and do anything. I mean a couple of years ago you wouldn't have seen this happening.

Define a tough guy, away from the cage.

It's all mentality, man. To me, physical means nothing. The toughest person is in your brain. The mentality. The stronger you are mentally, the stronger person you'll be.

Are there any words of wisdom that you could offer to inspire others?

Be positive. Knowing what you want and asking for it. Not even asking for it. Knowing what you want and saying, "This is what I'm going to get." I think that's the best thing you can do because even asking for it, if it comes down in your mind that you won't get it, any negativity and it just won't happen. Whenever I do anything it's always like, "Okay, that's what I'm going to do, that's what I am going to do and this is what's going to happen." And I know the outcome because I'm so sure of myself, so confident that it's going to happen that I don't doubt myself at all.

How far ahead can you see your future in MMA?

I take one day at a time. Every day is different. I can't tell you where I'm going to be every month.

JAMAINE FACEY

At Elephant and Castle, southeast London, I meet Jamaine at his office beside the Imperial War Museum. Wearing a blue shirt and black trousers, Jamaine suggests that we sit outside as it's an unexpectedly sunny day. Got to make the most of the weather while you can! We eat pasta salad and drink smoothies, while Jamaine shares his thoughts on life and fighting, love and family.

Standing at six foot one tall, and fighting in the welterweight division, Jamaine's debut wasn't a success. He was beaten by a devastating TKO, but has bounced back with some great entertaining bouts which have drawn followers to him. Having trained in Thailand he admires Anderson Silva and bases his techniques on him.

Jamaine what were your schooldays like?
Hectic, mate. Fighting every day, train for football, doing your lessons, tuition. Going to the girls' school across the road from the common where we were at boys' school, and living day by day.

Was it hard for you when you came to London from Birmingham?
Coming to London I noticed the tension between people. I had to compromise. How I grew up, you could have a fight and the next day you see the same guy and you're playing football with him. What I found out when I moved to London was it was more the case that if they can't deal with something with their fists, then it goes down to the weapons or it's a gang fight.

Can you name three people who have inspired you?
My mother, and the family around me really, so there's more than three, but it depends what type of person you're asking about. Today I would say Barack Obama. People were trying to put him down saying that he wasn't going to do it, that black people are not ready to be depended upon. Why shouldn't we be ready? We were ready at day one, we've been ready from day one. As I was growing up, I was always into sports so it was always people like John Barnes or Muhammad Ali, Mike Tyson.

What are your favourite MMA fights?
There's quite a few, but the one that really got me watching it very deeply before I even started training was Santos, the Cyborg, versus Melvin Manhoef. That was an incredible, intense fight, yeah.

What about your own most memorable fight and why?
Maybe my second fight after my loss was against Scott Rogan. He was a pro underground boxer, with 75 bouts. He'd come to rip my head off. I just had my game plan, took him downstairs, ground and pounded him all day long. Took my time and slipped him in an arm bar with ten seconds to go.

Was there a turning point in your life and how did you deal with it?
Probably when I moved to London when I was 16. I left school. My mum left me in Birmingham to do what I needed to do for about six months while she moved and got everything set up and ready in London. Then she brought me up. I didn't want to come to London, I was happy where I was. As I moved to London I really kind of matured straight away. Because I've had my childhood in Birmingham and my adulthood in London, I matured straight away.

How do you take your pleasure away from the cage?
I go out partying, but that's what most of us do. It's more when I'm at home with my son, Tyron, and I'm just chilling and kicking back. That's more intense and more pleasurable for me.

Do your childhood ambitions still exist?
I always wanted to be a football player, so no, it doesn't exist really. I'm 32 now, so a 32-year-old footballer is old, as they say. But I've got a long way ahead of me in the MMA, so that's my new ambition.

What is your philosophy on MMA?
Hit and don't get hit.

Do you think MMA could help to reduce violent crime among young people?
I would say yes, definitely, because it's more of a discipline and a learning curve. People from the outside will look at it and think it's a violent, thuggish type of sport. There's all different types of skills you need to learn. Learning them will give you discipline. Take a young kid from on the street going to learn jiu-jitsu. He can't just go there thinking he can go beat up everyone. You start from the ground level and from working at your grades you will learn respect for the people who you're training with. That brings out the respect

when you fight, because you have to always respect the person you're fighting.

How did you get involved in MMA and why?

I used to watch it on TV, but I wasn't really into it until I actually went to a live show. When I saw the fights live I wanted to get in there. I was still immature to the fact of what you needed to be and do to be a cage fighter. Then I got banned from football. Someone decided to do a rear neck choke on me for some crazy-arse reason. So I got up after he was choking me and I knocked him out. Then one of my other boys was doing it, and I decided to go training with him at Elite Fighters. I met Dave O'Donnell down there and he introduced me to everyone. Marvin Arnold was the guy who actually told me to come down to Elite and I just fell in love with it. When I was there, I was seeing people like Brad Pickett and Dean Bray training. Quite a few guys went there, actually. I thought, "Wow, this is good." I just fell in love with it. It felt natural to me. I grew up watching WWF, so I was always rolling around with my friends growing up, but now I was learning the techniques. It all felt natural.

What are your emotions about winning and losing?

I lost my first bout. I was okay until I saw the cage, then I just went into psycho mode and the composure wasn't there. That's why I feel that I lost my first bout because I wasn't composed and I wasn't mentally ready. Physically I was 110 per cent, but mentally I was probably 50 per cent ready for that fight. That taught me a lot and I appreciate it, and I'm glad that I did lose that fight in the way that I did, because that matured me. It took about three weeks to understand what I did wrong, and to understand how and why and what I needed to do for my next bout. But my wins, I've just stood there composed and shook the guy's hand, "Thanks for the fight." And just been ready. One of the guys had me in a guillotine and I knew just what I was doing.

Do you have a favourite MMA technique or personal style?

If I was going to mimic somebody it would be Anderson 'the Spider' Silva. That guy is unbelievable, trust me. When you watch Anderson Silva's fights you don't see him getting beaten up, do you? You don't see him get beaten up, but you see him beaten. His style is unbelievable. I like fighting. I don't like getting hit. The style that he's got, it's really hit and move, hit and move, and that's what I like. He's my best fighter of all time, bottom line.

Define a tough guy.

A guy who doesn't need to go round bullying and hitting people. You don't need to be physically strong to be a tough guy. It's more of a mental thing. But you've still got to know how to bang, just in case.

Have there been any frightening moments in your life and how did you deal with your emotions?

I haven't really had many except for when I was younger, my mum used to deal with me, man. There's one time when I used to get suspended from school. I've never been expelled but I've been suspended from school due to fighting. At school, some people probably saw me as a bully, but I wasn't a bully, I was more of a judge and jury. I beat up the bully, that's what I used to do. If a guy beat up the little kids, I'd hold them up and let the little kids whack them. I used to get in trouble for things like that. So I used to get suspended. And then I knew my mum. She never used to be, "Come on son, let's talk through it." She used to pick up the stick, bang, bang, bang. She was tough, but she was fair. And the only person I feared in my life was my mother really, while I was growing up. Now, I appreciate what she did, because she had six kids to deal with, she was working two jobs, being a mum and being a dad. We never made it easy for her, so when I knew I was in trouble, school didn't scare me, but my mother did.

I was the second youngest of six children. I had an older brother who is five years older than me. Then I had three sisters in between that and one younger brother, so it was always a house of mischief. Everyone was fighting, causing trouble with each other. But once we stepped out the door, if one of our brothers or sisters was in any trouble, then the person would have the whole house to deal with. As I had three older sisters, many times I would have to go and sort certain people out, and I guided my little brother through his life as well. But he can handle himself. Schooldays were a bit crazy, because as my older brother's five years older than me, when he went through senior school he kind of left some crazy-arse legacy for the Facey family. When I turned up people thought, "Oh, you're Stretch's brother. Yeah, you're tough." And so I had to go round beating up people because my brother was the hardest in the school, they wanted to test the name, the Facey name. And a lot of people got hurt.

Have you ever been in trouble with the law?

My brother's always in and out. His second home is the prison. That's where he's living right about now, shame to say. But you know he's a big man, he knows right from wrong, and he is still with the life that he leads. Myself, I don't need to have that type of relationship with the police. I see them as people who are there to do a job. So I respect them so long as they respect me. I've only ever had maybe one crazy encounter with the police, where I had 12 of them rush me and brutally attack me and take me down to the ground and rough me up due to them thinking I had a gun because I'm a black guy and I'm wearing a hood. It was a proper, typical example of the way they do things – stereotyping. It got thrown out of court because the guy said I punched him and I hadn't. It was a nasty time in my life. I run a sports centre; I deal with kids and teach them to respect their elders and stuff like that, respect the police, they are there to do a job. Yet the next day I'm getting manhandled and roughed up and brutally beaten by police officers. I still have respect for them because I know not all of them are like that, because I've dealt with them, I've talked to them, I've had business with the police in work and the life that I'm living now. Maybe ten bad ones out of maybe 1,000.

Are you religious?

I grew up being religious, but I'm not a Sunday runner, going to church every Sunday. I do believe there is a higher being up there looking down on his creations. I had a trip over to Thailand and the culture of the Thai people really caught me and so did the Buddhist spirit. The people over there really taught me, so although I'm not a practising Buddhist, I'm looking into the religion and their way of life. I find it really calm and peaceful. It's righteous for me, so that's one religion that I am looking into. I'm open. There's a lot of people saying their god is the best god, but I feel that everyone's god is God. There's only one God. No matter how you look at it. Everyone can wish and believe that their god is a cow, a monkey, you know, a guy with eight arms. I believe there's only one God and no matter how you look at God, everyone is preaching and praying for the same god. So I'm open to listen to interpretations of people's beliefs and I'm willing to listen and learn.

How do you see MMA developing in the UK?

Regarding the MMA scene in the UK right now, I feel the English media needs to start portraying us in a better light. Because there's a lot of good fighters out there, and a lot of good organisations trying to put on good shows and big shows and we're not getting the recognition on TV and through the newspapers. I really feel that it is a big sport, it is a new sport still, and it needs more publicity. It needs more recognition as a sport instead of just guys getting together, wrapping a cage round them and having a fight. The boxing scene now is dead and buried, but there's so much money there it's unbelievable. I can watch ten boxing matches and fall asleep in probably nine of them. MMA fights are so exciting. You've got body shots, arm locks, chokes, arm bars, everything. So I feel it's more exciting, there's more ways of winning a fight than in boxing and it's just an unbelievable sport.

How would you like to be remembered?
For treating people the way I would like to be treated; firm but fair when I'm at work. At home, loving, with my friends. I'm a nice person. I just treat people the way I expect them to treat me.

3

The Pain Game

Training for a bout demands total commitment from a fighter. For any bout, fighters need to be at their peak both mentally and physically. Most fighters train three times a week, regardless of whether they have a contest in the offing or not. As a fight approaches, the training becomes more frequent and more intense. Ronnie Mann speaks of pushing himself to the limit while training, as do several other fighters. They work on each technique separately as well as building up their basic fitness and strength. Without a high level of basic fitness, the pain can really start to kick in as the skills and technique practice gets underway. In order to maintain the basic level of fitness necessary, fighters must establish a solid training regime and become mentally disciplined enough to stick to it. Without these things fighters cannot have the necessary confidence to believe that they can get into a cage and win. Training combats nervousness. It teaches fighters to control their adrenalin, so that the fight becomes a professional rather than an emotional experience. A good training camp is essential to those who wish to compete.

Matt Freeman, fighter and commentator, has very definite views on the pain of training and fighting:
   A level of pain comes with certain things in the MMA environment.

When you're training with any combat sport anybody can hit anyone, but that's not the art. The art is hitting without getting hit back. There comes a stage in any combat sport where the student is going to have to get hit. Whether it's controlled, semi-contact, or light contact, you will get hit. That immediately gives you a respect and an appreciation for pain. When you have that through your own body, that respect is transferred to your opponent and other people. Why do we keep saying that martial arts give you discipline and respect? You end up by not wanting to bash someone because you've been bashed yourself. You know how that feels, you know how that hurts and you become less inclined to go out and bang someone yourself.

Mustapha Al-Turk:

With regard to MMA in general, and the amount of work we have to do, sometimes boxers, or wrestlers, or fighters in other disciplines don't appreciate what we do for MMA. We have to train so hard in so many different areas and have to strike a balance between the different disciplines and what's needed for that particular opponent. It can be very, very hard and very, very draining. In MMA you have to concentrate on so many different things and aspects.

And while we're on the amount of work needed, a word from Henrique Nogueira:

I train about 3,000 hours for three hours of fighting. I'm up every day at 5.30 to train, and after that I teach. It's a hard life. But I still want to fight.

'Dynamite' Dean Bray agrees:

I think you have to take it seriously because it is a serious sport. You have to train 100 per cent. You can't go in under-prepared because if you do that you're going to get yourself injured. If you're a hundred per cent prepared for all your fights, then you should come through them with flying colours. There's a lot of safety in MMA as well, so as long as you adhere to the rules, it's always all good. Some people who don't understand the sport think the cage is a bad thing, but it's there for safety, and that's that really.

THE PAIN GAME

Joe Turner, who originally trained in judo and jiu-jitsu, needed to amend his regime when he switched to MMA:

I introduced three or four grapple sessions a week on top of the regular kickboxing and conditioning, just to get up to speed, with no de-grappling. I also needed to get used to some nice big guys rolling around on me and to the heavier weight compressing me. It's hard work.

Buzz Berry talks about fitting training in around a fulltime job, and echoes what other fighters say about the need for hard work:

I work as well, so I fit my training around my work. When I'm finished work, then I go training. So my bread and butter is my daytime job. This is more a hobby. My friends where I live say it's unbelievable what I've achieved in my fighting life when I've got a fulltime job and considering where I train. It's like you look at all the top pros where all they do is they get up, go for a run, go home, eat, rest, go to the gym, go back again and then go to the jiu-jitsu, or boxing, or whatever. That's all they do all day long, every day. Where I've got to go, I'm a foreman at work. I lay tarmac on footpaths, drives, roads. I run a gang and make sure our daytime job's right. Then when I go home I get changed, washed, shower, whatever. Then I'll go and do my training for my fighting. At about one, I'll have a shower, get something to eat and I'm ready for my cot. It's time for bed.

Brad Pickett:

When you're in the gym you push yourself as hard as your body can take. Even if someone else is saying, "Yeah, you're doing well," you feel that you're not doing as good as you could. You push it a bit more and you reap the rewards at the end of it. I say, "Train hard, fight easy, and never give up." If you lose, train up, you fight another day. This sport is hard. There's so many ways of winning and losing in this sport, you will suffer a lot. Don't take it too bad. Don't accept a defeat either. Throw all your cards on the table and fight, fight to the death. You keep trying as much as you can with different techniques and stuff, but it's hard to go on. The heart and the will to win, that comes from within. Try and get it inside yourself and try and give yourself that tenacity to fight to the end.

Mark 'Baby Face' Smith talks about how they prepare for a fight at Team Titan:

The week before a bout, Brad and I walk around a lot. I usually weigh about 72 or 73 kg, when we're training. If I know I need to cut weight through that week I do the same things: from the Monday we stop eating carbohydrates and then we go for runs, just to burn excess energy off. By the Thursday morning we like to see what weight we are. Brad likes to be under 70 kg, and I like to be as light as I can. We rest all day on the Thursday, because the night before the weigh-in we dehydrate ourselves. We do this in the least possible time for the weigh-in the next day. I might still be 69 kilos on Thursday morning so I've usually got to lose three kilos overnight. I'll do that in the sauna and by running around. The team help by sitting inside the sauna with us. It's very, very draining. As soon as the weigh-in is over, I eat. The last time I weighed-in I had two guys with me, holding two carrier bags of groceries. They just started feeding me fruit, the right type of food, carbohydrates, to get into my system so I'd be ready for the next day. If you're slightly heavier, you've always got your eye on your weight. Everybody's body is different, but as a general rule, this works pretty much from what I've seen.

For Ed 'Smasher' Smith, fitness is the key:

You need to be fit to fight. That's what I've got to fit in. I've got the skills, I've got the tools, it's just the time to get the fitness in – get the morning runs in and stay flexible. I was fighting at a weight of 91 kg, that's middle range of lightheavy. I'm now looking to come down to middle-weight. I'm not that ripped as a fighter anyway, so I'd like to get ripped and come down to middle weight. I can keep all my muscle and lose the fat. I'd like to fight at 88 kg.

Most fighters these days have a healthy diet. Weight is crucial. Fighters have to pay attention not only to how much and what they eat, but to the quality of the food they consume. Hidden additives can not only affect the quality of the food, but could also put a fighter accidentally in breach of the rules. Harmful substances can be hidden in even the most innocent-looking piece of fruit. For part-time fighters, or those without sponsor-

ship, maintaining the right diet can be a financial struggle with difficult decisions to be made. Mustapha Al-Turk, who fights for UFC, talked about his training regime:

> With regards to my training, my diet hasn't changed that much. I had quite a healthy diet anyway. I do have off days here and there, but generally it's quite good. I steer clear of refined foods. I try and eat a lot of fresh vegetables and fruit. I do make a conscious effort to eat red meat every now and then, because my body craves it. But I eat a lot of fish, salads and vegetables. I try and drink juice whenever I can. I stick to fresh organic produce whenever I can afford it, really. I can't justify an organic chicken, man! £9 in comparison to £3. But with regards to carrots and lettuce, I stick to organic. It's very difficult to weigh up what substances are in our food, especially for the layman. I have a pharmacology degree, and my sister's into alternative medicine and knows about food. In the society we live in food's always going to be messed about with.

What about the psychological aspects of MMA training? Each fighter has his or her own different techniques to make sure that they develop the right mental attitude to the job. But what is the right attitude? Henrique Nogueira shed some light on this:

> Mentally, you have to be boss. If you're no good mentally, then you're no good physically. Mental control is first, then body, and from that, life. I love discipline and respect. I will respect the other guy, but he must respect me too, that's very important.

MMA fighter Daijiro Matsui agrees with this. He says that his chief rival is himself. He believes that if he can't beat himself, then he can't beat anyone else. Joe Turner also talks about the importance of good mental preparation for a fight:

> What scares me is me, because if I stick to my strategy and do what my trainers tell me, I will win, and do it comfortably. The moment I step outside of what I should be doing, it gets messy. So I'm more afraid of myself than of any opponent.

Many fighters talk about the need for mental resilience, and this seems to play a large part in their understanding

of what makes a 'tough guy'. Mustapha Al-Turk says that, for him, a tough guy is:

Someone who's tough, not only physically but mentally. Mentally relentless, not going to back down because of a knock from losing a fight, or getting punched in the face. There's a lot of mental aspects to being tough. It's very little physical actually.

James Thompson uses Neuro Linguistic Programming as part of his training. This is a psychological approach to life based on positive thinking and visualisation of the future outcomes of your actions. James uses the approach to stay calm and positive during the run-up to a bout, as he explains:

I was training a lot. I wanted to do something more with the mental side of training, because that's the side that gets overlooked. So I started looking at different things and Neuro Linguistic Programming is one of the things that came up. NLP helps me more with the mental side of the game. It's a different way of looking at and approaching things. There are different aspects to it. One aspect I use a lot is about 'self talk'. You might be telling yourself negative things. Perhaps in a fight, you'll be thinking, "This is hard," or "This is fucking hell." Obviously that's not going to do you any good. With positive self talk you tell yourself good things about what you're doing, let go of the negatives and concentrate on the positives. That has a massive effect on your attitude and performance. I think that this kind of approach is getting more popular. Everyone's looking for a bit of an advantage wherever they can find it. People who fight realise that the mental side of the game is overlooked; it's such a massive part of it.

Many fighters talk about the sacrifices they make for their love of MMA. They miss their families, and especially their children, while they're on the circuit. This doesn't change if they're at home but still doing intense training in the run-up to a bout. Jean Silva talks about the sacrifices he makes for his career on the international circuit:

It's a long time since I left Brazil, three or four months. I live with my family over there. It's really hard for me. A lot of people think,

"This fighting, it's very nice." But it's not always like that. I leave my family and my children. I live all my life in Brazil with all its culture, and here I live in the gym just to follow my dream. This is one dream, it's not easy. It's really hard. And you can imagine, you sleep in the gym and wake up in the gym and train. Every single day, the same thing. You have a couple of fights and you think to yourself, "Why am I here? Why did I leave my family in Brazil?" But I'm sure, at the end of the day, it's going to be fine.

A lot of fighters are the same as me at the moment, because they follow the dream as well. Some British fighters go to America, or different countries, they leave all their families and everything in your country. It's completely different to come here and train in your country for a long time. It's not like coming here for a couple of weeks just to fight, and then go back. That's okay. This is my dream, that one day I'll do this as well. At the moment a lot of fighters live like I do, that's the truth.

For some fighters, like Afnan Saeed, MMA has helped to cement relationships:

My girlfriend had started watching me fight before I started going out with her. I think she must have fallen in love with me when she saw me in the cage!

Other fighters report a little more difficulty in convincing their friends and family that they're just doing a job and following a career like anyone else. Ed Smith says that his family were a bit worried at first:

People who don't know cage fighting haven't seen the skill. I think especially when you bring people for the first time, especially girls, the first fight they see, they're in shock, its like when you see a fight on the street, and it's, "Oh, shit!" Then, all of a sudden, they see the technique. It's not like guys on the street kicking the shit out of each other, it's two guys who know exactly what they're doing. They're both trained, and they've got technique, and they're competing in a cage. Once the family have seen a few fights and they've got used to it, they can appreciate the technical side.

Dean Bray talks about the overall positive effects that training has on his life:

I'm a much calmer person now. I never get involved in any

road rage or anything like that. If someone cuts me up, I don't care. I just let them do it – I just let them get on with it. MMA really does take the aggression out of me. I'm tired because I'm training so hard all the time. I wouldn't get involved in any conflict outside the cage. I would do my utmost to walk away from anything that came up unless I really had to protect myself or one of my friends.

Ed 'Smasher' Smith seems to feel pretty much the same way:

In modern-day inner-city life we've got strain. Most guys who come to training are in a foul mood – they've had a row with their bird, there's shit at work. They get to training and it's all let out. It's like a pressure release valve. By the end of the session, everyone's got smiles on their faces and we go back home in a happier state of mind. Most people's perceptions of fighters are wrong. If you speak to them, most of the guys in my gym are the nicest guys there have ever been – they're funny, a laugh, charismatic. I think it's the discipline you get from fighting. It's only a certian type of people who keep going back. All the loons and the nutters, they are idiots, they try to start fights on the street, they're not disciplined. We are, it makes us better people. We're a lot more passive in our everyday lives. We're not gonna go mad and explode and start smashing people up, because we're disciplined.

Henrique Nogueira again:

With MMA there are no more nightclubs, no drink. You concentrate, you sleep well, you're happy. I used to love to party and to drink, but I've stopped. MMA has changed my life and it's better now. I am more focussed and have more concentration. Now I love my life and respect my body more.

So, does all the training, sacrifice and lifestyle change pay off in the cage? Steve Dossett's dad, a former competitor himself, thinks so:

To beat a jiu-jitsu man at his own game in his first fight, with all the nerves and everything, is a really good achievement. He's only had three jiu-jitsu lessons, and he got the guy to tap out with a guillotine. Steve only learned the basic techniques over the last couple of weeks. We were hoping to knock the guy out with boxing techniques, but obviously the guy knew that Steve is a kick-boxer and tried to take him to the floor. Steve beat him at his own game, his strength has got him through and he's held the guy on.

Ed Smith talks about how the training stands him in good stead on fight night:

I'm quite calm before I fight, I sometimes think that I'm a bit too calm. I think when I'm backstage and I see a few of these boys, that some of them take it too seriously and they work themselves up too much. By the time they get into the cage, they're fucked, they're mentally and physically exhausted. Whereas me and a few other boys, we'll have a little sleep before we go out. I'm relaxed, I'll have a sleep after the rules meeting, put my hoodie up, put my things on and just have a little sleep. When it comes nearer to the fight, that's when I start focussing on the job in hand – and that is to smash this guy up. To me, when you're in a fight, that's about damage, it's not about winning points, not about submission; it's about maximum damage. What can I do to this geezer to fuck him up so the referee's gonna pull me off him? That's what fighting's about, and that's what I train towards. That's what I like to do.

That's what they like to do, alright. Almost every fighter talks about how much they enjoy the training, the fight nights, even the travelling. Here's Ed Smith:

At the end of the day I enjoy it, that's what people sometimes forget when they get into the cage. I like to fight. That's what we are. We're gladiators. We like to put on a show and give the crowd what they want. They want brutality, they want blood and that's what we want to give them. Standing there in front of thousands of people cheering for you is something else, it's an experience that's difficult to describe, unlike anything else in the world.

Afnan Saeed:

I just love fighting. I used to fight all the time at school when I was younger. My dad always encouraged me. If I was bullied he'd say, "Get out there and sort yourself out." He knows a lot of travellers, and I've been to a few fist fights with them, and I just grew to love fighting. My mum started me training, then I did Thai boxing and MMA's a natural progression.

FIGHTING CAMPS

Since MMA first hit England, a large number of fighting camps have started up. Some have come and gone, while others have managed to survive a number of changes as their fortunes have risen and fallen. Lee Hasdell, the godfather of British MMA, sums up the whole thing:

"A real warrior understands the meaning of victory and defeat; it lives inside the mind on a daily basis. Only now, after many years of martial arts and meditation training, am I starting to see the meaning of the way of the warrior. It's in the continued relationship with fear and the near-death experiences that one feels inside the mind and body during training and competition. Moment by moment one must not be defeated by the voices of doubt. I look back and see clearly that defeat is never from the sword of the enemy, but from falling down on one's own sword during the bout."

ELITE FIGHTING SYSTEM

Elite was the first ever mainstream MMA organisation in England. It was started in 1997, but really became the organisation that we all know now in the following year, after the first open combat demo in February 1998. Lorraine Campbell says that when Elite started they met a lot of people who were less aggressive martial artists, who felt that the Elite style of self defence looked violent. But some clubs understood the system, although at first they were unsure. As time has passed, more people from soft martial arts have begun to incorporate mixed martial arts in their training. While some of the London Elite clubs still exist, Chris Cummins has gone on to start another Elite club on the Old Kent Road in south London. He also teaches the system in Barbados. Paul 'Psycho' Griffiths runs a club in west London, and Lorraine and Chris are both instructors.

The Elite Fighting System style lives on. From the beginning of MMA, through its heyday and still today, Elite fighters are fixtures in the eight-sided cage, whoever the promoter may be. New fighters get support from the veterans, and are still trained by them.

THE PAIN GAME
TEAM TITAN

Team Titan was started by Mickey Papas and Gary Cornwall in a garage in Enfield in 1995. When they reached the day where 20 fighters tried to cram into the space for training, the operation was moved to an industrial unit. Even though Team Titan has never advertised, and relies entirely on word-of-mouth, they now have about 50 people training with them. Not all are competitive fighters, some come just for fitness or to lose weight. Nevertheless, the training regime promoted by Team Titan has become more popular with fighters, and the competitive fight team has now grown to 15, all young men whose preference is to train in mixed martial arts rather than in a single discipline.

Mickey Papas developed a system called wingjitsu from his background in pancration and wing chun MMA. Pancration is one of the oldest mixed martial arts; it was part of the Olympic Games in 648BC. Gary Cornwall met Mickey through Brad Pickett, who loved the techniques that Team Titan had shown at Wembley, and especially the approaches to stand-up and groundwork.

Gary's background is in wing chun and kickboxing. Mickey used to compete in pancration, where you could do anything in competition, including kicking and punching, except strike to the head. It's an amateur sport, so he claims to have never fought any famous fighters. When they launched Team Titan, Mickey took redundancy from his work as a city business analyst doing computer networking. Working in the day and training in the evenings was becoming too much, even for a bloke as fit as him.

You are attracting fighters from other clubs. Is there a particular element to this club that's causing that, or is it just the good food?
What we have here is a good strong bond with each other. We have a strong team, and that's important, because it's not only that the instructor helps the team, but that the team helps the instructor. It helps to work with each other, because people make each other better, and as the team grows everyone improves. We have a good, solid technique and the team is still young. It's like having good footballers that haven't quite bonded yet, so they don't start as a team, but once a team works and fights together more regularly in the cages, they get experience and the team grows. That's what's happening.

WARRIORS OF THE CAGE

You've got 15 fighters. Are they difficult to manage?
They're all from different backgrounds, but they're a team. They all help each other in everything. We just keep pushing at them all the time. No matter what style they've trained in before, they become moulded to the way we do things here. What they did before wasn't wrong, but maybe where they had one way to do something, now they might have four ways.

What about the social and psychological differences between the fighters?
I don't think that's important. We haven't got a military style of doing things here. Everyones's a mate, a friend, it's like coming to a social club. You're not gonna get to the point where you say, "I've gotta do this, I've gotta do that." Everyone's having a good time, and when you're having a good time, you not only pick things up better, you can understand it a little bit more because you can interact with everyone there.

How do you know when a fighter needs a fight? He may say he's ready...
If they're not 100 per cent fit we don't let them fight. We don't put them in if they're not ready. We know when they're ready. If they can technically handle themselves in stand-up and technically handle themselves on the ground and are guaranteed 100 per cent fit, then they can fight. Fitness and cardio are 80 per cent of the fight.

Who prepares the fighters mentally?
Gary, I think. I do the more technical side, I get the guys ready with stand-up, the ground, clinching, how things are done and the way to fight. Gary works more on their fitness. He'll leave his house at five o'clock in the morning to get them running before he has to go to work. He's right there in the ring with them during the fight to get them through the fight mentally: wrapping their hands, talking to them between rounds to make sure they're ready for the next one.

Do fighters need to be both physically ready and mentally focussed?
Yes, but sometimes they might lose that after the first round. I maintain that by talking to them and putting my eyes into 'em and saying, "Come on, you've gotta do this, you're gonna do this." They

148

seem to snap out of it and just come back round to what they learnt in training.

How important is it for a trainer to understand the dietary needs of the fighters?
With the guys who want to make this a proper trade, to become fighters, the trainer's got to watch everything in terms of technique, but also has to understand that the right fuel in the fighter's body will create better, more successful training. So food and diet is important during training and, obviously, getting towards the fight it becomes more important.

How important is it for a trainer to be in regular contact with the fighters?
The fighters always need guidance in the gym and sometimes away from the gym, in terms of their social life. Here at Titan we try to keep things as close knit as possible. We're a family here, so anybody who has any problems, no matter what, can come to each other, and especially to me. If people come to me I give them the best advice I can, and that keeps us close. Not only do we understand what happens outside in terms of our own private lives, but also within the gym.

How hard is it for you to tell the difference between the effects of ordinary medicine and banned substances?
The UK associations seldom have drug testing because it's very expensive, but they do have it in America and it's important for the fighter, if he does get ill, to be able to understand the lists of banned substances. They need to know what banned substances are on the list and also to find out what is in any food they eat or in any medicine that they're taking. That's the only way to be sure that a fighter doesn't violate the rules.

How are the fighters looked after during and after a fight?
The most important thing is that there's a medical crew at the side of the cage. The quicker you can get to a fighter who's injured, the better it is. After treatment, you still have to keep an eye on him. His whole team should be vigilant to see whether he needs to go to the hospital, even if he says he is okay. You've got to keep an eye out on him really. I believe that there should be two sets of medical crews, one at cage side and the other upstairs in the changing rooms. The

fights cannot continue unless and until the medical crew have come back to cage side. Obviously that gives them a bit of pressure to do what they have to do in such a small amount of time. You cannot always diagnose and treat an injury in such a small time interval and it's better for the fighter if he has treatment continued in the changing rooms.

Have there been incidents in the past?
I have seen a fighter who'd had some attention and then had been left. He said he was okay, but, because I've been in the sport for such a long time, I knew that he was still concussed. He didn't know what he was saying. It was obvious that medical treatment was needed, so we advised him that he needed to go down to the hospital and somebody took him.

Why train guys to fight when you could be home with the family?
Mickey: Everybody has a profession and I've chosen this one, and it also provides for my family. My dad used to say to me, "Even if you sell tomatoes, you be the best you can be," and I'm being the best I can at what I do.

Gary: It's the same thing. It's the fighters. The guys phone me up and say, "Are you there tonight or can you be there at five in the morning?" And I say, " Yeah, I'll be there for you." It's my fix. I don't drink or anything like that. I train with the boys and they keep me young.

Is it hard to carry on? Who inspires you?
The fighters inspire me because they're there to train and I'm there to teach them. It's a kind of symbiosis. We need each other. I thrive on the success of my students.

Do you follow any religion?
I believe in God, and my family does go to church. But, I believe that I control my life and if I don't make a move, nobody else will help me. We have knelt down, all of us at Titan, and we've had a chat. I haven't specifically asked God to help us, but as a team we all help each other, and we're here for each other. Everything that we've trained for and all the stuff we've done throughout the preparation for the fight should, hopefully, guide us through to a victory.

THE PAIN GAME

Why do you think that MMA has become so popular?

MMA has just left everything else behind and has overtaken boxing in popularity. There's still a lot of kickboxing up in the north of England, but down here in London kickboxing is just dead. They don't have it at York Hall in Bethnal Green anymore. I think MMA's a fascinating sport, it exhilarates the crowd that watches it because of its excitement as a fighting art. It's not only just hands, it's everything that a fighter can possibly do that makes it exciting.

LONDON SHOOT FIGHTERS

Paul Ivens and Alexis Demetriades founded London Shoot Fighters in 1997. They are part of the world elite of MMA. Having gone to study in Japan, to progress his skills in martial arts, judo, boxing and wrestling, Paul also worked in nightclubs for six hours a day, frequented by the US Marines who came in to drink … as well as pursuing other diversions! Paul came back in 1996 and involved himself in Pancration, and then began working as a cornerman during fights. Paul has also trained at a club in Beverly Hills in the USA, where he first learned the technique of the double leg lock as displayed by Pride UFC champion Mark Kerr. Known for his wrestling abilities, Paul has also won National GB Freestyle Wrestling titles.

Alexis has a background in boxing and wrestling and is two-time National GB Freestyle Wrestling Champion. His brother Marios was taught by Eddie Bravo, the jiu-jitsu black belt turned MMA commentator, while he was in the USA.

Alexis, Paul and Marios grew up together and went to the same school in northwest London, three brothers in all but name. Their gym – which is the largest in the country at 30,000 square feet – is a training base to many stars and champions, including Lee Murray, John Hathaway, Jean Silva, Andy Zajac (European Kickboxing Champion and World Kicking Silver Medallist), Kathy Gifford, Francis Heagney, Michael Johnson and Marius Zaromskis, Dream Welterweight Grand Prix holder 2009. (This guy is one tough motherfucker – well, they all are!)

Gaz Roiston fights out of London Shoot Fighters. He talks here about the benefits of a good training camp.

How did you get into the fight industry?

Similar story to a lot of people. The first MMA I saw was UFC2. I saw

Little Royce Gracie bashing everybody, submitting everybody. It was about 1993 or 94, I was about 13 years old. I'd already had an interest in martial arts, had been training, and to Thai boxing. After I saw UFC I just knew what I wanted to do with my life.

Were you being bullied at school?

No. I'd love to have that classic story: that I started training in martial arts because I got bullied. I was pretty good at sports, I always liked it. A lot of the mainstream sports and team games didn't really appeal to me, like football and rugby. I was always interested in sports because I wanted to see who was the best, who could jump the furthest or the highest, who could run the fastest, who could throw the furthest, who was the toughest fighter, who was the best.

How did you start with London Shoot Fighters?

I started training first with Andy Jardine because that's who Alex Reid was training with. I met Andy at a sport jiu-jitsu class run by Gary Turner in about 1996. I'd been doing the typical thing, training down our local squash court with my mates after watching these UFC shows and looking in magazines and books and trying to copy the techniques, because there was no-one out to teach us. Anyway, I met Reidy and he said to me, "You're not too bad, you should come down and train where I train." So I did.

Which fighters have inspired you?

James Zikic is somebody I really respected when I was coming up in the sport. I used to watch Jamie fight and he was amazing. He was the reason why I started amateur boxing, because I saw how well he used his hands in fights and how confident it made him. He wasn't scared, he wasn't glove-shy. You know he was willing to stand there and trade. And not just trade, but do it skilfully. I thought, this guy's the business, he's for real. I knew he'd been away to train with Frank Shamrock and I wanted to be like him, so I started training the way he did. I tried to emulate and copy him. I went to America because I knew Jamie went away to train. In Las Vegas I stayed with my cousin for a few months and trained with a Brazilian jiu-jitsu team run by John Lewis. I'd seen John Lewis draw with Carson Gracie Junior and he was good and had great jiu-jitsu. When I came back, I started training at London Shoot.

THE PAIN GAME

London Shoot Fighters is very well known. Who else trains there?

Jamie obviously. There's Alex Reid, he's a fantastic fighter, and we've got Michael Johnson too. He's a fantastic athlete. He always raises my game whenever I train around him. We've got up-and-comers like Marius Zaromski and Suley Mahmoud. And, of course, we've got Mustapha Al-Turk. He's beaten Mark Kerr who's a two-time Abu Dhabi champion, he's a world Vale Tudo champion, and a Pride UFC veteran. He's got all the credentials he needs. It just shows Mustapha's class, and where his dedication and time have taken him. Mustapha's a guy that's given up a well-paid decent job as a chemist to train fulltime and it's paid off.

What keeps MMA so popular?

It could be all sorts of elements, whether it's the excitement of the actual sport or the way it's been marketed is a question of interpretation. I think in the early days, lots of people heard about this sport because it was advertised as a big spectacle. You know, "It's in a cage, it's brutal, it's a street fight, we're actually going to do this for real. It's like *The Running Man*, but for real." But now, it's emerged as a *bona fide* sport. Anything that people take seriously gets complicated, it becomes hard. Take football. It was just a question of kicking the ball in the net originally. But now it's a strategic game with athletes getting paid millions of pounds, training hard, and having to think about what they're doing.

Do you think that boxing will make a comeback?

Things always come around in cycles. Boxing had some golden years and now it just seems to be lacking stars, enthusiasm and interest. It's hard to say. I'll always respect boxers and their talent because I've boxed myself. There could be a revival, it might make a comeback. The way Cage Rage is growing at the moment, it's got such popular interest, it's a threat to boxing.

Some people say that MMA is barbaric. Do you agree?

No. It's essentially the first sport ever, isn't it? One human being fighting another.

I think pretty much all sports, especially contact sports, are influenced by instinct. Human beings, especially men, like to take risks. We like to test ourselves physically and a fight provides the opportunity. You have to think about what you're doing when you come across another skilled opponent. You have to be fit and in shape, strong, to have endurance, and to have well-drilled moves. All this stuff comes about in one package, in one event. It's not just a question of who can jump the highest or the furthest or the fastest and whatever, it's who's smart enough to use the tools they've got. I've heard it said before, but it's like a game of chess where your arse is on the line.

Which bout would you organise if you could put any two fighters in the world together?

If you get two great explosive fighters – for a great fight you've got to have two styles that gel. Sometimes two styles can cancel each other out, they can make for quite a boring fight. For example, at the last UFC everyone was excited about this Costa Diago/Sanchez fight, the second one. It wasn't exactly a barn burner for anybody who saw it. What is going to be a good fight is James Zikic versus Cyborg. I'm predicting the second round, late second round knockout for James Zikic. He is highly underrated in terms of his stand-up and his skills. I mean this guy can box, kickbox and he's slick. He cuts angles, he's good. Right now, coming into this fight, he's got fitness. I think we're going to see James cut some angles, land some big right hands and pepper him with shots. He's going to have to weather a storm if Cyborg comes up throwing everything. He's not an idiot, but he only throws everything for, let's say, three or four minutes. That's less than round one. Late into round two, Jamie's going to knock him out, I'm sure of it. It's going to be exciting.

What's your favourite technique?

There's a special secret ground and pound position. It's gonna be the new twister, mate. And it's called 'the Gazatron'. You wait and see it.

Tell me about Kamal Lock.

You used to have a sort of hardcore elite which consisted of guys like Kamal Lock. He was in his late thirties, but in fantastic condition. It's a shame that he retired before the sport really kicked off, because he would definitely be a major force in Cage Rage. In some of those earlier shows, the Millennium Brawls and the Ring of Truth type of events, he was one of the main draws. He always fought well. He was a big guy, with a little man's style. He had small man's jiu-jitsu, small man's kickboxing on this huge frame. He must have been about six foot two, or six foot three; a muscular, athletic heavyweight fighter. He had it all, everything.

THE PAIN GAME

Who else was part of the old hardcore?

James Zikic was one of the old mainstays of the original shows. Then there was John Thorpe, who will always be remembered for his fight against Tengiz Tedoradze. Tengiz was not really known about that time, about 2000. Nobody knew that he'd been a former Greco-Roman world champion. When you reach such a high level in an Olympic sport, you stay in shape. Tengiz used to say, "Yeah, I don't train so much anymore, I just play rugby." But he is a highly conditioned world-class athlete. He hit really hard and John had to eat a few in that fight. That fight was a real test for John. It was highly contested. He was a big, tall white guy, a heavyweight, but athletic and strong. He had every attribute that you expect from a decent, natural athlete. And he came in. He got Tengiz to the rug. He was a former Greco-Roman warrior coming down. John had a very hard time. He was constantly on his back throughout that fight. What Tengiz wasn't versed in was submission. He could hold a man down, he could pin, he could hit him, he could do all this stuff, and eventually, after the fight of his life, John hooked him up in a triangle and tapped him out. That was a happy day for us.

What was it like fighting in those early days?

We were competing at the High Wycombe Judo Centre. It's only a small venue but there was a loyal, hardcore crowd that used to come down. You'd see the same faces in the crowd each time, same athletes or other guys from the same team. You didn't really know who you were fighting. Your best guess of what your opponent would be like would be based on what gym he was from. You'd be thinking, "What's the last guy like that I fought from that gym? Yeah, he's pretty tough, he had a judo background. That means that this guy tonight, he's probably pretty much the same." So you had to base who you were fighting on whoever you'd seen from the same gym.

So that was all due to the London Shoot Fighters?

Yeah, that's all down to the training here. There were a few names in those days, some tough guys. There was a guy I fought called Mark Day. He gave me the hardest fight of my life. I fought him to a draw at Millennium Brawl. Afterwards my face looked like the Elephant Man. I had lumps all over me and he had such a tough head. I hit him as hard as I could and everything bounced off him. About three years later, three years on, we fought again in Extreme Force, and luckily I won this fight – but testament to Mark's tough head, I actually broke my hand on it. I don't know what he's got in there, but mate, he's got a skull like a horse. He's tough. Mark also fought Alex Reid who's now at Shoot Fighters. Reidy was training out of Andy Jardine's gym at that time, I think. I can't give you an exact date when Alex started training here. I think I started training here shortly before him. I moved out of my previous gym because I felt the training here was just more structured.

I believe Mark Epstein, the Beast, is also with Shoot Fighters?
That's right. He came over here through his connection with Lee Murray, who was training here. Lee put London Shoot Fighters in the spotlight. He's always been an amazing athlete, naturally. Will of iron, absolutely – he's one of those guys who will not tap. You could break his arm, he won't tap. He wants to fight, he wants to hurt you when he fights. He wants to knock you out. He wants to win and nothing will get in the way of that.

Lee's been in the UFC, and has fought the UFC champion, Anderson Silva.
You know that was an interesting fight, because that's where Anderson Silva showed his true class. He always respected Lee Murray's ability to finish a fight. He always realised that Lee Murray was dangerous. Lee's great, he's a team member, but Silva got taken to school in that. You know, he worked him up and down; low kicks, punches, but it was always in the move. Another guy, perhaps not of Anderson Silva's calibre or class, might have stepped in. But he never did with Lee. Lee always looked dangerous in that fight. Every time he threw a right hand, it looked hard, sharp, crisp and powerful, and he knew Anderson Silva didn't want any of that, so he stayed back, he low-kicked him, side-kicked him to the legs to keep him away. He just carried on and worked it to a decision, which is the smart thing to do. For me, Anderson Silva really showed his class in that fight. And Lee Murray proved that he was world class as well. There was always a moment in that fight, no matter how badly he looked like he was getting beaten, where you know when he landed that punch it would have knocked him out.

Does London Shoot Fighters succeed in tournaments?
Yeah, we fight in a lot of submission tournaments. A lot of the up-and-comers and the pure scrappers enter tournaments before they

move up into main MMA competition. We usually do pretty well. Sometimes the boys win gold.

When are we going to see you in the cage again?
I'm due to fight in the States on a show called TFC pretty soon. I'm signing a contract shortly which puts me on a wage. They keep putting the show back, which is frustrating.

MUSTAPHA AL-TURK OF LONDON
SHOOT FIGHTERS

What were your schooldays like?
It was a mixture really. I got a bullied a few times, but nothing major. I always stuck up for myself. I would never really back down. I did bully a little bit, but not too much. I've always been a good person like that. I've never really been a big bully. School was generally good for me. I went all the way through school. I did A-levels, I did a degree. School was a positive experience.

Do you still have your childhood ambitions?
No, no, I thought I was going to be a doctor. But no, the most I could actually stomach in education was a degree in pharmacology, so no.

Do you accept that cage fighting is a brutal sport?
It can appear to be very brutal and I wouldn't recommend it to everybody. However, it appears more brutal to the untrained eye, because it really is an amalgamation of three or four disciplines: kickboxing, boxing, jiu-jitsu, wrestling, if you segregate the disciplines; boxing, wrestling, jiu-jitsu, judo, would you say they're violent and aggressive? A lot of people say, "No, they're not brutal." But put them together and then people misconstrue it as being brutal.

Can MMA be a positive thing for young people?
Absolutely. Same as boxing, karate, judo, table tennis, for Christ's sake! Anything that will get kids off the streets and channel their energy in a positive way is going to be good. I see it in everyday walks of life. You go down to the boxing gym in Tottenham, KO Gym; the police actually work with the young people down there to channel their energies and their strengths. I've done a bit of work for

them and it's always good, because kids lose their path very easily with regard to drugs, women, alcohol. So it's a good thing, all sport is a good thing.

Do you think that the UK media should pay more attention to MMA?

Absolutely. The sport is still in its infancy. If you look in the back pages of any tabloid newspaper you can see clearly that they don't have MMA included even when there's been a big event like the UFC or Dream. It's never included, but you always see boxing, football, rugby. It will be one day, though. Let's hope it's sooner rather than later.

How has MMA affected you personally?

It's made me a lot more confident. I'm a hands-on man, I'm a physical man. People can say to me, "You've done well, you did really well." But no, in physical endeavour you know how well you do from inside yourself. The physical and mental confidence it's given me is unsurpassed. You can't really buy that.

Are you religious?

I am a practising Muslim. I try and pray as much as I can. I don't fast because my job doesn't allow me. But I'm more religious than people let me show. Saying that, I don't really enforce it on the kids. I don't ask them to pray, but they see me doing it. I do it every day, as much as I can. I tend to stick by my religion. Fighting has made me a bit more religious because you put yourself on the line.

Has there been a turning point in your life and how did you deal with it?

A real turning point in my life was when I decided to give up work. I had a very good job, working for a very reputable pharmaceutical company. Because of the nature of the work I could come training every time I got frustrated. I could stop, train, compete and win. Every time I took it a step further. Until I decided that you only regret the things you haven't done in life. So that's when I decided to fight fulltime.

What does your trainer say to you before a bout?

"Switch on, you can do this. You've trained hard, you've trained with so many people. You've sparred." Dave generally goes over the last 15 weeks, or whatever, of training, really just to switch me on.

Define a tough guy.
Someone who's tough, not only physically but mentally. Mentally relentless, not going to back down because of a knock from losing a fight or getting punched in the face. There's a lot of mental aspects to being tough. It's very little physical actually.

CHUTE-BOXE

Recently, the Brazilian training academy Chute-Boxe has been bringing fighters over to the UK. They come with an impeccable reputation for jiu-jitsu, hardly surprising since their style is based on traditional capoeira skills. Chute-Boxe competitors are highly respected wherever they go.

Chute-Boxe was started by Augusto Oliviera, Rudimar Federigo and Rafael Cordeiro. Augusto and Rudimar began training together in 1982 in their home town of Curitiba, Brazil. Rudimar taught and worked with Augusto for seven years, by which time their friendship had become indestructible. In 1987 Augusto graduated, and was awarded the prestigious Chute-Boxe Official Instructor Certificate. Rudimar and Augusto remain the longest-standing Chute-Boxe Masters and are both among the most respected coaches in the world.

After graduation, Augusto went to the USA in order to train at the Muay Thai Academy of America, in Los Angeles. He was the first Brazilian Muay Thai fighter-instructor to go abroad for an exchange training program from Thai instructors. He stayed in the USA for around six years and was involved with Muay-Thai fights and training.

Augusto did not forget his friendship with Rudimar, or his commitment to developing the sport in Brazil. All the time that he was in the USA he stayed in contact, keeping Rudimar abreast of everything that was happening in the fight world and especially sending him information about Muay-Thai. As a result of receiving a constant supply of up-to-date information, Chute-Boxe became a lot to be more professional.

Rudimar Fedrigo was run over by a truck when he was 13 years old and his leg was severely damaged. He was looking at a year-long recovery period and the doctors advised him to take up a sport to strengthen his leg muscles. He chose Muay-Thai, which was then a new martial art, practised in Brazil. With some reluctance, he started training and quite surprised himself by getting very good at it. Instead of using the sport simply as physiotherapy and giving it up after his leg was working normally again, Rudimar found that he couldn't give up!

After some years, Rudimar stopped taking classes from the instructor and started teaching. His first classes were held in the open air, in a park in Curitiba, Brazil. These were successful and the classes moved to a club, and eventually to Rudimar's own gym. This he called Chute-Boxe. Rudimar is still unable to give up. Nowadays he's a manager too. Among the stars that fight under the auspices of Chute-Boxe are Wanderlei Silva, Mauricio Shogun, Murilo Ninja and Evangelista Cyborg. Rudimar is known as one of the world's best MMA managers and coaches.

Rafael Cordeiro started training with Chute-Boxe in the early 1990's. It soon became clear to Rudimar and Augusto that he was on track to become one of the most skilled fighters ever to pass through the doors of their gym. He started fighting in local Muay-Thai tournaments, then in national tournaments, but all the time he was also working towards his instructor qualifications. He got his Chute-Boxe Official Instructor Certificate in 1994. In 1993 he had been chosen as one of three elite Chute-Boxe fighters to face a challenge against three fighters from another Brazilian martial art called capoeira. This turned out to be one of the first professional Vale-Tudo tournaments to be held in Brazil.

Augusto Oliviera says:
> At that time it was still one martial art against the other, it was not MMA then, so the only thing that was forbidden was kicks and punches to the genital area, bites and poking the eyes. Everything else was valid. There were no gloves either. So, it was Muay-Thai versus capoeira and Rafael won by a knockout within a very few minutes of the first round. After that event, Chute-Boxe, which was already famous in Brazil for winning almost all the Muay-Thai tournaments in the country, started being famous for the Vale-Tudo fights as well. Rafael fought in other Vale-Tudo tournaments.

Rafael Cordeiro no longer fights. Instead he's become one of the best coaches in the world. He, like Augusto and Rudimar, has remained loyal to Chute-Boxe. They have developed a distinctive style of MMA fighting at the camp – one that demands absolute commitment from the fighters, and a determination to achieve success.

Augusto Oliveira:

> Since the beginning, Chute-Boxe fighters have been known for having a very aggressive way of fighting. At the beginning of MMA, jiu-jitsu fighters had a huge advantage over those fighting in other styles, but the victories were kind of boring. Chute-Boxe showed the world that stand-up fighters could win fights too. And they gave the audience a nice show, full of knockouts. At Chute-Boxe we try to instil that mentality into all of our fighters. We always tell them to be aggressive, to use their stand-up skills, to use their Muay-Thai. We train them to fight until the end, to never give up and give the audience their money's worth. That's what we've taught our fighters since the beginning, and that's why most of the fights you see a Chute-Boxe fighter in are very entertaining.

As the reputation of Chute-Boxe has spread high-prestige fighters have grown up through the camp, while other established fighters have sought out the Chute-Boxe methods to improve their game. In the very early years these included Nilson de Castro, Fabio Piemonte and Claudio Popeye. Later they were followed by Wanderlei Silva and Murilo Ninja. The more recent crop of fighters included Mauricio Shogun, Daniel Acacio, Luiz Azeredo, Jorge Macaco, Jean Silva and Evangelista Cyborg. This is surely an awesome contribution from one camp to both a single discipline and Mixed Martial Arts.

WOLFSLAIR

I'm in two minds either to go by train or jump in the car with Alex Reid. Fuck it, I jump in the car with the Reidernater. I met Alex at Ascot station where we started our journey to Liverpool. It's after 10pm and Mr Reidernater has just finished teaching his class. At Oxford we stop at the services to take a piss, but mainly because Alex needs something heavy to sustain himself on the journey until we get to the hotel. Before he unwraps his sandwich, I ask him if he would like some food that I'd prepared at home earlier. Politely, he enquired, "OK, what is it?" I have some fish, bream, in one container and mutton, rice and peas in another. Mr Reidernater was more than delighted when he saw it, and we finished the lot between us.

It's 1.40am as we leave the motorway. Welcome to Liverpool. I've never been here before, although back in the days of John Barnes, Ian Rush, Peter Beardsley, Jan Molby and Alan Hansen, when they were sponsored by Crown Paint, I was a Liverpool supporter. I probably still am somewhere. I have to say, though, that as I grew up and got wiser I became a Gooner.

At the Radisson Hotel, Alex confirms with a duty man that it's OK to park here. The bloke's looking at us like we're foreigners. I can't wait to get past him, as I'm about to meet a great veteran of the MMA scene. Ricco Rodriguez welcomes us at the door of Room 2404. I stand by the window facing Liverpool docks, a nice view from up here but no better than many views in London.

We are all tired. Sean Salmon, a professional wrestler, takes up the biggest settee, which leaves me with the shortest one. As he sleeps his right arm is extended and overhangs, and I wonder briefly if it's worth the fight for a comfortable sleep. Should I finish Sean with a guillotine, leg lock or arm bar? It's not for me, I decide, I like to look a man in his eyes as I lay him to rest.

The next morning we head to Wolfslair MMA Academy, picking up Mario Sukata on the way. Paul Kelly and Tom Blackledge are already there and Cheick Kongo is on his way. They are all preparing themselves for the session ahead. In walks a true soldier wearing a black and white tracksuit with matching trainers. Forget Duracell or Ever Ready, this man always has enough energy to light up the arena and more watts than a power station. It's Michael Bisping, a.k.a. The Count. In footballing terms, it's as if Bobby Moore just walked in.

As Ricco, a.k.a. Mr Suave, takes the class, I sit and watch eagerly. I strip into my MMA shorts, ready for some fun, only to find myself sparring first with – guess who? Sean Salmon, the wrestler. As I see his stance and feel his punches I think, "He ain't going to be so easy." It's a good experience. Sean's a very cool and interesting guy. A man you would definitely want on your side in times of war. A man you wouldn't try to take a settee from. A good sweat is worked up during Ricco's session, and I truly enjoy the occasion.

I introduce myself to Cheick Kongo as he's probably thinking, "Who the hell are you?" I tell him, "I'm the baddest black man on this planet, so don't even think about fucking with me." The old song runs through my head, "Dreeeaam, dream, dream, dream." This man is made out of granite. Cheick has finished his session and has agreed to an interview. As he takes a seat, I notice two tattoos, one on each calf. One is a spider, the Spider-Man logo, and the other is The Punisher. Ever seen that movie? He's a man not to fuck with. No mercy and certainly no remorse. Sitting very nonchalantly, I absorb his energy. Cheick's eyes penetrate, yet Cheick is polite, even humble in tone, as he answers my questions. He's one of a few on the scene with no fight name.

CHEICK KONGO

Where is your name from?
It's from Burkina Fasso in West Africa, where my father is from. I've taken this name because my father gave it to me. I use Kongo for my mum because she's from Congo and of course it sounds the same.

What were your schooldays like?
I was a regular student. I can't explain to you exactly what I did, because it's very different from the English system. I got a good level of education, you know. It's not the best, but it's good. It's alright, because I trained at university in engineering and computers. It's what I did before, now I work in a different way.

Name three people that inspired you when you were growing up.
My brother, my mum and God because you have to be redeemed, you have to do everything by yourself and to be strong, just to realise all your projects.

Do you still have your childhood ambitions?
The ambition I had when I was a child was to be an astronaut. I thought it would be fantastic to work out in the sky and try to get to the stars and planets, see some new worlds. But I wasn't good at mathematics. Of course, now I just have to earn some money. I'm just a guy that tries to make his own business. I never thought that I would be a fighter one day. But now I am, so I just have to do something great.

WARRIORS OF THE CAGE

What brought you to MMA?

I did MMA a long time ago, but I stopped fighting because I was tired. I fought in different organisations: The Ring, King of Frame, doing Thai boxing and MMA. One day I got an invitation to fight in UFC in the States. I thought, "Why not?" I knew that in the USA I would start like a beginner because nobody knew me, which is unfortunate, but it's alright. I did a good job and it's going to be good for me.

Which was your most memorable fight?

The one I lost because I was in good shape. I did too much stuff, and when I came to my fight I was tired. I underestimated the opponent. It was just a mistake and I haven't made it again.

Do you have a favourite MMA fighter?

No, I haven't a favourite fighter. All the guys I train with. They train me every day. They give me the skills and they kick my arse.

How do you spend your time away from the cage?

It's simple. I share this time with my friends and family, that's all. I don't need to be crazy or do crazy stuff. I like to laugh. I have a good time with my friends. The rest of the time I just train.

Have you had bad moments in your life? How did you deal with them?

I think that when I lost my brother and friend also. I miss them. Friends, family helped me. I believe in God. Now I'm spiritual, you know. I changed my life. God exists and does everything for me. My mother was for the Qu'ran and I grew up with the Qu'ran. It was like that in the family for six generations. If we were at home we just followed this way. On the surface you're tough, but whatever happens between fights, you deal with it.

Have you been in trouble with the law?

Like all guys, yeah. I was a bad guy, in fact. When I started to become famous, and people started to show my face in magazines and on TV, it made me change. I wasn't in big trouble but I just tried to be smart, very smart. Like the guys who make trouble or bad business. But I don't like trouble with police and the law.

THE PAIN GAME

What work did you do before you became a fighter?
I was a commercial agent. I was selling clothing and I kept going for ten years. I stopped to fight, but now I'm trading my own stuff a little bit again, like I did before. I get different stuff between my fulltime work. Commercial clothing. Now I'm working like a designer. It's very good – it's not a bad thing for me and of course it helps my family and friends. And if it works, very good.

What would you like to be remembered for?
I don't know what people are going to think about me. If I can do great things, of course, people will recognise me a lot of times. I respect the fans and just want them to have good memories of me, that's all. I just want to do my job safely.

I get talking with Eddie, father of Paul and Gary Kelly. Eddie takes a break in the office as he tells me to get stuck in with some pasta, fruit and bread rolls that have been prepared for the fighters. He tells me that the academy was founded by Antony McGann and Lee Gwynne who are also the gym's owners. Eddie tells me about the ladies who work in the office organising the other functions of the academy. Wolfslair now has a section for merchandise, new showers and a diner upstairs. I was impressed to hear of such great achievements, and honoured as Eddie gave me his own Wolfslair t-shirt. Fits perfect!

Having trained there, I can tell you that Wolfslair has everything a fighter needs to become a legend. Quinton Rampage Jackson, who feels very comfortable there, Mario Sukata who is the overall head coach and heads up jiu-jitsu, and Dave Jackson, who's the head of Thai boxing, all agree. The fighters who continue to train at the academy include The Count (Michael Bisping), Gary and Paul Kelly, Tom Blackledge, Paul McBride and even the precocious Jack McGann, who's still a teenager and has a gold medal. Watch out guys!

Wolfslair is considered to be one of the best academies in the UK, whether you want to gain self-confidence, keep fit, box or move into MMA. But make no mistake, it's a place for the dedicated, so be sure that you want come out as a winner.

When I return to the Radisson Hotel, Alex and Ricco are in high spirits, parading round the apartment singing and bantering. They're about to cologne themselves and are ready to hit the Liverpool night spots. But they delay the start. Ricco sprawls on the couch, flings out his tattooed right arm flamboyantly, and answers my questions in his L.A. accent.

WARRIORS OF THE CAGE
RICCO RODRIGUEZ

What were your schooldays like?

I grew up in Patterson, New Jersey and I did get picked on quite a bit, being a little chunky and funny looking. I was bullied a lot and learned how to fight real quick. My family moved around a lot, so I always had to make new friends. I got into a few fights living in New Jersey and New York. I had a very rough childhood, but it made me who I am today.

Can you name three people who have inspired you?

I really look up to my mother, because when you're a single mother raising two children in the ghetto people don't understand. To be a responsible parent, involved in your children's life day in and day out, is hard. She came from Puerto Rico and raised me and my sister on her own on the East Coast, which was very difficult in the eighties, we were pretty much poor and broke. So she was definitely someone that was a role model to me.

A second person is a guy called John Jack Marshardo. I met him and his brothers in 1997 and he was just a phenomenal guy. He's a man that sticks by his family through thick and thin and respects marriage, doesn't cheat on his wife and isn't disrespectful. When he's with the boys he's a different person than he is with his wife. He's Brazilian, and he was born with one hand. His daughter was born with her face on one side and her mouth on the other side. When his wife didn't even want her, John Jack raised his hand and said, "Well, look what happened to me." He's been through things in life that no man, not even myself, could bear. He's just a great person. I would fly out to the school and meet him and he would teach me jiu-jitsu.

The last person is Carla, the mother of my two children. She was a woman who believed in me before anything in my life was positive, who has really had a lot of respect for me whatever I've been through. So I've got a lot of respect for her as well, she's very good fun and just a great person.

What's your favourite MMA fight?

Kazussi Sakowaba and Hanzo Gracie. That fight was the best, because Hanzo Gracie really is one of the greatest guys I've ever met and he invited me to his home and his school. I got to train with Hanzo and Sakowaba, I know both of those men and what they're capable of doing. Hanzo never taps out; you could dislocate a body part but he'll never tap out. That fight in Japan was one of the most amazing I've ever seen.

What's your own most memorable fight?

That would have to be beating Randy Cotour for the vacant title in UFC 39. It was really an epic battle and I was losing after the first three rounds. I won the fourth and the fifth. Being there in Mohican Sun, Connecticut, with my family and friends, winning that fight in tears, was the highlight of my career.

Has there been a turning point in your life?

When I was 16 or 17, I graduated from High School in Tottenville. I didn't want to go to college, I didn't want to fall into the cracks of New York City and I didn't want to collect money for the Mob. I wanted to do something better. I was at Staten Island, so I took $150 and I moved to California. I didn't know what I was going to do or where I was going to end up. But I knew that I was going to do something with my life. I was going to travel the world and be famous and live a life that people can only dream of. And that's what I did. I took a chance.

How do you spend your time away from the cage?

I spend every moment I can with my children. Having a family completed the way I wanted my life to be. I realised that children are a lot like glass: you mould them into the shape that you want them to be and, if you're not careful, you can shatter them. So it's really important to educate children and spend time loving them, because if you don't they can end up like me.

Do you still have your childhood ambitions?

I've completed everything in my life that I ever dreamt of. If God comes to take my soul or the Grim Reaper comes to get me tonight in my sleep, I'm the happiest man in the world. I've been rich, I've been poor, I've been well known, I've been hated, I've been loved, I've been disrespected. I've finished pretty much everything I've ever started. If I chose to complete the cycle one more time then I could. But if I choose to just be happy and just enjoy my time with my children, then that's what I'm going to do.

How did you get involved with MMA and why?

I wrestled in high school. It opened doors for me to wrestle with the Machardos. I took odd jobs in the beginning to pay for it. I've always been blessed, like an angel helped to give me opportunities. In 1997, when I was 19, I flew to Brazil to compete in the Jiu-Jitsu World Championships and won. I went back in 1998 and then I competed in Abu Dhabi and won. Doing wrestling competitions at a very high level put me in touch with some good people. The first guy I ever trained with was Eric Parson, he was training and fighting Rashudo who was a champion. He didn't have time to train me, so he pushed me over to the Machardos. I wound up with Mark Curren in Arizona as his training partner, he was fighting for UFC in Pride. Then I went to Japan on a contract and also trained with Sakuraba at Takado dojo, where I met Tito Ortiz. Training with so many people has led me around the world for the last 18 years. I got into fighting because it was a way of making money, and it was something I loved doing. I always wanted to work with children and I was wrestling in high school, but there was no money in it. It wasn't about money in the beginning, it was just a passion, it wasn't about the glory – but as you get older and get into the fame and everything else, things get twisted.

What's your philosophy on MMA?

There's no real philosophy that's a proper one. One of the greatest movies I've ever seen is *Fearless* with Jet Li. There's a point when the Japanese and the Chinese sit and have a cup of tea: my philosophy is the same. I'm not saying my style is better than any other style. I believe that karate, kung fu, wing style, jiu-jitsu, Brazilian jiu-jitsu, wrestling, they're all phenomenal styles. I believe that karma is real and that karma is everything. Everything in life has some piece of karma, energy flows in a pen or a cell phone or in a human, and I believe that whatever energy or karma you put out will come back to you tenfold. With styles in mixed martial arts it's very similar. If you're a guy that's a dick on the street, that's going to come back to you. Karma is about the way you treat people and the way you carry yourself. I don't say my style's better, but if you use my philosophy and my theories you'll find they work. If you train your mind it will make you that much better.

Can MMA help to reduce violent crime among young people?

100 per cent. People can say that MMA is just fighting, but this is truly a competition of athletes that fight. There's a mutual respect between

fighters. Sure, there's a lot of people at the top that don't get along, but when you learn martial arts at a very high level you become very, very good at it. You'll respect people even when they don't respect you. If you walk the streets and someone spits in your face you might think about bashing their faces in, but we know better. We can control ourselves. Children could have that same philosophy, that same respect for themselves, the same courage or belief that they can control it, and that's what they need. Children that have been in trouble, look at their upbringing – this all comes down to not having their parents in their lives. They need role models. Everyone's done something bad in the past, but it doesn't mean that they're not allowed to have another chance to make changes in their lives, that's what important. Children need some structure in their lives. Martial arts can give them that.

What are your emotions before entering the cage?
The same as at camp and in training. When you become very deep in your philosophy, you understand that you must keep your emotions very flat. You don't want to have highs that are so high and lows that are so low that you're just going up and down. You want to keep that flow nice and straight. It's important to keep your emotions inside, because if you're not in control of your emotions then you've already lost the battle. You have to keep your composure at all times. If you allow someone to disrespect you, it's your fault. You have to respect yourself before you can go out and ask anybody else to respect you.

Have you ever been afraid and how did you deal with it?
I think that everyone should respect fear. The only thing I fear is that my children will not have a father, or I can't provide for them the way they should be provided for. The most important things in life are your children because they are going to carry on your name, your philosophy and repeat the way you treat them. They remember every moment with you more than you remember it, especially when they look up to you and they know you've done things in your life. It's important to not let fear set in. All you have to fear is fear itself.

Are you religious?
Very religious, yeah. I'm a Catholic but I've met plenty of other religions and philosophies. Every religion is good, whether or not

people want to fight over it. They all have a God and they believe in right and wrong and some don't eat certain things. There's no right or wrong religion. What are you doing? You're meditating and you're praying. It clears your mind, brings your body and your spirit together. You can have as many religions as you want but they all believe in good things and promote meditation and really good karma. It doesn't matter if you believe in an afterlife or not. I've seen things that I can't explain, and believe there's something bigger than what we're living on.

Define a tough guy.
A person who knows when to use his force and when not to. A man that knows right from wrong at that moment and is able to control his anger. A man who takes care of his responsibilities. He does the right thing at the right moment.

What would you like to be remembered for?
All the high points in my life and all the low points, and for doing something for the sport. We're all sinners, and if you've never sinned then cast the first stone. The truth is that everybody makes mistakes. What's the difference between a hero and a regular person? A hero does something at the time when it's needed and a regular person just stands there and watches it happen. So my thing in life is, when this is all said and done and I walk away from this, I'm going to be the better man, I'm going to be the tough guy and go raise my kids and do the right things. Where's the fun, to go out and chase strippers and do drugs or go out fighting instead? I've accomplished many things in my life, I've done things that people will never forget, submitting Nogara in Abu Dhabi, winning the UFC world title, moving to California with 150 bucks in my pocket. I looked at my sister when we were living virtually on the streets in a cracked apartment, and said, "One day I'm going to travel the world and be famous." I followed my dreams. When I was a kid I watched movie stars on TV. Now they're coming up to me and saying, "Yeah, Ricco, love to watch you fight!" Everybody goes through highs and lows. It's what you do to come back when you're down that matters. Everybody can make comebacks, it doesn't matter how old you are or how many things you've been through in life. Everybody can do anything they want as long as they put their mind to it.

THE PAIN GAME

Who named you 'the Suavi'?

'Ricco Suavi' was a song that came out in the eighties and then it just kind of stuck; you know, always being smooth with the ladies and everything – not that I take pride in being slick. There's no reason to raise your voice, there's no reason to be disrespectful. I learned a long time ago that you get further being polite and respectful, I think it goes a long way. I used to be that guy that was from New York and I was arrogant and cocky. You have to know when to put that charm on and when not to.

4

Fight Night

It's fight night. You've been looking forward to it all day. Rushed home, grabbed some food, had a quick wash and brush up, checked the wallet, found the ticket, sorted the cab-fare home. It's time to head towards the venue. What do you prefer? Some leap into cars and steer a path through the crowded streets to find a spot down some dodgy side street or in an arena car park. Others choose the edginess of travelling by train and waiting for a bus to get to the Troxy or York Hall. Whatever the chosen route, as the journey progresses we see others heading to the same place, the pumped-up steroid freaks, the wannabe glamour girls, the guys from the different training camps, a few celebrities. We get to rub shoulders with them all at the door, and with security if we don't keep our wits about us!

What's your favourite venue? The one that makes your blood rise with anticipation? The purpose-built sports arena or the converted cinema your granny used to go to? Does it even matter? Some don't give a shit about the surroundings, the sticky floor in the bar or the state of the gents, when they've got a seat waiting. What *does* make a difference is the size of the crowd and the mood they're in. The fuller the better. A good card means a good atmosphere.

Oh yes, the tickets. Some fans think it's pretty expensive just to see your favourite fighter bash the fuck out of his opponent. Maybe you'd prefer to stand in a football stadium mid-January for your £50, seeing your team lose in the rain. Take that into consideration and think of what you're getting at MMA.

You've finally forced your way through the crowds, the police and the door boys, got in, met up with friends and sunk a few sherbets, exchanged numbers with some half-pint bimbo, had a fag, and now your stomach is crying out for the next meal. Is the food good value for money, or just another drag on your already stretched wallet? The cheaper the venue, the cheaper the grub, generally speaking. Does the food really taste good or are you just thinking that because you're starving? Maybe you prefer to escape to a near-by KFC or Maccy D's. It's only about the money, the quality's about the same everywhere.

What else might fans want? More concession stalls would be good. All MMA events should have action figures of fighters, t-shirts, jewellery, videos and photos of champions, bookstalls and calendars. Merchandising is the future of the game. Something to take home for the kids that is also a source of much-needed additional income for the fighters. These gladiators need more than just black eyes and aches and pains. They need their faces on our chests! Get those tees printed! Ian Freeman, Mark Weir, Lee Murray and Michael Bisping have all made it to the elite. Don't you believe these sportsmen deserve the respect and recognition within the UK that only good merchandising can bring? Come on Britain, what are you waiting for?

So much for out front. Meanwhile, behind the scenes, while we're having a drink and a chat, hundreds work to get the show into the arena. The fighters, psyching themselves up in the noisy backstage environment or dealing with pre-fight nerves in a quiet corner – if they can find one. Cage builders do their final safety checks, wanting to keep MMA's reputation as the safest fighting environment in the world. Doctors prepare the first aid and recovery rooms, check that the ambulances are outside, just in case. Ring girls put the final touches to their costumes and makeup, the dancers warm up, the ref finds his gloves and the MC runs through his lines. Lighting men, sound technicians and camera operators grab a few minutes for a last run-through: "One, two, three, testing. Can you hear me at the back?" The promo girls pass through the crowds, making sure everyone gets a fight programme and a friendly smile. Outside the police wait for the trouble that's unlikely to happen.

The future is bright ... The future is MMA.

FIGHT NIGHT

ANGRR MANAGEMENT – CAGE BUILDERS

The Angrr Management cage was designed by Chris Payne and Mark Stanton with fighter safety in mind. The deck is padded with 40mm high-density foam, cut into interlocking jigsaw mats. The uprights are padded with the same foam, and filleted with foam at the top and bottom. The deck, the uprights and the fillets are covered with non-slip vinyl, which has been ultrasound welded to flatten the seams and protect the fighters. If they get injured in the cage, it'll only be by their opponents!

The second requirement for the cage is that it is easy to assemble and remove from the venue. This is a tall order for a piece of kit that has a diameter of 24' 6", but which can also be extended to 32' for larger arenas. An optional one-metre-wide aluminium walkway can be fixed on to surround the cage and four portable podia for cameras – or ring girls – can also be added. The design and prototype trials took eight full weeks and resulted in a cage which can be assembled by the team inside two hours, and which requires no nuts or bolts. A truly great feat of engineering!

The cage is built upwards from the ground. The basic structure for its support resembles a spider's web and is constructed from a 50 x 50 x 3mm Mig-welded box section, with the cross members sitting inside folded 3mm steel cups. With the legs dropped, this supports the deck. Uprights are inserted into channels around the edges of the web. These uprights carry the perimeter panels. The side panels are made of plastic-coated galvanised chain-link, and are clamped to the uprights with flat steel bars. Then the uprights are dropped into holes and fastened with cleats and spring-loaded plungers. They don't even move when 200 kg of fighters fall against them.

The next step is to lay the deck. It's made from interlocking MDF panels, which fit onto the basic web structure. The deck is padded, and covered with the 'canvas' which is held in place by ratchets. Padded panels are attached to the uprights, and top and bottom fillets laid in place.

Two hours work for the team. Everything interlocks. All clips spring-loaded. No tools needed. Nothing here to hurt or cut the fighters.

Two middle-aged family men, Mark Stanton and Chris Payne, self-professed adrenalin junkies, bump into each other at a training session. They chat over old times, devise an MMA promotion, discover that they can design and build the cage...bingo!

CHRIS: We've gone from strength to strength over four years. We've got one of the best cages in the UK. Cage Rage ring us up now; they know we've got the goods.

MARK: It's a fulltime job now. There's six of us and it's bloody hard work, but we all enjoy it.

CHRIS: For me, it's more than a job, more than a hobby. It's a passion. Better than my daytime job, engineering. It's very fulfilling – I can't describe the stress and emotion involved in the build-up to an event.

Their inspiration comes from their shared history in martial arts; both retired early because of injury. They devise and build everything themselves: two 20-stone guys thrashing and clattering about need proper support.

CHRIS: For big shows we hire in about ten riggers, and discuss with the promoter where the cage is to be sited. We have to think about the lighting rig too. It's built like a spider's web – centre pin, folding legs. The flooring goes on the frame, then the mats. That's followed by the side panels and then the canvas is stretched over the top. Ready to go!

They usually arrive at the venue on the Friday, complete all the discussion and arrangements, socialise and then start the set-up at 10am the following morning. Everything is ready by lunchtime. After the show they drop the cage and journey home. It's a 20-hour day.

CHRIS: We're aware of safety issues – we can't have fighters falling out of it, or bits breaking off and injuring people. 7,000 people at Wembley are not going to be happy if after ten minutes they've got to go home, no entertainment or money's worth. We have to comply with safety regulations within the constraints of all venues – it's imperative that we wear hard hats and high visibility vests; that's one small issue. The cage has to be constructed within British Standards; the seal has to be within British Standards. The small cage is 24' 6" across flats and the large cage is 32' 8".

FIGHT NIGHT

The main event is a Christmas show, on home turf at Weston-super-Mare, followed by a big promotion in Kidderminster. Just about every UK promoter has used an Angrr Management cage.

MARK: One of our best fights was at Weston, just before a big event in Bristol, McNally and Wallace. It was awesome, I wish we'd started filming shows then. There's a hand-held version, it's wicked. They were beating hell out of each other, on the floor, grappling back up again ... In the end Wallace knocked McNally out, second round. Everything was electric. The fight, the building – electric!

CHRIS: Competitors have shown interest in the cages, they snoop around, trying to work it out. It's not a closely guarded secret but we don't want to give too much away – it took me three weeks to work it all out, sketches and cardboard templates. I've quoted for people if they've wanted a cage, but it's unlikely I'll build one for anybody else.

Sponsorship is an important element in putting on any event. In the past, these have included Budweiser, Golden Wonder, *Fighters* magazine, *Combat*. Local businesses sponsor local shows, using the fight card.

MARK: One of our directors, Al, runs a brands studio, working for companies like Coca-Cola, Somerfield, Safeways. He was doing a promotion for Budweiser at the time. With Golden Wonder, we approached them. We did a big international show in Bristol about three years ago and they've both come on board. Al does the promotion. He's always contacting people. It works well with his other business, he asks if they want to come on board. We've done some deals for cash and some where we've swapped interests.

Angrr Management have also established a good relationship with Cage Rage, built on mutual confidence and fair dealing.

CHRIS: All the fighters and promoters – and Grant Waterman, the referee – think our cage is second to none. They know they're safe, that it's unlikely there will be a mishap, that if there is we'll be there to back it up. So far we haven't had an incident we've needed to address.

MARK: Apart from one. One fighter leaned against a door that wasn't there. Somebody had left it open and he fell through flat on the floor.

CHRIS: It wasn't properly constructed at the time and he fell through.

MARK: What it was – there were two doors, one for the camera guys to come in and one for the fighters. The camera guys went out and left the door open. Lee bashed on the wire mesh, to warm up, and there was nothing there – the door was wide open.

The success of Angrr Management's designs have led to appearances on television, most notably in the BBC programme *Casualty*.

CHRIS: They contacted us, asking about cage availability. We came up with a satisfactory deal and went to Bristol. We put it up in an old church hall and we ended up taking part as extras.

MARK: They thought that you just put up the ring and then it's the same old stuff – dark and dingy and behind closed pub doors. It's not that, it's a growing sport. The first thing I wanted was to see the script to make sure nobody was actually injured in the cage. I wanted to push the sport forward rather than keeping the dark image. We said, "Right, where's the judges, referees, boxers, paramedics?" All they had was two girls who wanted to fight and a ring announcer, so we offered our services to help them along. Chris played a doctor, me and Ollie played judges, and my boy took the part of the referee.

There is a great future in MMA. It has still to peak. Mark Stanton speaks of how his own initial perception of MMA was as something brutish and primitive, until his understanding of it expanded. He believes a similar process will occur in society at large.

MARK: I didn't really understand MMA. The first time I saw it, I thought it was really odd, these guys rolling around on the floor. You need to watch it, and learn; it's very intense and complicated, but it's not a game of chess. It's more like cat and mouse, it's real. It happens every day to people in fixed situations. I'm not condoning that, because it should take place in a cage. That's what's happening now and that's why it's growing. People can see it as a real sport. I don't think any promoter has reached a peak yet, a lot of people still don't know MMA exists. Some of the tabloids are picking up on it – men read the back pages first thing on a Saturday. It's on some Sky Channels. It's a growing sport – in America it outsells boxing on pay-per-view every time.

PULLING POWER

Girls are an important part of the night. No MMA bout is complete without a group of scantily dressed ring girls who accompany the fighters into the ring and remind the punters of which round they're about to watch. It's a coveted position because it guarantees photographs and even television coverage, and this can be an important opportunity for girls wanting to pursue a career in modelling or acting. Competition is high. Those who work outside the cage for the promoter are known as 'promo' girls. You can meet them selling programmes and drinks; their job is mainly to make the whole event better to look at, and they succeed. For the dancers, who have already spent years training, the fights may be just another gig. It takes all sorts!

JOANNA TAVERNER – RING GIRL/ORGANISER

How did you get involved in MMA?
It was in Cage Rage days. I was offered some free tickets on *Star Now* [the modelling auditions website] and they were looking for some girls to try out that night. I went down to Wembley and bumped into Dave O'Donnell who said, "Oh my gosh, you should be a ring girl here, why don't you work tonight?" Well, I couldn't do that night, but I did go to watch. It was the first time I'd even heard of MMA. I really enjoyed the whole show and everything about MMA. They didn't have dancers then, just the ring girls. Dave asked me to

do some promo videos the following week. I went back to the studio to see the film *Cage Fighter* and take some pictures. Everyone was really friendly. I thought it was great.

You became responsible for recruiting other girls. What do you look for?
Pro Elite put money in and wanted to make the show look more professional. They wanted a team of about 25 girls, half of whom would be professionally trained dancers, which is what I am. I was operating under strict guidelines. Pro Elite had a contract with Sky Sports and wanted the show to have more general appeal, they didn't want it to look like a show with a bunch of strippers out of the local pole dancing club. When they used to have dancers at the Troxy, there were complaints because the girls obviously weren't professional dancers and it annoyed the women and half the blokes. They wanted me to choreograph the show. They also wanted another 15 girls as promo models, wandering around, giving out leaflets, looking sexy and stuff. I would try to get a mixture of races and body shapes. I needed experienced girls who weren't shy on camera and were very sociable, but obviously I didn't want to have slapper girls. The girls I looked for would be as attractive as possible.

What was the audition process like?
I'd go through all the girls' pictures and details and they'd come to meet us at, say, Pineapple studio, or the Troxy so that they could dance for us. Most of the girls were fine, but then you'd get the girls from the strip clubs who would strip almost naked. I've had girls kiss me in the audition, crawl across the table and try and seduce me. We've had all sorts. Then we would take them to the studio and see how friendly they were. If they had a boyfriend it didn't work in their favour. That was not from my side, but from the guys' side. They preferred single girls. For me, as long as you get the right girl it doesn't matter if they've got a boyfriend or not, but I did get the feeling that the guys wanted them to be single. Maybe for extracurricular activities.

Is abuse of the girls a problem?
At one fight, we had a lot of fans who were sexually harassing a lot of us, which was a nightmare. I wouldn't say there's an awful lot of verbal abuse normally. In the team that I worked with, everyone was very blunt, but then it was a straight-talking male environment. I

feel comfortable working with that and I can give as good as I get. I think a lot of the girls found that very difficult. It wasn't too bad from the fans though. You sometimes get some glimpses of the girls in the audience and they might give you some dirty looks, but that always comes with the job when you do anything glamorous. Most of the guys are very nice, wanting pictures taken with us and stuff like that. It was only every so often that the fans would get a little too feisty. I've had arguments with security because they'd refuse to let me go down the middle to get to the cage (which I needed to do as the event manager). I'd say that the MMA events I've worked at it were completely disorganised from the girls' point of view.

Do you think that ring girls should be escorted to their vehicles after the event?
I think that would have been ideal. When Cage Rage was at its height we were always booked into the hotel. There were always people around, but now it's Ultimate Challenge the girls don't even have hotels. The girls have to leave late at night on their own to find their car or public transport, which I think is disgusting. The guys that are there, well, the majority are there for a drinking night, so the guys get really drunk, mess around. I definitely didn't feel safe. So whenever I worked there, I had people come with me so that I was never on my own at the end of the night.

Did your boyfriend like you having the job?
I was mostly single, so it was fine. A lot of the girls did have issues with their boyfriends though, because they weren't happy with them doing that sort of thing. Some of the girls used to lie and say that they did other jobs. Some of the girls I know were actually strippers but their boyfriends didn't know, so Cage Rage wasn't too bad to them. I think you need to be in a strong relationship because if you've got a boyfriend and he knows you're half-naked on stage and there's thousands of guys there drunk, he might feel uncomfortable. Whenever I had a boyfriend I used to invite them down. Because I was managing the girls at the beginning, I was dressed more in a sexy sort of way. I dressed in a slightly more sophisticated way when I became part of the management team myself.

What don't you tolerate?
I found it very hard when I was told that I had to use certain girls. For example, I was told I was the manager of the girls, but I could

only choose *some* of the girls and they would choose the rest. A lot of the time, those girls were people who members of the management team had picked up from local strip clubs. So if so-and-so was shagging that girl then basically that girl got the job. It annoyed me because I've been dancing since I was 13, and I've had dance troupes that have opened shows at Wembley Stadium. I once won £100,000 on a television programme because of my dancing. I've always been proud of what I've done. I didn't like it when I couldn't choose the dancers because I didn't want people to associate me with that tacky side of things. I think being a woman didn't help, even though I was quite a feisty woman. If you look at Ultimate Challenge now there are no women left.

How could you have improved your team?
I would have been completely in charge of the girls. I don't think the guys needed to be involved. I think they used it to add to their marital situations, let's say. Being an older woman and with my professional experience, I could pick different types of girls, different faces, different figures that would suit all the different types of men in the audience, not just the two at the top.

What's the lifespan of a promo girl or ring girl?
Being a ring girl is what the promo girls aim to be, that was the big thing. I'd say most promo girls were lucky if they lasted two shows. Those who did had a chance to end up being a ring girl, but when I was there the four ring girls were there for a year. I think one of them had been there for 18 months and she was the longest standing ring girl ever. So it's very short lived. I always used to tell people to enjoy it while it lasts. You never know how long it's going to last. Even though I was the manager, if I was told to get rid of a girl, I had to. It wasn't the way that I would normally do business because I'm a very open, upfront, honest, straight talker. I'm rubbish at lying and I don't like it. I used to feel quite uncomfortable having to sack girls that I knew were wicked dancers, but maybe they weren't ten out of ten looks-wise.

Do you have to compromise to get to the top?
When I first started I would have said "no," but looking back I would say "yes." I think it depends on who's in the management team and who's in control. With guys that have that sort of money they're used to being able to buy things. Most of them are married,

most of them are fat, bald, with beer bellies. If they can pay a girl a couple of hundred quid to do something to see them up that night, then they will. I didn't appreciate that side of things, and to be honest, as a trained dancer with a modelling background, I think I've been lucky not to come across it before. But I saw it in the cold light of day. I actually had a couple of young girls that I was told had to work for me, going round different parts of the audience trying to sell themselves and then meeting guys in the hotel at the after party and sleeping with them for money, and more than one guy in a night. They were blatant about it. They didn't care. Literally touting around in the crowd. I'd never seen anything like it.

Do ring girls feel intimidated by their peers?
Yeah, definitely. I was a bit older when I started, and a mum, so I felt I was past that kind of thing. There were girls who were all friendly to each other's faces, but as soon as their backs were turned on each other the knives dug in. It was really quite a backstabbing environment. I've still got a few good friends from it, but certain girls were really bad. In the first six months that I worked there, my purse got stolen, my car and house keys got stolen. It took about four days to get my car out of the hotel because of it. I couldn't leave anything around. I had problems with a couple of girls that had been there longer than me; I didn't go down well because they wanted my job. I think that was why certain things of mine used to keep going missing. Even my stereo got nicked because they told me to bring it so I could do run-throughs for the Sky Sports show; my birthday present got nicked at Wembley. Nobody gave me money for it. That's the sort of thing that I didn't like. It used to wind me up. I put a lot of effort into what I did and things that I didn't get paid for.

Would you go back?
The girls used to get paid at around £200 a night, now I've heard it's like £75, which is one of the reasons why I'm not there. I wouldn't work for that sort of money.

JUANITA – MISS BLING BLING

Southeast London, Lewisham station, and it's around 12.30pm. Anyone would think I'm selling myself, as I've been standing there for a while. A sleek blue BMW pulls up with its window drawn down to broadcast the thumping bass of funky house music. It's Juanita. She invites me into her car with a smile and a greeting, "Sorry to keep you waiting!" I could get used to this. (The car, I mean!)

We tour her manor in southeast London. We're heading to a restaurant where she adores the food, only we're too early, so Juanita drives to West Norwood to a Caribbean shop for jerk and fried chicken with salad and patties.

This woman has standards, I mean she even stopped off to get her nails done. She's not your stereotypical cage glamour bimbo, an empty shell parading around the MMA scene. Juanita is a very considerate, educated and genuine woman, but her looks, cor blimey!! It feels dangerous, as if, when she smiles at you, you could be hypnotised and fall under her spell. A weapon of mass seduction. As the hours pass, I realise that Juanita is the same outside the cage as she is inside. She takes no shit from anyone – what you see is what you get.

Her day is tightly scheduled, I even get the privilege of meeting her daughter when we collect her from school. While I'm wondering where we're heading next, she pulls up and we're outside her home. Whoa! I did say standards earlier, didn't I? I could definitely get used to this. As we adjust to the stylish comfort of her luxurious leather suite, she flings on her pink slippers with 'Bling' printed on the sole of each foot and says, "Hit me, babes" .... meaning "roll the tape!"

How did you become a Cage Rage girl?
I was filming and Andy Geer and Dave O'Donnell were at the same studio. They asked me. I don't think they had many girls from ethnic minority backgrounds, so they thought I could change the game a little – add some black glamour.

What were you doing before?
Estate agent, fulltime, but some acting, modelling, dancing. I was with a couple of agencies that provide extras for film and TV, so did some walk-ons and commercials. I wanted to pursue a career in entertainment and everywhere I went it was like – you should be on TV, there's something about you. When I was told Cage Rage was going to be live on Sky Sports I thought it was a good opportunity to get my face known, get some TV experience.

FIGHT NIGHT

Was the clothing comfortable?
Some of it I loved, but I've had a child so there are some stretch marks. If men want you wearing hot pants – I call them 'batty riders' – then that's not really appropriate. Some things were too revealing for me, showing parts of my body I didn't want to be shown, but they made allowances for the fact that I'd had a baby. I have a large bottom and some things looked transsexual on me, and it's for TV, live TV. I'd prefer a dress, but for the other girls the shorter the better. I've just got some parts I'd prefer to be covered.

What kind of attitudes did you encounter?
The usual – wolf whistles, as if we're all bimbos and we're all up for it. We're there to entertain people, to look good, eye candy. At the same time it's cool because you get your own following – they come to watch the fights but they come to see you as well. You always know the ones who are following your progress or looking for your pictures on the website, supporting you by buying your pictures. You get some guys who just shout this and that. They just want a quick leg over.

What would improve the job?
Include more people from different ethnic backgrounds, not just blondes with big tits. I know that's probably what most guys like, but they should have people from different walks of life. I'm sure they didn't think I'd be a success, didn't think people would respond to me, but people loved me. They still ask, "Where's that black girl?" I feel that the racism that was there at the beginning, changed. They thought that in order to make people watch, they needed a load of blonde Europeans with big tits, but they're watching for the fights. Everything else is second.

What were your duties? Did you serve drinks?
Yeah, but only once. It was fantastic because I made so much in tips, but the Wembley Arena staff took over. We used to meet and greet, mostly at the ringside. We'd bring the celebrities through, make sure they were OK. We'd dance with them, nothing too much. No telephone numbers. We were there to entertain, good eye candy.

Were you looked after once the show was over?
The ring girls were well looked after. I was allowed to park in the car park, alongside the owners. I had good perks, people accompanied me to my car and hotel.

Has working in MMA influenced your career?

I get offers for modelling jobs – we were sponsored by *Nuts* magazine and the *News of the World,* and I was on *Nuts TV.* I was on Sky Sports, so it opened up opportunities. When I go to casting or audition interviews and they ask if I've done glamour work, I can tell them I've worked different places. Being on Sky TV gets your foot through the door. I believe everything is an opening; it just depends how far you want to push yourself.

Can you do it for the next five or ten years?

I believe it's short-lived. I had a good friend, she's over 30, but looks 25 – she's been doing it for years. She's still got a career and still looks amazing. It's all stereotypes – you'd look at her and think 'bimbo', but talk to her and you see she's got some class, some education. It just depends on what you're willing to do for it. Some people sleep their way to the top, some people can act their way to it, some people have a lucky break and get spotted, and some people may have to work that little bit extra. For me, being the only Afro-Caribbean girl, at photo shoots they always have to build everyone else around me – because they're not going to stick me on the end. They have to centre me, so I'm always seen. They build all the European girls around me, so I'm always spotted and always in the centre of everything. I'd love to see the next black girl they bring along. She'll be my competition. English girls aren't competition for me because we look nothing alike. So – yeah, I'm cool.

Highs and lows?

When there's been a really amazing show and everything looks good and everyone is happy with you. Lows can be people's perceptions – people may think I'm mixing with drugs. Actually, I'm drug-free. Also, I don't have anybody to relate to, so if I need hairspray or mousse there's nobody there. There's also guys that think that because you're in hot pants, a low cut top with your tits out, it's OK for them to look only at your chest when you're having a conversation, instead of making eye contact. I find people are having conversations with my chest, or constantly looking at my backside. I suppose if you're dressed like that, it's what people are going to do, but afterwards, in a conversation, they can assume you're dumb or an airhead or a bimbo. I wear a long hairpiece but I'm not trying to be white, or copy the other girls. I like that look. I'm an educated young professional black woman. I've been an estate agent, worked in offices, been a PA. I have good qualities and skills and I don't want people to think I'm just glamorous, although I am beautiful. Have a conversation with me!

Is drug use common among the girls?
I've never seen it, but I've heard sniffs in the toilet. I don't know if they've got a cold, but when there's more than one girl in there and they're sniffing … if you're on the circuit you know what takes place. A lot of people use cocaine to be able to perform, some of the ring girls want a personality they don't have naturally. They use it to get through the night, give them more confidence. People aspire to be us, and some do that because of how the girls look on television … you wouldn't know if they're coked up. Maybe somebody will offer and you might think, "Okay, I'll try that." I want people to know I've never been coked up, never done any of those things. What you see with me is what you get. If you aspire to be like me, come and talk to me. I'll tell you – no to drugs.

What would you say to girls starting out?
Do it, but don't get sucked in by it. Don't make it the be-all and end-all. Don't sleep around with fighters. Be yourself, have a natural personality. Be well groomed. There is a future in it – just be yourself, follow your own mind, be headstrong. Go out there and do your thing. The world is your oyster.

REFEREES

Unlike any other professional sport, MMA doesn't require any professional qualifications to referee a match. This sport can be a case of life or death, but there have been minimal deaths within MMA due to the refs' regard for the safety of the fighters. It is vital for these guys to know and understand the techniques, the moves and most of all the codes for submission. Most have previously refereed boxing matches, or bouts in other forms of contact sport. With their experience, they have as much right to be in the cage as any qualified boxing ref has to be in the ring.

WARRIORS OF THE CAGE
HERB DEAN

Herb is one of the top referees in the UFC. He started back in the late 1990's, in the earliest days of the sport. He's a very recognisable figure, easily identified by his dreadlocks, but is otherwise a very humble, quiet guy who you wouldn't necessarily identify with a contact sport. I approached him at a Cage Rage weigh-in, where he had no problems about making himself immediately accessible for interview. Similarly, his UK counterpart, referee Leon Roberts, made himself available for interview when I approached him on the night of a Cage Rage event.

Herb, this is your debut in the UK for Cage Rage. How are you feeling about it?
I feel great. I mean Cage Rage is a great organisation and I'm happy to be here.

You're very well known in the UFC. How did that come about?
I'd been refereeing for a while before I went to the UFC and I was licensed in some of the States as a referee for the UFC big fights and I got assigned to the UFC.

Were you ever bullied or harassed at school?
I went to school in Pasadena, in California. I didn't have much trouble really, I mean nothing out of the ordinary. There were a lot of rough kids in the school that I went to and you all test each other out.

So you began as a referee and now you've become a fighter. What inspires you to fight?
Oh, I train, I love the sport. I'm a referee who fights every now and then. This is probably my last fight. I like fighting, it's fun. It's the reason why I got into refereeing, because I like to train in the sport and every now and then, even if you're just a referee, sometimes you want to get in there and do it.

How do you spend your time away from the cage?
I spend most of my time doing MMA stuff. I used to work in the medical industry and then I slowly started changing, doing different jobs so that I could have more time for refereeing. Now mostly what I do is referee, or other jobs within MMA.

FIGHT NIGHT

What would you say to the kids out there today to inspire them?
I'd ask them to think long and hard about the things that they do and to take a real good look at what makes them happy and what they're going to be doing in life.

Does morality play a part in fighting?
I'm not going to say it plays a part in fighting because people do the same things for different reasons. We're all getting in here and fighting in this cage, but not everybody gets the same thing out of it, or has the same style about it. Myself, I'm a moral person, so I'm going to have morals about what I do, that's my personal style. But this is an intense sport and whatever someone has to do to get in there, I don't blame them for it.

What are your emotions and thoughts before a fight?
Usually different before every fight. It depends on how far before a fight you're talking about, because they change by the day. Entering the cage, I'm usually pretty good and pretty focussed. Sometimes in earlier fights I've been nervous the night before, just constantly thinking about what I've been going to do and what's going to happen. These days when I go in the cage I'm focussed and happy to get in there and do my thing.

Are you religious?
Oh no, I don't really want to talk about religion. I just do my thing.

Would you be happy for your children to take up MMA?
Well, whatever makes them happy. I'm going to expose them to as many things as I can and whatever they decide they like to do, I'm going to support them.

Does the fact that their father is a fighter affect them in school?
A little bit. I think that a lot of personnel at the school, especially my daughter's school, they know about the UFC so they watch out for her and help her out. They respect what I do and they look out for her. Other than that, no difference.

How do you spend your time away from MMA?
Mostly with the family. We have a lot of interests in common with our kids. We have a good time. We watch movies, do outdoor

activities. We just set up a trampoline the other day and what I did most of the week before coming here is jump around on a trampoline with the kids. We had a good time.

So you've got a soft spot then?
Oh yeah, definitely.

LEON ROBERTS

Standing over six feet tall and heavily built, Roberts is an imposing figure. These characteristics are useful for a referee of international standing and experience – though, with the level of respect that his knowledge and experience command, he rarely has to resort to his physical capabilities in the cage. In fact, any fighter who's worked with Leon will tell you that he's kind, considerate, polite, caring and generous – unless you fail to obey an instruction!

He's the first man in and last man out of that cage. The ref's decisions are crucial to the outcome of the fight, but also to the safety of the competitors. Sometimes it can even be a matter of life and death. Outside the cage, Leon works with young people, assisting them on their journey through life.

You work as a Programme Officer for the Youth Offender Service. How did you get involved with that?
I always wanted to work with young kids. I did a lot of voluntary work. Took a lot of inner city kids on holidays. I ran an after-school and holiday club in the local primary school, and did some residential social work as well, working in a seven-bed unit for young people that couldn't be housed at home. Then I worked in a Youth Justice Centre, which was run on Saturday. We had between 20 and 30 young people come in and I ran programmes with them regarding their offending. That led me on to get into the Youth Offending Service.

What age group do you work with now?
They're aged between 11 and 18. Once they turn 18 they go onto the probation service.

What have you achieved from that?

This is going to sound a bit clichéd, but it gives me a purpose, a reason to get up in the morning. It's like being a fireman or a policeman, somebody that has something important to do. I think if I don't go to work then I'm not actually going to be helping anyone. I don't want to go and sit in an office or be an advertising rep, which I've done before. I want to go home at night and say I've tried to make a difference. That's what my job's about.

Have you changed anyone's life?

The work I do is about long-term change. I see young people who I worked with five or six years ago, and they've got a family, kids and a job and they come up and ask to take me out for a beer. Some of them come up and thank me for what I did. I had a young lad from a traveller community who I did a lot of work with. He found me when I was working a door in Gloucester and he actually broke down in tears, thanking me for what I'd done with him. So you do change lives. Some young people are too far gone to do anything with, which sounds negative but that's the fact of it. Some of them aren't so entrenched and you can do something. You have good days and bad days with young people.

Are most of the offenders from a similar background?

They're from different backgrounds. I work with young people from inner city homes, with one parent and who are living on the poverty line. I also work with young people whose fathers own businesses and they've got mansions. The diversity of the people I work with is huge. Every sort of culture, background, ethnicity, somewhere along the line there's somebody of each group offending, and then they come to us.

Do you get your young people involved in MMA?

I can see the positivity of a combat sport, whether it be MMA, boxing or Thai boxing. I get my young people now, if they show an interest, down the boxing gym or weights gym. Because of the TV, a lot of my clients see me on the telly and they think it's really funny that I'm a referee. I talk about the discipline that you need and I help them find a discipline in a sport. Maybe they can't read or write, they're not very capable in school, but put a pair of boxing gloves on them and they can prove to themselves that they have got something. I use sports, especially MMA, to get in with a lot of them.

Could MMA be a way forward for them?

I think it can be. Fighters come from different social backgrounds. It's a cliché that a lot of boxers come from broken homes and poverty, and they've worked their way up, though Mike Tyson is an example. We know a lot of white collar athletes as well. I'm not saying that every young person I work with is going to become a fighter, but I think there's a potential for some. MMA can show them that they can be creative in other aspects of life, whether it's being the best builder or being a fighter.

Do you get support for your refereeing?

In my personal and social life everybody supports me. By nature I'm a very introverted person and I don't like being in the limelight, it's just not my way. When I coach the fighters I like to stay at the back, and not be anywhere near the cameras. Everyone laughs, and pretends we're not doing this in front of cameras because they know how much of a struggle it is for me each time. So everyone says, "You know you're doing a really good job, keep it up," which encourages me to battle with my nerves.

What's been the worst incident you've seen as a referee?

There are two that spring to mind. They both happened at Cage Rage arena shows. One was Tom Black against Tom Howard, where Howard took a shin kick to the head. I dived in and stopped the fight. He had a huge gash down his forehead, very, very deep. Everyone knows that you can get injuries when you're fighting, but that sticks in my mind because it was huge. I actually put my hand over his head so the camera couldn't see it and my finger was going into the gash, it was that deep. The second was at a world title fight between Shaolin and Nakamura where Nakamura's arm popped. I stopped the fight. It wasn't until they showed the slow-mo that people stopped booing because they thought I did the wrong thing. I could actually see his arm twisting the wrong way and it just snapped. He couldn't fly home for ten days after the show, it was that badly damaged. So those are the two worst incidents that I've been involved in.

How do you deal with it if you feel you've made a wrong decision?

We're human, and mistakes can and do happen. As refs we have to limit the mistakes. In the UK, the refs are competent and mistakes are rare. We have a split second to interpret a situation that can make the difference between winning and losing and, more importantly, between a fighter being seriously injured or not. If I have erred on the side of caution and stopped a fight, then at least the fighter is healthy and still able to train and earn his living.

What happens if you and the doctor disagree?
My role is not to question a medical professional about his decision. Nor would I expect him to question my decisions as a ref. I do make any concerns I have clear to the doctors, though. As referee, I can stop a fight at any time if I feel that a fighter is not intelligently defending himself when standing or on the ground after a restart. We all work together to keep the fighters safe.

Have you ever had problems after a decision?
Some corner staff, friends and family members can get very vocal, and sometimes aggressive. I've been approached a few times after a bout by angry supporters who do not always understand the complexities of our sport. I try to take time to explain to them, but sometimes alcohol consumption can be a barrier. I have seen refs run from the ring, and once saw a ref get hit, but as the sport becomes more professional that seldom happens now. More people realise that we're employed as referees because we know what we're doing.

There's been a lot of criticism of MMA. Is it justified?
Unfortunately, people that want to ban the sport or don't like it are very ignorant about it. As soon as they see a cage they automatically think street fight, underground fight, or whatever. A cage is the safest place a person can fight in, because you can't fall out of it. In the late 90's when this sport first started, a lot of councils wouldn't have cages. I went to MMA events in rings and MMA events on mats. When you're on a mat and somebody shoots in, you come off the mat and you hit the floor. In a ring you can fall through the ropes. Having a fenced environment means you're safe, you can't fall out and it's difficult for anybody in the crowd to get in. So the fighters are in no danger. There's two fighters and an official. And that makes it the safest environment for fighters to compete in.

Why do you think it's taking so long for MMA to get established?
It's still new. The first event in this country was 1996, which is only 13 years ago. When you look at it in the context of how long

football and boxing have been around, it's a very short time. It's going to take us years, but each year you can see a growth. There's more events, more people getting involved. People from different disciplines are crossing over. Boxers are coming to MMA because they know it's the sport of the future. I think MMA will overtake boxing. I can't see that MMA would ever pack a stadium every week with 30, 40, 50 thousand like Arsenal, Liverpool or Chelsea do, it would be silly to think that. But we can have our own targets and our own goals. I do believe we can reach those targets and goals and make MMA more mainstream.

What do you do away from the cage?
My fulltime job. Monday to Friday, I finish that anytime between 4.30 and 5.00pm. Then I go training five nights a week. So my week's taken up. If I haven't got a show on at the weekend, I like to spend quality time with my wife and my god-kids. I haven't got any children of my own but I've got three godsons who I love spending time with. I love getting out and about. My family's quite tight, we all live in very close proximity, so we have Sunday lunch with my granny, things like that. Have a chat with her, see how she's doing. I'm not a party man – I don't go out drinking, I don't smoke, I don't do anything like that. It's not in me, I'm a very quiet, reserved person and I like to live my life like that.

I can sense a spiritual element within you, am I correct?
Yes. There is a spiritual element in there, yes. I wouldn't say I'm overpowering about my belief, because it's not in my nature, but I am religious. I am a Christian.

Does religion have a part to play in sport?
I believe so. There's a lot of very religious people involved in sports. A lot of MMA fighters pray or thank God when they've fought. I think that if you've chosen a path that you're happy with, it's the right way to go. MMA's not out on the street you know, it's not randomly attacking people or unnecessary violence. It's about people whose job it is to go into an arena and fight. Afterwards they'll embrace each other, thank each other and have a drink. A lot of people that have a religion, whether it be Christianity or Islam, who use their religion to criticise sport show their personal shortcomings.

Crime and violence are increasing, can MMA be a way out for people?
Yes, it provides them with another option. Quinton 'Rampage' Jackson, whenever he does an interview, talks about how he used to be on the street, fighting all the time. He says that now he can go into an arena and get paid for it, of course he's going to do it. He's an example of somebody who has become very famous from using his hands and his legs rather than reading and writing. So yes, there's avenues and options for everybody there.

Would anything stop you being a referee?
It would need to be something very significant to pull me away from a sport I've been involved with for 15 years. If I ever got wind of match fixing in MMA, or was ever approached, I would have no hesitation in refusing to referee that. Also, if I ever went to an event where the necessary measures to safeguard the fighters were not taken, then I would not ref that promotion. Integrity is worth more than money.

DR YOUSEF RASHID MBBS, DFFP, RCOG

Dr. Rashid has been in practice since 1991. He first became involved in boxing the following year, and has since extended his interest to include cage fighting. He is often to be found ringside, as well as at the pre-fight conference and in the dressing room, when he is in attendance as medical adviser. Dr. Rashid is trusted and respected by all who have been subject to his care, and by promoters and officials.

Do you have an official title, or position?
I don't have an official title, but I suppose I'm the Chief Medical Officer. I did all the 'doctoring' for Cage Rage for five years.

How did you get involved?
Dave O'Donnell contacted me – he'd either had a cancellation or somebody had let him down. I was recommended because I'd worked in boxing, kickboxing and Thai boxing since 1992. That was about six years ago, and he was quite happy so we carried on.

Why MMA?
I didn't know very much about it – I'd done a couple of bouts for

other promoters – but the injuries are very similar to other sports. It's not too different from the doctoring and ambulance side of things in other sports.

What are the main types of injuries?
Concussions, cuts and lacerations, some fractures and dislocations. Most injuries are concussions from heavy impact.

What checks do fighters undergo?
They usually see me for a medical examination the day before a bout. They fill in a form which lists their medical problems – if they have any – so that the team is aware of the fighter's history. Then they undergo an examination to ensure they are fit to proceed. I'd say 99 per cent of these guys are fit – they train for months. Generally, their medical condition is tip-top.

What on-site medical facilities are provided?
Right. Well, there's me and the paramedic ambulance crew. We have two vehicles – not just one – on standby. If needed, we can transfer a patient to hospital without delay. There's a medical room in the venue, so we can keep somebody for observation. Most injuries are dealt with inside the cage; after initial observation, we take them back to the dressing-room for further observation, and neurological observation by me and the ambulance paramedics. If we're not happy with their condition, we transfer them to the nearest Accident & Emergency facility, preferably one with neurological facilities.

Have there been serious injuries?
Concussions can be quite serious, but the majority of fighters come round after about 30 seconds. As long as the neurological observations are OK, that's fine. We generally do two or three sets of those observations at ten to 15 minute intervals. If the fighters are OK, they can go home. We did have a chap who went to low-kick an opponent, ten seconds or so into the bout, and actually had a double fracture of his lower leg. Clean break. He didn't realise, but it looked spectacular. It wasn't really serious because we were able to stabilise him in the ring and then transfer him to hospital. People misunderstand the effect of repeated blows to the head, it's something I've seen much more in boxing.

In cage fighting and MMA, the gloves are not so padded and there is evidence that a short, sharp burst of trauma is much less damaging than repeated blows that are cushioned. If somebody gets hit quite hard the shock probably prevents them from continuing, and sustaining more damage.

Boxers wear 16oz gloves...
Amateurs wear 16oz gloves, I think professionals wear 12oz. The gloves in MMA are very much lighter, a maximum of six ounces.

Would you continue your involvement if some injuries proved to be fatal?
We've not had any fatalities in MMA in the UK. I've not heard of any, and the sport has been going on for many years in America and the Far East. Having said that, anything can happen in contact sports, and all fighters know that. They're fully aware of the implications. This is a hypothetical question, but I'm sure I wouldn't feel very happy if something like that happened. We'd have to review our procedures. In terms of my position in the sport, my view is that it is a dangerous business. If you're involved in something, allowing it to go on, then surely it's better to have all the medical coverage you can. This ensures that if something did happen, you'd be able to deal with it as quickly as possible; try and minimise the harm and get the fighter to hospital as quickly as possible.

How do you respond to criticism of MMA, given that deaths have occurred in Russia?
Most of that criticism seems to come from the boxing fraternity; I'm not sure they're fully aware of the rules that govern MMA. I've spoken to people who think that it's a free-for-all – that anything goes. They aren't aware that there are quite strict rules. The main thing is education, people need to know what the sport is about. That's key for the future.

Is the cage more protective than ropes?
Definitely. I saw a show that took place in a standard boxing ring; the fighters had to be pushed back into the ring. It's not like boxing, other moves are involved. If two fighters are in a grapple hold and get pushed against the ropes then it's easy for one, or both, to fall out. In the cage, they have more support and don't suffer injuries by falling out.

Brain scans are taken in America. Are there any plans for the UK to follow suit?
I'm not sure about the long-term checks that are done on fighters. I haven't personally been involved with MRI scans on any of the fighters I've seen. It could be argued that it should be developed for the future. The British Boxing Board of Control insists on yearly MRI scans and, although the pick-up rate for abnormalities is very, very low, they are seen to be pro-active in doing this. I think MMA, Cage Rage and other organisations should look to introducing it as a requirement.

And blood checks?
Checking for hepatitis B and C, and for HIV, is the norm for the BBBC. I haven't been involved with that in British MMA. A lot of injuries that bleed are not too serious – nosebleeds, for example.

You have four children. How would you react if any of them wanted to become MMA fighters?
I'd be happy for them to get involved in the training, I think that's excellent and keeps one fit. Cardiovascular exercise and the ability to defend one's self are very important. Allowing them into the cage for full contact bouts is another matter. I don't know how I would feel about that – as a father, sometimes logic flies out of the window and the protective instinct takes over. Nobody is going to take away from the fact that it's a full contact sport which can be dangerous. As a father, my protective instincts would take over.

FANS

Who are the fans? Mostly men, although an increasing number of women are watching MMA. Mostly young, apart from the older guys, of course. Mostly knowledgeable, either about a single discipline or MMA. Mostly ordinary people, apart from the famous ones. Some have never thrown a punch in their lives, while others are wannabes or actual contenders. They're me, you and the person next door. Their noisy support for their favourites creates the fight night atmosphere. Fans are also the people who put their hard-earned over the counter at the concession stalls and into the box-office. They like to get their money's worth, and presumably do.

FIGHT NIGHT

10,000 people travelling to Wembley can't all believe that they're wasting their money!

Like the fighters themselves, each fan has his or her own reasons for going to the fights. Some fans talk about having started to watch MMA at home when the Sky TV broadcasts began, which led them in turn to the video and DVD market. One fan said:

> I loved the fact that it was real fighting, not just boring boxing bouts. Watching Royce Gracie demolish guys 200 pounds heavier than him was a real inspiration because I've always been small, so he showed me that technique will always beat size. He also put jiu-jitsu on the map for me.

Fans also say that they like the excitement and variety of the contests, and enjoy seeing the fighters compete, seemingly just for the thrill of competition, the adrenalin rush and to test how good their skills really are. Many fans now resort to recorded material only between live events, as they have moved away from the screen and into the arenas for the live experience. For some people, there's a personal connection with their own experiences:

> I once won a fight, and the adrenalin rush you get when fighting is amazing. I believe they do it not only to get that amazing rush during the fight because anything can happen, but also to get that feeling of invincibility when you win, it's unique.

Every fan has a favourite technique, the one they wait all evening to see:

> I like the head kick knockouts. Doesn't happen that often but when they do it's usually spectacular.
>
> My favourite technique is the triangle choke, simply for the fact that not only is it a technical submission, but your opponent has to face falling asleep with their head in between your legs.

And everyone has their favourite fighter:

> Randy Couture/ Chuck Liddell are the main guys I would look out for...
>
> My favourite national fighter has to be Michael Bisping.

He's the best at ground and pound and possibly the best at submissions nationally, although I don't know many British fighters.

My best international fighter is Fedor Emelianenko, who is the best at everything!

My favourite international fighters are, first of all, Fedor Emelianenko, because he is just a whole level above every other fighter, and secondly, Georges St.Pierre, because he is one of the best all-round Mixed Martial Artists ever to grace the octagon or ring.

If fans could meet their favourite fighters, there seems to be no limit to the type of questions they would ask:

I'd probably ask about his training regime, most effective street techniques, and what other stuff they do besides MMA.

I would ask Fedor Emelianenko: could I please have a copy of your training regime?

Like supporters of other sports, MMA fans are interested in what could be, as well as what is. They put together their own fantasy bouts, ignoring weight divisions, age and travel difficulties:

The Pride guy – Fedor Emelianenko – against Randy Couture.

Fedor Emelianenko vs. Anderson Silva – it would be the most technical bout in history!

The fans debate every aspect of the sport. Some prefer the rules more as they are now, while others are more old-school and hark back to a time with less restrictions. Some people still have a taste for eye-gouging or head-stamping. I prefer MMA as it is now – a sport, rather than human brutality with no rules.

Lots of fans have ideas about how to improve the national and the international scene. Suggestions include:

Allow UFC fighters to fight Pride fighters – maybe some kind of team contest.

First of all, I would make just one MMA company and have all of the best fighters from around the world there. Then I would change the rules slightly, I would make the first round of a fight ten minutes long and then the following two rounds of five minutes each, like Pride used to do. Then finally I would allow knees to the head of a downed opponent but not kicks. Apart from that I believe MMA is perfect.

Would any fans consider participating in MMA themselves?

I would love to do MMA, it's always been a passion of mine to learn the technical side of fighting and I always love to compete anyway.

I would – for fitness, confidence, just to learn a new skill set.

As if you couldn't have guessed, the actor and television celebrity Danny Dyer became a fan of MMA from watching the TV shows. Now, he too has started to go to the live events:

To see it live! It's a fucking brawl, but it's so technical at the same time. It puts boxing in the fucking bin, I've got to say. No disrespect to boxing, but MMA's a powerful fucking sport. I'm blown away by the power of these men, the spirit, the heart. I've got to take my hat off to every single one of them. They're proper fucking people.

Danny's TV shows include *The Real Football Factories* and *The World's Deadliest Men*. He obviously thinks that some of the MMA stars qualify for inclusion in his hard man hall of fame:

I'm probably going to do a film about this. I'd like to try and get into their nuts a little bit and understand a bit more about it. It's not about the pound note, because these men aren't driven by the dollar. I think it's more about the spirit – if you've got it in your veins, you just like to fight. These are men, who if they're not doing it on the terraces, they're doing it in the streets, they're doing it outside pubs, clubs. So why not put them in a cage and let them fight it out? I think with this sport you're taking it to the line. It feels like it's just legal.

I know it's not the same as street fighting, but I hold my hands up to any fucking man that gets in that ring with those small gloves on. But it's that walk down the aisle to the cage, that is a walk of fucking death!

WARRIORS OF THE CAGE

How do the fighters react to their fans? Paul 'Semtex' Daley has mixed feelings about how some fans react:

You know I've had props from everybody and I say the same thing to all of them: I don't want to hear it. One, because I don't want to let myself outgrow who I am. Two, because it's expected. It may come as a surprise to *some* people when I take the big wins and when I'm winning big fights, but I expect to. To hear congratulations is a bit of an annoyance because it sounds to me like you didn't think I was going to win. From day one I've known I was going to win a hard fight. So when you're telling me, "Oh well done, well done," it sounds like you didn't think I was going to win, so I don't want to hear that. I just know – you know what it's like when you've got a feeling? Like I say, this is my path, this is where I'm going, this is where everything, all my energy, goes. So I don't want to hear when I've done well. Once I've made it and I'm sitting up and my family's good, everybody's good and I'm able to do the charitable work I want to do, then I'll listen to it. When I've got a house, and I've got a car, and a nice family, congratulate me then because I'll have made it. When I'm able to help other people, I'll have made it. Right now I'm just trying to help myself and the people around me.

Matt Freeman has been impressed by the fact that fighters are willing to spend time with their fans:

But once it's all over, you see the MMA guys back in the arena talking with the fans. How many times have you seen a boxer in a 12-round war do that? Then walk into the arena, sit down and take photos and shake hands with people. Where else do you get that unity? Where do you get that feeling? The reason is after every fight the fighters come back out, they sit at the tables, they come in the audience, they take the photos.

And that's the other thing about MMA fighters, they put the crowd first. They come to please, and that's so important. The overall vibe I get from MMA is of a close-knit community where the fighters and the crowd are so symbiotic, so together. Because the crowd appreciate the fighters, and the fighters are big enough to go out to their fans in the crowd, sit down, have a beer and go, "Sorry I let you down, man."

They go, "No, you didn't let us down, it's just the way things are." The fans believe they're part of it. They're not isolated or alienated. They're an important part of it. It's that whole community feeling. Can you imagine Mayweather or Hatton doing that after 12 rounds? Hatton is that sort of lad, but it's just not protocol in boxing. How often do we see smashed-up fighters still laughing, joking with their fans, taking photos? I cannot believe how many injured fighters come out to their fans. I sometimes think, "Oh my God, what's he doing here? He should be in hospital," and he's sat there after the fight with his fan club chatting away.

MMA stars are accessible and are seen by the fans as blue-collar people, they're blue-collar working men who have not lost sight of their roots and they're willing to get back in the trenches with you after their fight. They're saying, hey, I'm just one of you guys, now let's go party. I hope to God that that actually never changes and we don't see the day when Chuck Liddell's brought up in a stretch limo with 48 bodyguards, led into the arena with his shades on, and after the fight he's swished out the back door to China White's with another 14 security men. I love the fact that you can see the top of the bill wandering around the show afterwards.

Long-time fight fan Darryl Jackson:

I was invited to MMA at Wembley in 1994 and jumped at the chance, not really knowing what to expect at a live event. When we turned up, there was Ian 'the Machine' Freeman walking around and I had the opportunity of meeting him. There was also Anderson Silva, Lee Murray, James Zikic and many more – all the people whose progression in MMA I had been watching on video for years! I became completely star-struck. I was on a high from meeting some of the fighters, and couldn't wait for some of the bouts. I saw Lee Murray fight Anderson Silva that night. It went three rounds, with Silva winning by judges' decision – but Murray was the first guy to go a full three rounds with Silva. It left quite an impression on me, with an electrifying atmosphere and very professionally organised.

THE POLICE

And what of security at an event? At the entrance and inside the venue, this is the promoters' business. Outside, it's another story. Here, the police have that responsibility. Their duty is to consider all proposed events from a public order and public safety perspective. Judgements are made on the basis of the size and nature of an event, and the history of the venue. For the police, it's about managing risk. Thus, a venue with a history of attracting disorder will attract increased policing, even if the event itself is a church tea-dance! The aim is to keep safe those attending the event and those living and working in the area.

Police training uses some techniques which MMA fans may recognise. A spokesman said:

> Officer safety training involves defence and disarming techniques, including 'empty-hand' techniques and hand or arm holds. Some of these may have their origin in martial arts techniques.

The police have three levels of public order training. All officers are trained to Level One, while more specialised officers undergo Level Two. The Territorial Support Group receives Level Three training, with a routine refresher course every five weeks. They often train with the other specialist units, so they can co-ordinate in a situation with the Dog Section or the Mounted Section. Every kind of situation is rehearsed including riots, 'angry man' scenarios and terrorism. They maintain peak fitness and are always ready to deal with any eventuality. Just think about that next time you have a dispute with the bloke on the door!

MMA fans know of at least one officer who trains and competes in the cage. It would seem, however, that this is not encouraged as a hobby for officers, as our anonymous police source makes clear:

> Individual officers need to consider whether their personal hobbies and interests may have a negative impact on their career. The perception of violence and the glorification of violence associated with cage fighting might be considered to be a negative indicator to taking part. There is always the viewpoint that any form of contact sport is violent. The other

issue would be the knock-on effect of any injury sustained making an officer unfit for duty. Fighting, by its very nature, may be associated with a higher risk of injury.

While senior officers in some forces are on record as condemning cage fighting, and may decide to police events as potential public order problems, others are more enlightened. Overall though, it does seem that the force's attitude is more about the perceived violence inside the cage and the 'message' it gives to spectators. The fear seems to be that the audience may take up street-fighting! Where an event could be thought to increase the risk of crime in an area, extra police are deployed to prevent crime and reassure the public. Generally speaking, MMA, as a regulated sport, is policed at about the same level as boxing. On a potential hazard scale of one to ten, it is considered a three. When asked whether MMA had ever been linked to an increase in street crime, the spokesman said:

> It would be difficult to link MMA with any increase in street violence, or among any particular age group.

The police are involved in various projects intended to provide direction for young adults and keep them off the streets. Among those projects available are football diversion schemes aimed at 'hard-to-engage' youngsters, fitness and boxing schemes with ABA coaches and junior citizen schemes intended to prepare young people to deal with emergencies and to teach them to make a contribution to their communities. While none of these projects directly involve or promote MMA techniques, the spokesman observed that:

> For young adults, developing discipline and respect for them-selves and others is a positive. As with alternative forms of training, including martial arts, if it provides people with a means to defend themselves, and the confidence to do so without resorting to weapons, it is a step in the right direc-tion as long as those skills are not misused.

Mixed messages, then. The police use MMA techniques in their training, but do not encourage officers to take it up as a hobby. They promote football and boxing for young people, but not martial arts, even though they wish to find activities which can help young people to develop discipline and respect for others. There would appear to be no evidence that MMA events encourage crime in or near venues, or that those who train in martial arts use their skills on the street, yet the police look on MMA events with suspicion. Baffling!

5

The Future

So, what's in the future for MMA in the UK? At the time of writing, there are too many fight clubs to list. Children as young as four are taking up Mixed Martial Arts training, and men in their 40's are still fighting in public. There has been a huge growth in all aspects of the sport, with gates increasing, more media coverage, hundreds of websites and, recently, a resurgence of events at major venues. These events are organised by dozens of different promoters in venues all over the country. American promoters organise over here too, and an increasing number of fighters from all over the world are choosing to develop their careers in the UK. They bring new fighting styles which, in turn, help the development of both the sport and UK fighters. Overall, it's looking bright.

However, fans are caught between feast and famine – no events for weeks, then two big ones on the same night. They say that they'd like to see some changes in the way events are scheduled, with better co-ordination and fewer clashes. There's a suggestion that there's too much competition between promoters and too little opportunity for competition between fighters. This starts to sound as if fans are feeling that a useful development for the future would be some kind of national co-ordinating body.

Notwithstanding these difficulties, BAMMA: The Fighting

Premiership was launched on London's South Bank in June 2009 in conjunction with Bravo Sports Channel and Giant Film & TV Ltd. It's an attempt to re-launch MMA on UK television, extend the fan base and enable the fighters to earn decent wages. Two events, each of six bouts, will take the winners through to a grand final. At this final, BAMMA belts will be awarded to the winners of six weight categories.

Andy Geer comments:

> Dave O'Donnell decided that it's the only business for him and he's got the rebirth going. He'll build it up again. I have absolutely 100 per cent faith in him. There'll be another show as big as Cage Rage. I've decided to focus on my other businesses that have been steady all my life. I lived the dream for a few years and it was a great ride. Very stressful, but it was a great ride.

The fans, the fighters, the promoters and the old hands are all ready for a rebirth of UK MMA. So what's holding it back?

One thing is the stance taken by the British Medical Association. Boxing has long been seen as a dangerous sport at both amateur and professional levels, and there is some evidence to support this. Studies have been made of the long-term effects that the sport can have on fighters. It's the blows to the head that is at the core of the debate, as this can cause not only cuts and abrasions but sight and hearing injuries, or, it is claimed by some, brain damage. From time to time a serious injury occurs, and there have been famous cases of boxers who have never fully recovered from damage sustained in a fight, or as the cumulative result of receiving punches to the head over many years. We all remember what happened to Michael Watson in 1991. Doctors say that the possibility of suffering brain damage is a real concern for all involved in contact sports. Some people think that those who take up these arts must already be suffering from brain damage! The BMA claims that research shows that those who have boxed have a greater susceptibility to Alzheimer's and Parkinson's diseases in later life. The sight of Muhammad Ali in his later years is one which may have made many a young fighter think again about his own career path. The British Medical Association is still calling for a total ban on both amateur and professional boxing, a position which it has held for nearly 20 years.

MMA is generally perceived by the British Medical Association to be more dangerous than boxing, having the additional possibilities of joint, limb and bone injuries. Since 2007, the British Medical Association has included MMA in its campaign to ban what it considers to be dangerous contact fighting. The World Medical Association supports this position.

Ed 'Smasher' Smith gives the fighter's view on this issue:

> There have been deaths at boxing, back in the days of bare-knuckle fighting. Since the gloves were introduced, it's been very safe. They're always trying to improve the rules and make it better. The thing I worry about in England is, because there's not that much money in MMA, there's no brain scans or blood tests. After a fight in America you have to have a brain scan straight away, in case you've got any problems in there. I think it's only a matter of time before someone does die unless they get legislation to protect the fighters. That's what they need, proper blood tests, if someone is bust in the head, and they've got a clot there, it only takes a lamp round the head and bang, they're gonna fall on the floor and die. There's no governing body for MMA, which I think there needs to be. I know Andy Geer's talked about this before, and about getting licences, like in boxing. There's still that underground element, it needs bringing out. There are all these different rules and organisations, for example in the UK they've taken out elbows to the head on the floor, which in a way is a good idea, because in UFC lots of fights get stopped early because of this. It means that by adjusting the rules like this fighters can have longer fighting careers, as they build up less scar tissue. In American fights people get really cut up and scar tissue opens again every time they get punched.

Despite the medical controversies and the public image of MMA, many fighters are still changing disciplines or, increasingly, starting their careers with multi-disciplinary training.

LARRY 'THE WAR MACHINE' OLUBAMIWO

Among the fighters who are coming over to MMA from single discipline martial arts is boxer Larry Olubamiwo. At the time he was interviewed, Larry was undefeated in the ring. He'd had four fights, and had won each of them by KO. Larry started boxing when he was 18 years old, then turned professional in 2008. He's promoted by Frank Mahoney. The War Machine fights in the heavyweight division, not surprising for a man who weighed ten pounds at birth and trains in Tooting, southwest London. Larry is a sportsman to be reckoned with. He trains with 20 oz gloves. When he's not training, the War Machine is either working or spending valuable time with his fiancée, Alex Muresan, and his loved ones.

We met at the Sobell Leisure Centre in Islington, where he works as an adminstrator. Sitting with the War Machine in his office, you can feel the power of his presence. Like most athletes in an aggressive sport, Larry is very polite and well spoken, one might even say humble. Offering me some nutrition bars and a bottle of cranberry juice, the War Machine lets *roar*.

Has MMA had a negative impact on the popularity of boxing?
No. But I'm biased because I love MMA and boxing. I've got a lot of friends, such as James Thompson, a great friend of mine, who's an MMA fighter, so I follow both sports. The consensus among a lot of boxing pundits is that MMA has weakened the sport a little bit, but boxing will see a resurgence. My take on it is that it's made a lot of people take notice of what boxing lacks, which is basically all the top guys fighting each other without all the politics. This is something the MMA has now brought to the fore and which boxing greatly needs to learn from. For years we've had people bucking each other, saying because I'm on this cable TV network and you're on this cable TV network we can't fight each other. With MMA there's none of that. The best get it on and that is what boxing needs to start doing if they want to get all the fans back that they've lost because of MMA's popularity.

Has boxing been supportive towards MMA?
I think a lot of boxers resent MMA because they think it's taking business away from boxing, and a lot of boxers, promoters and managers feel that the skill element is missing from MMA. I disagree with that, because having done a little bit of martial arts myself, I know it takes great skill to do what those guys do in MMA. A lot of people make fun of their grounding, saying it's like they're messing around like little kids. But the ground game is extremely skilful. People don't realise until they've actually been in there and tried it,

how much technique you need on the ground in MMA. I feel that boxers have a lot to learn from MMA in terms of knowing more about the sport so they can make an informed judgement. On the whole, I would say boxers are quite positive towards MMA because they're contact sport combatants too. They have to go through the same rigours that we have to. In that respect they are respected by boxers.

Why do you think boxing fans stay so loyal to their sport?
Boxing appeals to the general public, and especially to the guy in the street. That's because everyone loves a fist fight. You know, just going at it hammer and tongs with your fists. It's only since the martial arts became popular, such as with Bruce Lee in the 70's, that the other elements of kicking and grappling started to become popular too. While MMA's got a lot of popularity, there's always that sense of history with boxing. Before boxing was regulated, they used to have bare-knuckle fights for money. It's that entrenched history that keeps the boxing fans loyal. As time goes on and MMA gathers the same kind of history as boxing has, it will start to get the same kind of following. MMA guys are admired, but because there's the lack of history of the sport, some people tend to not want to get too into it. Within the MMA there are a lot of guys who are legends now, and a lot coming through who are going to become legends. As more guys come into the sport and achieve things, you'll get the general public really revering it as well.

Does boxing have anything to learn from MMA?
Boxing promoters and managers really need to take a leaf out of MMA in terms of the match-ups at the top level. MMA has pretty much shown how this should be done. It's the fans that pay the money and it's the fans that want to see certain fights. It's the fans that make the sport so if the fans want to see a certain fight between top boxers, that should happen, as it does in MMA. I really believe that in the next few years boxing needs to start getting the top boxers at each weight to fight each other, even if it's not for a title. Everyone in the sport knows who the top guys are regardless of whether they have a title or not. Oscar de la Hoya, towards the latter part of his career, never fought a title. He just fought the biggest matches against the top fighters. Bernard Hopkins did the same thing. They're now the new breed of promoters and other promoters need to follow suit.

WARRIORS OF THE CAGE
JULIUS FRANCIS

Peacock Gym, Canning Town, east London. I'm at the historic building where many great fighters have trained. The reception area is plastered with posters and photographs showing famous boxers, celebrities and even some underworld characters. I take a walk through the gym itself and witness the current generation of athletes giving their aggression to the punch bags, training with weights, skipping or sparring in the ring.

Having heard that a pro boxer was to convert his abilities to the cage, it was chance not to be missed. I watched through the window as Julius Francis was rehearsing his grappling skills for his MMA debut. As his session comes to an end, he acknowledges me and suggests that I wait downstairs in the gym area. In fresh clothing, he orders two orange juices and we find a table where he explains about entering the world of MMA.

Why have you chosen to go into the cage?
It's a culmination of looking, and watching, and seeing what's been going in the cage, and people will know me from my boxing. Most people will know I was given the chance to fight Tyson. I'd already become the British champion, winning the Lonsdale Belt outright. I've been the Commonwealth champion, and fought for two European titles. Plus I've fought, I think, five or six World Champions – guys that have gone on to become World Champions and guys that are former World Champions. So I've kind of built up my stuff in the boxing ring. Plus, I was a former kickboxing champion. I won the European title in 1990. I have defended my title three times, I think, up until the time when I became a professional fighter in 1993.

Who approached whom?
My trainer, Mark Rowe, was friends with guys that had been involved in the cage, and Cage Rage, and MMA. It's not just a case of six months ago they asked me if I'd get involved or if I wanted to fight, it's been over, say, two years. I boxed for 14 years as a professional fighter. I retired from boxing in not the greatest of circumstances, just because I felt things weren't going right for me. I took my time and said, "Alright, I'm going to retire from boxing." And then it was a case of seeing friends – a couple of my friends were cage fighters and looking at it, I thought, "Well ... maybe, maybe." Then people kept asking me. So then it just happened.

THE FUTURE

These days, how do you feel about boxing?

I would never knock boxing; I would never put boxing down. To me, it's an evolution of gladiatorial sports. Back in the Roman and ancient Greek times you had guys participating in things like this, in what they called the gladiatorial arena, like the circus. But it was much more brutal then, because the guys used to fight with ball bearings and glass tied onto their hands. We might think now that cage sport is brutal. Well, people said the same thing about boxing. Yet if you look back in history and at what people have achieved through boxing, there's a lot there. It's not just that they have become World Champions, and they became rich and famous, but there are a couple of people who have actually transcended boxing – like Muhammad Ali. People look at Muhammad Ali and remember he was the first heavyweight champion to win the heavyweight title on three different occasions. Maybe in another life, or if circumstances were slightly different, and he never had Parkinson's disease, maybe he would have gone on to become President of America.

What inspires you as a cage fighter?

I'm not really inspired. It's a challenge to me; it's not a challenge involving anybody else. I see guys coming out of there with broken noses and cuts and guys getting knocked out and I think to myself, "Do I want to end up like that?" No. But it's a challenge for me, because deep down I'm a fighter. And that's what fighters do, they fight and they look for challenges. I'd say I'm not just a fighter, but a sportsman. When I'm working with kids in schools, I keep saying to them, "Challenge yourselves because you never know how far you will be able to get in later life, regardless of whatever it is you want to do. Whether you want to be a footballer, doctor, nurse, challenge yourself and push yourself. Go for something when people keep saying you can't do it." That's what I believe, what I've always believed. I look for challenges for myself and that may be the inspiration for me.

How do you relax away from training and fighting?

I have children; I've got two boys, two girls. I have a girlfriend. You know, when we relax I tend to sit down in front of the TV.

So do you give it the tough nut outside, but at home you're the soft spot?

When people look at me the first thing they see is this big black guy who looks very mean. I think that as soon as I open my mouth and start talking to people, they are kind of disarmed, maybe by the calm nature that I have. Obviously, I can be aggressive because I'm in an aggressive sport, but I don't have to prove to people that I'm big, I'm strong. I don't have to prove that to people, because it's not about whatever I can do out on the street. So I am quite calm and love to chill and relax and watch films and go for walks in the park and picnics and stuff like that. That's what I like doing.

Are you religious?
I do believe that there is a God and I do pray before a fight, not just for myself but for my opponent. I pray after a fight too because, regardless of the outcome, win, lose, or draw, it's not about me saying, "Oh yeah, I've won," or, "Oh well, I've lost." It's about going home and knowing that my opponent is okay and I'm okay. I do dangerous sports, and I've seen bad things happen to some guys that I've been close to. You know I have thought that there is always something in knowing that you can actually turn to something other than the weights, maybe my trainer, just to say, "Alright, yeah, everything's going to be okay."

As a fighter, how would you describe pain and nerves?
I would say to anybody who wants to fight that you can't say that you're not nervous and you can't say that nerves are not an issue. I get nervous before a fight. I get nervous because I don't want to lose; I get nervous because I don't want to end up in a situation where the opponent gets badly injured. Yet, at the same time, I have to be wary, and it's a fear about protection. I want to go out there and do the best I can and come out with everything intact. I always keep telling myself that if I wasn't nervous that it would be no use me fighting, because I think if you haven't got nerves, there's something wrong. And if there's something wrong, then you shouldn't be in the ring.

Would you see MMA as a way forward for your children?
No, actually. None of my kids can box – I've got two boys and two girls. They're not interested in boxing. They kind of look at it and say, "Alright, dad is a boxer." My eldest daughter; "Yeah, daddy's a boxer." My youngest, because she was born just around the time I was fighting Tyson, all she's ever known is, "Daddy's a boxer." She's seen me box, she's been around boxers, that's all she's grown up

with, so she's the only one out of all of them that would ever lace up a pair of gloves. But oh no, I wouldn't let her box.

Now you're known to be a cage fighter, do you get much publicity on the strength of your boxing career?
Well, people know my name and say, "Oh yeah, he boxed Tyson." As far as publicity is concerned, it's not about me going round and getting on celebrity dance-offs and *Big Brother* and all that. It's not about that because that's not me. If people want to read about me, that's fine, because this is what I do. It's not who I am, it's what I do for a living. So there's a big, big difference.

MATT FREEMAN

Matt Freeman is a commentator, editor of *MMA Unlimited* magazine and has been a fan since 1997. He is very well known on the scene, an insider who is in a good position to know both what the fighters would like to see in the future and whether the promoters are likely to deliver it to them.

Do you see MMA mostly as a physical or mental discipline?
They all say it's physical chess, it's a cerebral game. You've got to go in there, know your ground game, your stand-up, your Muay Thai from your boxing. There are so many aspects that you have to live it every day. Also, because the outlet is so emotional and powerful, how many genuinely nasty fighters do you know? 99.9 per cent of fighters are the nicest guys you could meet. Why? Because it's all left in that cage. MMA encompasses the whole body, and these guys use that outlet. When fighters leave the cage they leave all that shit as well. You find morally superior men in MMA, because they've got that nastiness out of their system. It's a complete contradiction of terms: the animal in the cage, the nice guy outside. Why? Because they're the animal in the cage.

Is the discipline required by MMA a good thing for young people?
It instils so much discipline in the young lads that are coming through now that they don't get involved in drinking or drugs or doing stupid things on the street. Every night they're thinking to themselves, "Tomorrow I've got this training to do and I've got

something to prove." That gives them a target and a focus to keep hold of and allows them to live their life and to be honest. It's not changing criminals, it's stopping lads going down that path. There's so much posturing on the street. When we hear about gangs, it's about proving. Fighters prove themselves in the toughest arena, so they don't need to go on the streets and say, "I'm this, I'm that." When you look at street violence it's caused either by drunkenness or through rival gangs saying, "We're the baddest, the hardest, the nastiest." Fighters say that in the most emphatic way, in the cage.

Do you think that there should be more MMA training in schools?

Boxing was still around when I was at school, we boxed once a week and I loved it. In America they've got wrestling in schools. These are fighting systems, but it's all done in a safe environment. When we talk about fighting it sounds vicious, but it's not, it's a sport and it's run in a safe environment. When you look at American stuff, the depth that they've got is unbelievable. Whereas here, if you mention fighting everyone's up in arms – it's too much of a mothering society that we've got, where we can't do any of these contact sports which take away aggression. You can actually teach a type of martial arts in school that will instil discipline in boys and girls. It can change them. If you get it into schools, you get the discipline in too. What could be better then MMA outside of, say, gymnastics to teach an understanding of the whole body?

Do you think MMA is safe?

MMA is done in the safest environment. You've got a cage, so people can't fall out. You've got a referee who's the better judge and he's qualified enough to understand when a fighter is hurt and when he is safe. Some people just want to see a fight finish. In boxing, there's only two ways to win: a war of attrition, trying for a points victory, where both of you stay on your feet for the full distance, or a knockout. There's nothing worse than knowing that you are technically inferior to your opponent, but if he hasn't got the one-punch knockout power, you've got 12 rounds of pain because you're not going to give in. The great thing about MMA is you're getting battered upright and on the ground. Your brain, your ground skills, your submission skills come in. There's so many ways to stop a fight that don't involve being bludgeoned the whole time. That's a huge difference between boxing and MMA. How many times have we seen boxers win and then collapse? MMA is more sophisticated, and I think the reason that boxing is rounding like a dog on MMA is fear.

Why does MMA get a bad press?
The problem we suffer from with MMA is public perception. If you look at the history of MMA, the biggest problem we had was because, at first, they promoted MMA as a gladiatorial blood sport. When the UFC first started, they were happy to trade on that. The posters would say, turn up and maybe see someone get killed, it's that vicious. We have worked so hard to live that down. But you know how long stigmas stay attached. What we have got to do now is to fight social conditioning to let people know that, as combat sports go, you can't get safer.

Why do you think people still want to train as fighters?
The desire to fight, the aggressive nature, is something that's always below the surface in a large percentage of men. We talk of being civilised, that's true. But underneath, just scratch the surface and find the desire to fight. You can't take it away, it's inbred. Don't alienate it, don't make it go underground. Embrace it, make it safer still.

Could MMA training help to keep young people away from crime?
A lot of lads on the streets have got no outlets. If they had that discipline instilled in them, I believe that a high percentage would think twice about hurting other people, because they would know and respect pain. I think a lot of these crimes that are committed are by kids who have no respect for the consequences of what they're doing. I feel the government and schools really, really underestimate the power of martial arts and contact sports. The more contact you take, the more you respect it. You have to receive and feel the pain and know the pain, and then you think twice about giving it out. Many of these lads don't understand that. They haven't had that feeling; they haven't had that respect built into them. When they do this 'happy slapping' or street crimes, I don't think they fully realise the consequences of what they're doing to that person. If they were in an environment where they were sparring regularly, being conditioned, feeling that pain, they would think twice before going for that happy slap, before kicking a person. When you've been kicked in a Thai boxing class, you think, "Oh my God." That

appreciation, that understanding, would be manifested in a different set of principles when they think, "I'm just going to bang this guy."

Can you see a way for women to get more involved?

Yes. One of the biggest problems about boxing was the attitude towards women. Jane Couch comes from my neck of the woods, she's a Bristol girl. I remember having to go to court to get her boxing licence. I know that boxers still treat women like second-class citizens and there's no outlet for women. The problem we have with women in MMA at the moment is the public perception of brutality. When you see the men grounding and pounding, substitute that for two women and it's not an image that most of society would want to see. Those of us that are enlightened would say that when a society embraces race equality or gender equality, it means just that. That means women have the right to do what the hell they want. The problem at the moment is not society, but women themselves. Too few women want to do MMA, simply because of what they've seen. If I was a woman watching and I saw someone pounding away to the face to get the stoppage, I'd think, "Oh no." But the more women we get coming to watch, the more they will understand the technicalities of ground fighting, the skills required in submission, and the more women will start training. It will be a long, slow process, beginning with them coming to the shows as spectators. In terms of self defence for women, MMA skills, like a simple lock or a finger hold, can buy them the time. If women realised there was a self defence element, we'd bring them in.

What has impressed you so far being in MMA as a commentator?

I love the fact that so many skills are brought into play. I like the fact that safety is well advanced and that money is coming into the sport quickly. Fighters are modern gladiators and I think they deserve to be rewarded for that.

Another thing I love is that it's not just about the winning. Fight records are important, but they're not the ultimate because the fans are becoming so knowledgeable. They know there are so many ways to win or lose a fight, and that it's no disgrace to be tapped out by a fantastic kamura, by a fantastic triangle. It's not because you're crap, it's because of the skill of the techniques. A fighter's record becomes more of an irrelevance. It's your spirit, it's your ability, it's your desire to please the crowds that's important.

THE FUTURE

I also love the fraternity. It's such a great, close-knit society. It's a great bonding arena. The fighters are wonderful human beings. They switch, they're Jekyll and Hyde characters. Before a show, where else can you walk into the foyer and see the man topping the bill sat at a desk signing posters for you as freebies? They do the business in the cage, they come out after and they're so chilled. That's fighting at its purest.

Who are the up and coming young fighters on the MMA scene? We spoke to some stars of the future:

JOHN 'THE HITMAN' HATHAWAY

London Shoot Fighters. I've been greeted by Ollie and Jean Silva and told that the Hitman is waiting for me. Unaware of exactly what's waiting behind the door, I'm surprised to find that John Hathaway is sitting very relaxed. He invites me to join him before he starts his next training session. The room I've entered is only for the privileged and I feel very honoured to be among this company.

Since his earlier bouts in Cage Rage, this young man has matured in all aspects of his skills and stability. It's becoming clear that he will gradually become one of the UK's fight legends. The Hitman had drawn a sea of people to his fan base since his debut on UFC – which was a great success, due to his win by a technical knockout. John established himself with Zero Tolerance, which was formed by that great man, John's coach Sol Gilbert. John eagerly awaits his turn to be crowned King of Kings as he continues to go from strength to strength. Standing at six foot one and fighting welterweight at 77 kg, he might not have to wait long.

John Hathaway turned professional in 2006 at the age of 18, after only two amateur fights. He was nicknamed 'the Hitman' by Sol Gilbert and Ron White after his third professional fight. They said they liked the way he handled himself. His skill and talents have led him to become a star of UFC, where he's the youngest UK representative. He clearly has a bright future in front of him – at the time of writing he has 11 straight wins to his credit.

There's something unique about John that I'm unable to put my finger on. He's an emerging young talent with plenty of potential and ambition to match. Sponsors should be queuing up to get their names on the Hitman's shorts.

What were your schooldays like?

I had a pretty easy school life. I went to a private school in Sussex. I wasn't a bully or bullied.

Was MMA at the forefront of your childhood ambitions?

When I was growing up my whole family always played rugby. So I was more into rugby when I was younger. I didn't really know that MMA existed. I was 16 when I found out what MMA was, and since then succeeding in MMA has pretty much been my main aim in life.

Was discovering MMA a turning point?

I guess it was. I obviously enjoyed the way the sport was run, and how it looked and the rules in the competition. It turned my life around from not really knowing what I wanted to do, to actually having an aim in life and really having the drive to keep going.

How does it feel to be the youngest contender of UFC to represent the UK?

I think it's great, not only to be the youngest fighter but to be a UK representative for the UFC. It brings me a lot of honour and pride.

What do you do away from the cage?

Just relax. I like watching movies and listening to music and spending time with my girlfriend and family and friends.

Name some fighters that you admire in the cage.

My first person I fell in love with in MMA was B.J. Penn. He was always my favourite and he's always going to be up there. The way George St. Pierre carries himself is great as well, just because he's such a great athlete and a great role model for everyone.

Who has inspired you?

My dad, always. Just because he worked really hard from an early age and didn't have the good things in life when he was growing up. So, he's always been an inspiration. Then my whole family and everyone around me who have been round since I was young. They've all given me inspiration to keep driving forward. Also Sol Gilbert, my first coach, who helped me to understand how hard training should be and how you should be pushing yourself. Now, Alexis Demetriades, he's been like almost another father to me, and really helped me out and showed me what I should be doing and how I should be doing things.

THE FUTURE

Who keeps you firmly on your feet?
My girlfriend. She always tells me pretty much how I'm behaving and tells me what's really happening and stuff. So she always keeps me grounded and keeps me down to earth and helps me out a lot.

How would you define a tough guy?
I guess it's someone who looks menacing and can deal with people.

What's your philosophy on MMA?
My philosophy on MMA is that it's a sport. It doesn't always mean people have to be fighters all their lives. It's all about the best sportsman, and the smartest fighter and most well-drilled and trained at the end of the day.

Do you think that MMA can keep young people away from crime?
I think so. I think any martial arts will give discipline to a young person and could hopefully help some of them to clean up the way they act and are. It could give them a lot more discipline and hope.

What's your favourite MMA fight you've seen?
One of my favourites is Eddie Alvarez versus Joachim 'Hellboy' Hansen.

Which is the most memorable of your own fights?
Versus Charles Barbosa for Contenders 8 or 9. I won that on a decision.

JAKE 'BRUTAL' BOSTWICK

The man from Kidbrooke Estate, southeast London (for those who don't know). Back in the day, it was quite a notorious area, probably still is. You've got to be tough to survive around there and that's why he's named 'Brutal'. He's one hard bastard. Many may remember Jake with a Mohican, and what a menace he looked. But never take things at face value. Jake is a great guy to associate with, charismatic, humorous. But I've seen him rock his opponents in the cage. Still in his early 20's, Jake is a great competitor on the MMA scene with the potential to achieve much and become a champion. Born at only

7lb 10oz, Jake has grown over the years and now fights 'freestyle' in the middleweight division, carrying a fighting weight of 185lbs.

Jake's first MMA bout was at the Circus Tavern in Essex, at the suggestion of Jason, then Head of Blitz Sports. Jake's father Terry has been beside him all the way, right from his early days of training in judo and gymnastics, and has attended every one of Jake's bouts. They still train together in Swanley, Kent with Kieran Keddle, the expert Thai fighter. Jake is a respected warrior and he continues to strengthen his abilities.

What made you choose MMA?
I started training, doing a lot of judo. I used to play rugby. I've always been a contact sort of person, quite aggressive. So I started training and then last year a fight popped up and I took it and I knocked him out. Then another fight popped up, I knocked him out. Then from there I thought, "I can do something with this," so I just got into it that way.

So did you fight in school, were you ever bullied?
I was never bullied in school. I got a lot of grief because of my size. I couldn't say race really, but I did get a lot of trouble with black people. Just because I had a skinhead, people used to think I was racist. I'm not like that. I did fight with other white people, so it's nothing like that. I did fight quite a lot at school. It's the way it goes sometimes. I just used to get in trouble quite easy.

Where did you go to school?
Blackheath. I grew up in Kidbrooke in south London. It's quite a famous estate, people know it. People say it's quite a bad area, but I'm a good lad, I'm no idiot.

Did you finish school?
Yeah, I finished school when I was 16. I didn't go into college or anything. I'm not a learning sort of person, I don't like school. When I left school I just wanted to train. I was playing rugby for the school as well. And then fighting popped up.

What did your family and friends think of you taking up MMA?
They love it. They know I enjoy fighting so they support me. They're always helping me and trying to help me with training and egging me on. I've got a good crowd behind me. I'm not married, I'm still a young lad.

THE FUTURE

Who's your opponent today?
I'm fighting John McGuire. He's unbeaten. All grand. He's not much of a stand-up fighter. Tonight, though, I'm not bringing it to him standing up.

So have you lost or gained weight for this fight?
Just normal weight, middleweight. I weighed in at 83.7 kg. At the moment, I'm about 87-88 kg. I'm quite a lump, so I've done all right for weight. I can't wait.

What inspires you to fight?
I love the thought of hurting somebody, for some reason. In this career, in this business, however you want to explain it, you need to be able to fight and hurt people to get through it. And I enjoy it, I enjoy the training, I enjoy the pain and the sweat and the blood and everything that's involved in it. It's so hard to train for a fight, and if you win a fight you get so much from it – the adrenalin, everything – you're buzzing. Especially if you knock somebody out. The best way to win is knocking someone out.

Do you believe in any religion?
No mate, I don't. I've seen myself. I don't believe in anything. This world is this world and whoever's been made in this world.

What's your philosophy of MMA?
Great sport, good for fitness. It can help young adults to control and channel their aggression.

How can it help young people?
Knowing about the increase in violent crime, I think the fact that MMA takes young people off the street and into a controlled environment will improve their outlook.

What's life like for you away from the cage?
It's good. People come up to you if they've seen you on a DVD or seen you at a fight, "You're Jake Bostwick, blah, blah, blah." You start talking, you might have a photo with them because they think you're going to be someone famous one day, like a good fighter, a known fighter. I've got a bit of a name so far I'd say. I take it as it comes and people have been alright so far. I haven't had anyone call me anything bad.

WARRIORS OF THE CAGE

What do you work at away from the cage?

I was doing suspended ceilings. I was in Thailand for a couple of months training out there. That's where all the tattoos come from. Then I came home and what I've been doing is training twice a day for the next fight, which is quite important. I like to go out with my pals. I would usually be working, but I'm not working at the moment. I might meet up with a couple of mates, go for a run, spend a bit of time with my friends. I enjoy having a good social life, having good friends, because if you haven't got mates behind you to help you in this sport then it's not so good. You do need good support behind you, and I like to socialise with a lot of people. That's why I have a big crowd behind me because I'm a very nice person. I get on with a lot of people.

What are your emotions before a fight?

See red mist I suppose, like a bull. It's the way you've got to be sometimes. You have to think that you don't like this person. I know you probably are best mates, you could be mates. I've seen people in the UFC fight, they're good mates and they fight, but you need to see the wrong side of them, you need to see that red mist. You need to be able to switch on. I can switch on very well, from nothing to something. So when I'm warming up for the fight I do get very aggressive and I feel like I really want to knock this person out.

Who do you train with?

I train out of Eltham Warriors with people like Mark Epstein and Jason Barrett. Some good boys up there, good fighters, champions, European champions. It's good to be training round Mark Epstein. You know he can bang. So you're training with someone who can bang. When you come to someone your own weight, because I'm not Mark Epstein's weight, then you're ready to take them.

Define a tough guy.

A guy that will go all the way with no holds barred, a person that will get beaten up outside the cage and get up and carry on with his hands up, no tools, just fists. Or it can be a person who will say, "No," and walk away. In some situations you can't do that. A tough guy is someone who shows no fear.

What was your most memorable fight and why?

My first fight because it was a nine-second knock out, and I was very young in the sport at that time. It gave a really big boost to my confidence at a time when I needed to achieve some of my goals.

What's your favourite of the fights you've seen?
Melvin Manhoef versus Evangelista Santos ['the Cyborg'] at Cage Rage 15, it was a complete stand-up war. Also Ross 'the Boss' Mason versus Marius Zaromskis at Cage Rage 22, another stand-up war.

What was the most frightening moment of your life?
MMA Contenders 2, at Caesar's Night Club in Streatham in south London. My dad, Terry Bostwick, fought Marvin Arnold and lost to ground and pound. It was the situation that I feared the most in MMA.

Has there been a turning point in your life?
I started with three straight wins, and then hit the downside with seven losses and one no-contest. I was in a situation where I wanted to quit, but someone once said, "Never give up," so when I was offered a re-match against Marvin Arnold I accepted the challenge. I really trained hard for the fight because it was all or nothing for me. Winning the fight put me on a high and it made me see that not giving up pays off in the end. That was my turning point.

Why do you think MMA has taken off in England?
MMA is a lot more involved and interesting than single-discipline martial arts. Because of the mix of stand-up and ground skills, you need to fight. It's not just stand-up.

Do you feel that MMA suffers from lack of respect?
I hate the way people judge cage fighting, the way they judge a book by its cover. They hear 'cage fighting' and think the worst, but they don't know about the preparation that goes into a fight, the hours of training, diet and nutrition, learning the martial arts inside out, and learning self defence – which you need in this day and age. Cage fighting is disciplined and takes place in a controlled environment with a referee and a doctor. If you're injured and don't want to carry on the fight, you can tap out or verbally quit at any time. On the streets, you don't have *any* of these options. That's how a lot of young adults get injured, sometimes killed.

WARRIORS OF THE CAGE
MARK 'BABY FACE' SMITH

Mark 'Baby Face' Smith started to train in martial arts when he was eight years old, and had his first public fight at 16. After two years' training, with Elite Fighting School, Mark had learnt many techniques, including how to protect himself by knowing when to submit. Knowing when to stop is often one of the hardest things for inexperienced fighters in training to accept. His first fight against Lyon Dickens was at Caesar's in Streatham, south London. It was arranged by Dave O'Donnell, who showed faith and confidence in 'Baby Face's' capabilities and maturity. Mark had only two weeks notice before the bout, and dedicated those two weeks to intense training at Elite. His dedication paid off.

By the time he was 20, Mark was already starting out as an instructor, and looks forward to becoming a fulltime teacher of the sport after he's finished winning all the titles. He clearly has no intention of ever giving up his involvement in Mixed Martial Arts, and expects to be training others when he's getting his pension.

Outside cage fighting, Mark, who has a degree in software engineering, works in a bank in the City of London, which we are not allowed to name. When he's not training, fighting or teaching, Mark spends a lot of time recovering from his exertions at home in South London with his family, and especially his mum. She has supported Mark's fighting from the beginning and can always be found in the VIP section at events. Now 23, and with a dream of turning professional in the near future, Mark says that his time is too full for him to run a place of his own. For relaxation, Mark likes watching gangster movies. *Scarface* and *GoodFellas* are among his favourites, and he enjoys listening to funky house.

I met Mark at Liverpool Street Station in his lunch break from the bank. Only the tautness of his stylish grey suit, by Paul Smith, and crisp white shirt might have betrayed to passers-by his other life in the cage, for he looked every inch your regular City gent. He led me through the lunchtime crowds to his favourite place for lunch – fighting food, lots of carbohydrates and protein. Over lean meat and pasta Mark shared his thoughts, hopes and dreams.

What motivated you to start training for Mixed Martial Arts?
I was getting bullied, and I'd had enough. I was from Bermondsey and went to school in Lewisham, so I had to go a long way. Probably because I wasn't local they used to try to bash me up. I never

conformed – everything was street talk and I stayed cockney. I don't think they ever really liked me. I saw a notice that said that the Elite Fighting School was giving the first lesson free. Dave O'Donnell taught the class and he taught me how to get out of headlocks and some other basic techniques. I was hooked at once, and committed myself to the sport. After I found MMA the bullying stopped. I finally started to fight back and people realised they couldn't mess me around any more. MMA gave me direction.

How did you feel when you fought in the cage for the first time?

I was very nervous and naive, but my mum was very supportive. I won with a tapout – I got him in an armbar. It was the best feeling I'd ever had. I knew I would never be bullied again. There were over a thousand people watching. Backstage, they were suggesting names to give me, and Andy Geer gave me the fight name 'Baby Face' because I was so young. After that fight I became part of Team Titan and Elite.

You seem so fired-up. Where do you get your inspiration from?

Dave O'Donnell plays an inspirational part in my life and career. He got me started, allowed me to build my confidence and continues to be a major figure in my life. I've become a confident person, and turned into a role model for others.

Who are you training with at Team Titan and Elite?

Brad 'One Punch' Pickett, Dean 'Dynamite' Bray, Ed 'the Smasher' Smith, Mark Buchanan, Jason Young and Michael Pastou. The instructors are Dave O'Donnell at Elite and Mickey Papas at Team Titan. I have the utmost respect for both of them.

One of your defeats was a decisive knockout. How did you overcome that?

In my eyes it was nothing really to overcome. It's all part of the game. A knockout is a severe concussion, you ask anyone. I really, honestly don't care. It does sound a bit funny, but I wouldn't feel that way if I'd been really fighting. It's just that I walked straight into it, boom! I did the same thing to someone else the year before. It's very, very quick. People have said since that it was one of the worst KOs they'd ever seen. I think, "Good, I'll stay in your memory, mate!" There was a reason I got knocked out that day, I probably attracted it. I just went round the gym, trained harder and haven't lost since. I learned from it, and I've made myself a more ferocious fighter.

Have you planned where would you like to be in five years from now?

My ultimate goal is to seek perfection. In five years I will still be here, but with multiple belts. Cage Rage is expanding rapidly, but fighting in something like Pride or with another big foreign promoter would be the ultimate for me. If I were to go for, say, Pride, and make a name for myself abroad, I'd want them to appreciate my style of fighting. I'd love to turn professional and then to teach others in turn. I would love to challenge Abdul Mohammed to take the title, but I'll wait until he's a lot older! I'm on a journey, and he's an obstacle I may need to conquer. I respect him as one of the greatest fighters in Cage Rage because of his art and charisma.

What do you believe in?

I believe in God and talk to him, and I like Buddhism, which I read about on the internet. The Buddhist path is a way of life which is very relaxed, but it also teaches determination. I ask God for strength to keep me focussed and I acknowledge that my beliefs do help me to concentrate on my training and the discipline I need if I'm to reach perfection.

What are your favourite moves?

I love knockouts and chokes. It's a thrill and I get a buzz when choking an opponent, especially banging them out. It's great! I have no remorse. He wants to finish me off, so I make sure that I do it first. It's do or die. I have no enemies or rivals outside the cage. This is a sport, it stays in the cage and it has my ultimate respect.

So is the whole event a thrill for you, not just your own bouts?

Yes it is. I love the whole thing from start to finish. The atmosphere is pukka. My adrenaline pumps at the entrance of the other fighters at about the same rate as it does if I'm fighting myself.

Who are your current favourite fighters?

My favourite British fighter is Paul 'Semtex' Daley, sorry, 'One Punch'! 'Semtex' fights like a warrior and his record is phenomenal.

He goes from strength to strength, and I love the style of his fighting. He's a young guy who will become a legend in the sport, and he's another person who inspires me.

Do you think that MMA is a positive thing for young people?
I've seen a lot of kids come off the street and into the gym. They find direction for the violence they've been encountering, and it's a direction they can use to channel aggression. I think the way people are being brought up today, they need role models. I had a good upbringing and turned out quite well, I'd like to say – I do my mum proud! Any physical contact sport can help young people because these sports are so physically demanding that there's no energy left to muck around on street corners and start stabbing and killing each other. What MMA does give you is a pair of balls, confidence. People who train would be more likely to give someone a right-hander than pull a weapon out of their pants. That way, at least they're not going to get badly hurt.

You've recently started to train some young fighters at Team Titan. What does that do for you?
I feel an immense pride and fulfillment knowing I've taught somebody some skills and techniques. To become a fulltime teacher eventually would be a great achievement for me, and it would be a very positive thing for me to do.

You've been fighting for five years now. Do you fancy a new nickname now that you're growing a little more mature?
I will always keep the name 'Baby Face', however mature I get, as everyone knows me as that. I'll also keep to my own style of fighting because, throughout the journey of my life, I've been known as a gentleman and highly respected. I aim to keep it that way.

What do the fighters themselves think about the future of MMA? On the whole, they seem to be optimistic about the sport itself, their own fight careers and their post-retirement plans.

Tom Howard:

If it continues to grow at this level I think that within the next ten years it's going to be successful on a global level.

WARRIORS OF THE CAGE

Ed 'Smasher' Smith:

All walks of life are into it. Five years ago it was just the louts, the gangsters, those were the sort of people you were getting, but now you get businessmen, City boys, nice girls, because it's an exciting sport and the exciting element about it is what's attracting everyone now. All the younger generation are into it, you know.

Dean Bray:

It's nice to have a few rewards from fighting. We put in a lot of hard training and we deserve some rewards. As the sport gets bigger, then hopefully we can get a bit more money out of it. We don't get paid a lot of money. We all have to have jobs and it would be nice to be able to pay the mortgage just through fighting like the guys do in the United States.

Some are already planning to provide the fans with the next generation of fighters, as Dean Bray explains:

If I do have children my kids are going to be training in Mixed Martial Arts from the ages of two, three years old, trust me. I don't know if you've seen Dave O'Donnell's little boy, but he's gonna be an exact replica of his dad. My boys are gonna go to school knowing arm bars, chokes, everything. Any boys of mine are going to be able to wrestle, know how to take people down … they're gonna know the lot, without a doubt. I can't stand bullies and I would like my sons to not be bullies, but to be children who can stop bullies.

For some, the future is already here. Neil Grove and Abdul Mohammed both spoke about how the friendships made in gyms and fight camps have helped them to recover from experiences which they suffered half a world away from their MMA training camps in England. They are both men who have been justified at some time in their lives in thinking that, for them, there was to be no future at all.

THE FUTURE

Neil Grove grew up in South Africa. He says:

When I was ten years old, I was held at knifepoint during a robbery. I've also had guns pointed at me when people were angry with me, and shots were actually fired at me one time when I was out hiking. I decided to move out of South Africa and go to a safer country. Now I am happily married to Emalene and have a son, Ethan.

Abdul Mohammed came even closer to death in Afghanistan, where he was born in 1975. He grew up in an isolated village in the Panj Shayari Valley, which he left in 1997. He talks of the arrival of the Taliban:

My friend and I were locked up by them in Hairatan for two weeks before we escaped. We walked through the desert through the night until we got to the next town, Masari Sharif. This town had also been taken by the Taliban and we were re-captured and locked up again for three days. Fortunately for us, the balance of power changed and the Northern Alliance regained control of Masari Sharif and we were released. When we got out, we found that other people had not been so lucky, and as we walked through the town we saw dead bodies everywhere. The final death toll was 4,500. I have seen extremism tear nations apart and cause wars. I have seen so much I can't explain.

Abdul now lives in the north of England, where he is safe and happy, fighting MMA and living with his wife and child.

SOL GILBERT

You have been a cage fighter yourself and very well known for your gym, Zero Tolerance. How did that happen?
I came from a boxing background, like most people, then I stumbled across UFC when it began in the mid 1990s, and said, "I have got to have this." I went to London and travelled to various fight clubs to learn BJJ, Brazilian jiu-jitsu, which I started with Roger Brooking. I loved it and did it for a year. Then I got bored

with it because I like striking and knocking people out. I searched the internet to find where they taught MMA, then stumbled across an open-trials contest, which was held by ML Sports. That's like amateur rules on MMA. I entered, had two fights, won both in under a minute. I kept on competing on these tournaments, spread over a year, I had ten fights with them, won all ten – even the light heavyweight title. I then signed a contract to turn professional. Then Dave and Andy wanted me to feature on the cards, when they moved from Streatham Caesar's to Wembley Conference Centre. On my debut fight, I became ill and then Paul Daley stepped in to take my place. I then fought on Cage Rage 8, where Alex Reid and Lee Murray were on the same card. Lee Murray fought Anderson Silva and I had beaten Jean Francois Lenougue by an arm bar.

What impact can MMA have in relation to reducing knife and gun crime for the juveniles of today?

A huge impact. My car doesn't get done anymore, now that I'm an MMA athlete. I think it's about respect for one another. It takes so much dedication and focus, and you have to put so much into the sport, that once you're involved with MMA there's no time to be on the streets, hanging around with the wrong crowd, getting involved with drink, drugs or crime. I think the sport of MMA is a saviour to the community as it brings people from all backgrounds and nationalities together. When I stage a show and young guys get together and enjoy the event, many have come up to me with thanks, asking how they can get involved, which to me shows support.

Are there age limits?

My youngest is three and a half and he's wrestling and grappling. Not with great structure. Just look at young boys and girls, most like to play fight – it's burning energy that's used. When they are tired, they call it a day. As a father, I'm like a referee. Here in ZT, Zero Tolerance, we came up with a class called box-wrestling, where we have taken out the contact of boxing so there's no impact towards the face, nor any knocking each other out. They just learn the boxing techniques, know how to hold their hands up and when it comes to sparring, it's more wrestling and grappling based. If it is striking, it's only to the body – which is good conditioning. ZT take kids from as early as four up till 12, 13 years old.

THE FUTURE

How do you see MMA in ten years?

Taken over the world. In fact, it's almost there. UFC are doing a fantastic job of marketing MMA. A lot of fighters are more articulate than before, whereas in boxing there's hardly any. MMA fighters can be seen as good role models.

How much inspiration and confidence can one gain from MMA?

A lot. If you look back to the earlier days when Royce Gracie was competing in UFC, he was a small, light guy, compared to some of his opponents. But he showed that he could dominate those bigger and heavier guys, which provided his confidence and the belief that gave him inspiration, not just to him but to all, when he dislocated many joints on them. In MMA, the better people are, the more humble they are. Small or bigger persons can be inspired to gain confidence and self-esteem from many facets of the MMA world. In MMA when you train, you can dominate in one session, then submit in another. So it shows discipline and that's what I admire in the sport.

Is there a future for females in MMA?

Without a doubt. At the moment I'm training a ten-times Muay Thai champion, Julie Kitchen, who has shown great interest in MMA, where she can apply the groundwork to her skills. She's one to look out for.

Do you think many police are fans of MMA?

It's a massive part of the curriculum. I have a lot of civil servants, not just the police force but ambulances, fire fighters, security guards, they all come down to train MMA. They know that, unlike back in the day, when they used to go to the gym or karate or punch bags, now you can't just punch people in the street if someone was to steal your wallet or break into your car, you would get charged for assault. With MMA, there's a lot of grappling and a lot of close-up work on how to dominate without striking them. That's why MMA has become more popular, due to these guys coming to train.

Would you say there is a lesser police presence at MMA shows than at other major sports?

Most definitely less. We put on a show at the Hilton Metropole before. We went down to Hove police station and had a chat with them regarding our event. They said if you have any confrontation from other crowds we'll be supportive of your show, even if there happens to be a football game on. I was delighted to hear that. Zero Tolerance has had 17 shows and it's never required the police to use force. We have a good relationship with Hove police, so that all can come to my show and be truly entertained with their friends and family.

What can the community, government and other parties do to make MMA popular?

Get behind the sport more, realise that this is a sport and these are athletes. Maybe combat sport isn't for everyone, and maybe that reason alone is why they don't want to see it. So they turn the television channel over when it's on. I don't like gardening programmes. Not everything is for all, everyone has their own preference. People want to stop looking at MMA as being as barbaric as cock-fighting and respect these sportsmen and women as highly conditioned athletes. They work really hard to get to such levels, train up to six hours a day, six days a week. You try it, see how you get on with a good healthy diet and a fitness regime, then once they get to that stage that's when the sponsorships get involved and good media coverage comes in. Look at UFC when they came to Dublin, they sold out everywhere. The arena, shops, complexes were profiting, like Hove is behind me and ZT, but we need more support from everyone.

I think the general public shouldn't be afraid to come down to compete or train in MMA just because they see guys getting elbowed or kneed in the face. Don't feel that's what you're getting if you go to a gym/academy. We have a number of gyms, ZT Fight Skools, and are hoping to have many more by the end of the year. When guys come to ZT, there's no striking at first, as we work on technique and conditioning, then we see where they want to go from there. We want to make it appealing to the masses, it's not just about entering a cage but can be used as an all-purpose stress release. I train a woman who's around 99 kg in MMA techniques and she loves it. MMA is open for everybody, across the world, for any purpose.

Is MMA strongly associated with criminals or are people from all backgrounds involved?

I know a lot of people within my town, who walk around nightclubs, and want to start fights, and think that they are big men, and want to take liberties. They are bullies. But they could never walk into my camp as they will get exposed. I have a student by the name of John Hathaway, who could have pursued a career as a professional rugby player for the Harlequins. He trains at ZT and at an earlier stage he came up to me and said he wanted to establish himself in the world of MMA. He went to Shoreham College, which is a very good school. He's very intelligent, articulate, had a private education, his parents are terrific people, no criminal history. John is known as 'the Hitman' and is very polite and humble as can be. But when that cage door is closed, there's a reason why he is 13-0 and has fought twice in the UFC and remains unbeaten. He's a *monster*. Once he steps outside of the cage, John is the nicest person on this planet and he's never even stolen a penny sweet. If people do have a criminal background and want to change and channel their energy in a positive form, then MMA is here for you.

6

Further Information

RULES

There is a popular misconception that MMA has no rules. While its history can be traced back through styles which were subject to only a few prohibitions – for example, Vale Tudo and the 'no holds barred' school – modern MMA does have an agreed set of allowable actions. In the USA the sport is controlled through the Unified Rules, which were first ratified by the New Jersey State Athletic Commission in 2000. These cover every aspect of competition. (New Jersey State Athletic Control Board, 'Mixed Martial Arts Unified Rules of Conduct' can be found on: http://www.leg.state.nv.us)

When the sport came to Britain promoters adopted these rules too, although there is still no national regulatory body which oversees or controls the sport. Promoters in Britain are therefore still able to omit or introduce new rules for competitions, as they wish.

APPAREL

What's cool in the cage? Fighters are not really given a lot of choice in this, as all footwear is forbidden. All fighters must wear a gum shield and gloves, but additional body protection is gender specific – women wear it above the waist and men below! Gloves are lightweight and cover only the palms and back of the hands, designed to protect the fighters' knuckles rather than the whole hand. They usually weigh four ounces for professional fighters, but amateurs are allowed to wear gloves weighing a maximum of six ounces.

Apart from the gloves, fighters wear shorts, as all other clothing is deemed to interfere with grapple and submission techniques. (Some shorts are pretty flash though!) The only real opportunity for fighters to show their sense of style is during their entrance to the arena. Flanked by ring girls and security guards, swirled in all manner of capes, cloaks and gowns, they have this one moment to parade to the music of their choice, hear their fight name over the public address system and enter the arena dressed like a king.

After that, it's strip-down and focus.

RESOLUTION

A fight, which usually consists of three five-minute rounds, can be ended in any of the following ways:

Knockout (KO): one fighter becomes unconscious and the fight ends.

Technical Knockout (TKO): the referee stops the fight because of injury, because one fighter appears to be unconscious (even if he may later turn out not to have been) or no longer able to defend himself effectively.

Submission: one fighter submits to the other by tapping his opponent or the floor. This is also known as 'tapping out'.

Stopped by the doctor: the doctor considers that one of the fighters has been too badly injured to continue.

Towel thrown in: the corner men, usually coaches and trainers, can throw in the towel if they feel that their fighter is unable to continue for some reason.

Disqualification of a fighter: contestants may be disqualified after receiving three warnings about conduct, or if purposeful illegal actions cause the opponent to be injured and leave him unable to continue.

'No contest' declared: permissible if one contestant is injured following the accidental use of an illegal technique, or if both contestants are in breach of the rules.

FURTHER INFORMATION

Judges' decision: Should any bout reach the end of the last round without being resolved, then the decision as to who has won rests with the judges. There are usually three of them and they score each fighter at the end of each round; if necessary, at the end of the fight these points are added up and a result is declared. Judgements are based on two criteria: whether the fighters have shown 'effective aggressiveness' and the use of 'effective technique'. Each fighter can score a maximum of ten points in each round; the winner usually scores ten points and the loser nine. A drawn round usually results in both fighters scoring ten. Judges can deduct points if fouls have been committed, so the points total could be less than 60 by the end of the bout. However, the judges may declare only a win or draw. Since only the result and not the points score is announced, the detail of how a decision has been reached remains a mystery to most fans.

FOULS

There are over 30 ways for a fighter to offend against the rules. The following actions are not allowed:

Head butting
Eye gouging
Biting
Hair pulling
Fish hooking
Groin attacks
Inserting a finger into the opponent's injuries or orifices
Small joint manipulation
Striking to the spine or back of the head
Striking downward with the elbow point
Throat strikes and throat grabs of any kind
Clawing, pinching or twisting flesh
Grabbing the collarbone
Kicking a grounded opponent's head (see 'open guard')
Kneeing a grounded opponent's head (see 'open guard')
Stomping a grounded opponent (see 'open guard')
Striking a grounded opponent with the elbow
Kicking the kidney with a heel
Spiking to the canvas on an opponent's head or neck
Throwing an opponent outside the fighting area

Holding an opponent's shorts or gloves

Spitting

Unsportsmanlike conduct which causes injury

Holding onto the perimeter of the cage

Abusive language

Attacking the opponent in a break

Attacking an opponent when the referee has taken charge

Attacking an opponent after the bell has gone and the round has ended

Refusing to accept the referee's instructions

Timidity

Interference in the fight from the corner men

'Throwing in the towel'

A note on the 'open guard' rule: This short-lived rule was unique to Cage Rage and allowed a standing fighter to strike an opponent who was on the ground. As long as the referee decided that the grounded fighter was able to defend himself, he would declare 'open guard' and the standing fighter could then use techniques which would otherwise have been fouls if directed at a grounded opponent.

WEIGHT CLASSES

No national Board of Control has been set up in the UK, so weight classes are not governed by any external body. This means that individual promoters can set the minimum and maximum weights in the classes at any point they wish. The same fighter could therefore fight at different levels for different promoters without actually changing weight! However, when Cage Rage was originally set up, the organisers adopted six classes based on the nine then used in the USA, under the Unified Rules of MMA. In Britain, promoters have on the whole continued to use the classes adopted by Cage Rage, although none are actually obliged to do so.

What are weight classes for? To prevent unequal competition – to make it safer – to provide better entertainment – to give the punters a good show, and the fight the chance to go the full distance. The weigh-in is therefore an important part of any competitive event, and 'making the weight' is the first target for every competitive fighter.

FURTHER INFORMATION

Weigh-ins and classes in Britain are in kilograms. The equivalents in pounds are given for ease of reference:

UK weight class	limit (kg)	limit (lbs)
Featherweight	66kg	145lb
Lightweight	70kg	155lb
Welterweight	77kg	170lb
Middleweight	84kg	185lb
Light Heavyweight	93kg	205lb
Heavyweight	no limit	no limit

The weight classes used in the USA are set according to the Unified Rules, which include nine classes, three more than are commonly used in Britain. The three lightest classes in the USA (flyweight, bantamweight and featherweight) fall together in Britain as featherweight. The two heaviest classes used in the USA (heavyweight and super heavyweight) fall together in Britain as heavyweight. In the USA, weigh-ins and classes are in pounds; the equivalents in kilograms are given for ease of reference.

USA Weight class	limit (lbs) men	limit (kgs) men	limit (lbs) women	limit (kgs) women
Flyweight	125lb	57kg	95lb	43kg
Bantamweight	135lb	61kg	105lb	47kg
Featherweight	145lb	66kg	115lb	52kg
Lightweight	155lb	70kg	125lb	57kg
Welterweight	170lb	77kg	135lb	61kg
Middleweight	185lb	84kg	145lb	66kg
Light Heavyweight	205lb	93kg	155lb	70kg
Cruiserweight	n/a	n/a	165lb	75kg
Heavyweight	265lb	120kg	185lb	84kg
Super Heavyweight	no limit	no limit	no limit	no limit

Since the original agreement of the Unified Rules in the USA, the rules and weight classes have been adopted by the athletic commissions of many other states and have now become standard in all but a few. Despite attempts to increase the number of weight classes in recent years, it has proved impossible to obtain agreement for changes from all interested parties.

WEBSITES IN ENGLISH

http://www.twitter.com/ukmmanews
http://www.wrestling101.com
http://www.bamma.net
http://www.uk.ufc.com
http://www.sfuk.tripod.com
http://www.londonshootfighters.com
http://ultimatechallengeuk.com
http://wolfslairmma.co.uk
http://www.ringsidebygus.com
http://www.sherdog.com
http://cagewarriors.com
http://www.gowamma.com
http://www.mixedmartialarts.com
http://www.mmamadness.com
http://www.mmaunltd.com
http://www.mmajunkie.com
http://www.mmaplayground.com
http://www.mmauniverse.com
http://www.mmaweekly.com
http://www.fightnetwork.com
www.stephenquadros.com
www.thebeast.com
www.jeansilva.co.uk
www.samiberik.com
www.myspace.com/markepstein
www.myspace.com/onepunchpickett
www.myspace.com/rosspointon

And finally, remember that it's easy to overlook the obvious and the most simple search is often the most effective. So, if you're looking for websites belonging to individual fighters (rather than their training camps) or others working in the sport, try the following format: http://www.fightersname.com

AND IN CONCLUSION...

So a fan and a writer set out to discover what makes the people inside MMA tick. We wanted to know what goes on behind the sequins and the lights. We were tired of seeing the bodies in the cage, but never seeing the people.

We wanted to know what motivated the fighters and we found a lot of people who spoke frankly of the good and bad times in their lives. It's been a privilege to hear what they had to say. Johnny interviewed people who have fought both inside and outside the cage, to build lives for themselves and their families. He met people who are still fighting to build a future for MMA in the UK, who show commitment and optimism and emphasise the positive effects that training can have on the young. The younger fighters themselves feel secure that they can build real careers in an arena which offers a serious sporting discipline to them and entertainment to the punters.

MMA is about a lot of things: love, money, fame and power. It's just that each individual person has their own priorities, sets their own percentage target. For some, the balance changes as they go through their career: their kids grow up; titles are won and lost; relationships end and begin. For even in the cage, the love of one's fans can be dwarfed by the birth of a child, and fame can suddenly seem like nothing...